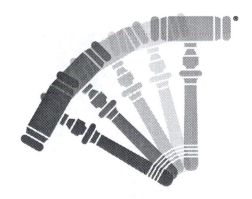

Casenote® Legal Briefs

FAMILY LAW

Keyed to Courses Using

Wadlington, O'Brien, and Wilson's
Domestic Relations: Cases and Materials

Seventh Edition

Wolters Kluwer

Law & Business

Copyright © 2013 CCH Incorporated. All Rights Reserved.

Published by Wolters Kluwer Law & Business in New York.

Wolters Kluwer Law & Business serves customers worldwide with CCH, Aspen Publishers, and Kluwer Law International products. (www.wolterskluwerlb.com)

To contact Customer Service, e-mail customer.service@wolterskluwer.com, call 1-800-234-1660, fax 1-800-901-9075, or mail correspondence to:

Wolters Kluwer Law & Business
Attn: Order Department
P.O. Box 990
Frederick, MD 21705

Printed in the United States of America.

1 2 3 4 5 6 7 8 9 0

ISBN 978-1-4548-3925-5

About Wolters Kluwer Law & Business

Wolters Kluwer Law & Business is a leading global provider of intelligent information and digital solutions for legal and business professionals in key specialty areas, and respected educational resources for professors and law students. Wolters Kluwer Law & Business connects legal and business professionals as well as those in the education market with timely, specialized authoritative content and information-enabled solutions to support success through productivity, accuracy and mobility.

Serving customers worldwide, Wolters Kluwer Law & Business products include those under the Aspen Publishers, CCH, Kluwer Law International, Loislaw, ftwilliam.com and MediRegs family of products.

CCH products have been a trusted resource since 1913, and are highly regarded resources for legal, securities, antitrust and trade regulation, government contracting, banking, pension, payroll, employment and labor, and healthcare reimbursement and compliance professionals.

Aspen Publishers products provide essential information to attorneys, business professionals and law students. Written by preeminent authorities, the product line offers analytical and practical information in a range of specialty practice areas from securities law and intellectual property to mergers and acquisitions and pension/benefits. Aspen's trusted legal education resources provide professors and students with high-quality, up-to-date and effective resources for successful instruction and study in all areas of the law.

Kluwer Law International products provide the global business community with reliable international legal information in English. Legal practitioners, corporate counsel and business executives around the world rely on Kluwer Law journals, looseleafs, books, and electronic products for comprehensive information in many areas of international legal practice.

Loislaw is a comprehensive online legal research product providing legal content to law firm practitioners of various specializations. Loislaw provides attorneys with the ability to quickly and efficiently find the necessary legal information they need, when and where they need it, by facilitating access to primary law as well as state-specific law, records, forms and treatises.

ftwilliam.com offers employee benefits professionals the highest quality plan documents (retirement, welfare and non-qualified) and government forms (5500/PBGC, 1099 and IRS) software at highly competitive prices.

MediRegs products provide integrated health care compliance content and software solutions for professionals in healthcare, higher education and life sciences, including professionals in accounting, law and consulting.

Wolters Kluwer Law & Business, a division of Wolters Kluwer, is head-quartered in New York. Wolters Kluwer is a market-leading global information services company focused on professionals.

Format for the Casenote® Legal Brief

Nature of Case: This section identifies the form of action (e.g., breach of contract, negligence, battery), the type of proceeding (e.g., demurrer, appeal from trial court's jury instructions), or the relief sought (e.g., damages, injunction, criminal sanctions).

Fact Summary: This is included to refresh your memory and can be used as a quick reminder of the facts.

Rule of Law: Summarizes the general principle of law that the case illustrates. It may be used for instant recall of the court's holding and for classroom discussion or home review.

Facts: This section contains all relevant facts of the case, including the contentions of the parties and the lower court holdings. It is written in a logical order to give the student a clear understanding of the case. The plaintiff and defendant are identified by their proper names throughout and are always labeled with a (P) or (D).

Palsgraf v. Long Island R.R. Co.

Injured bystander (P) v. Railroad company (D)

N.Y. Ct. App., 248 N.Y. 339, 162 N.E. 99 (1928).

NATURE OF CASE: Appeal from judgment affirming verdict for plaintiff seeking damages for personal injury.

FACT SUMMARY: Helen Palsgraf (P) was injured on R.R.'s (D) train platform when R.R.'s (D) guard helped a passenger aboard a moving train, causing his package to fall on the tracks. The package contained fireworks which exploded, creating a shock that tipped a scale onto Palsgraf (P).

🏛 RULE OF LAW
The risk reasonably to be perceived defines the duty to be obeyed.

FACTS: Helen Palsgraf (P) purchased a ticket to Rockaway Beach from R.R. (D) and was waiting on the train platform. As she waited, two men ran to catch a train that was pulling out from the platform. The first man jumped aboard, but the second man, who appeared as if he might fall, was helped aboard by the guard on the train who had kept the door open so they could jump aboard. A guard on the platform also helped by pushing him onto the train. The man was carrying a package wrapped in newspaper. In the process, the man dropped his package, which fell on the tracks. The package contained fireworks and exploded. The shock of the explosion was apparently of great enough strength to tip over some scales at the other end of the platform, which fell on Palsgraf (P) and injured her. A jury awarded her damages, and R.R. (D) appealed.

ISSUE: Does the risk reasonably to be perceived define the duty to be obeyed?

HOLDING AND DECISION: (Cardozo, C.J.) Yes. The risk reasonably to be perceived defines the duty to be obeyed. If there is no foreseeable hazard to the injured party as the result of a seemingly innocent act, the act does not become a tort because it happened to be a wrong as to another. If the wrong was not willful, the plaintiff must show that the act as to her had such great and apparent possibilities of danger as to entitle her to protection. Negligence in the abstract is not enough upon which to base liability. Negligence is a relative concept, evolving out of the common law doctrine of trespass on the case. To establish liability, the defendant must owe a legal duty of reasonable care to the injured party. A cause of action in tort will lie where harm, though unintended, could have been averted or avoided by observance of such a duty. The scope of the duty is limited by the range of danger that a reasonable person could foresee. In this case, there was nothing to suggest from the appearance of the parcel or otherwise that the parcel contained fireworks. The guard could not reasonably have had any warning of a threat to Palsgraf (P), and R.R. (D) therefore cannot be held liable. Judgment is reversed in favor of R.R. (D).

DISSENT: (Andrews, J.) The concept that there is no negligence unless R.R. (D) owes a legal duty to take care as to Palsgraf (P) herself is too narrow. Everyone owes to the world at large the duty of refraining from those acts that may unreasonably threaten the safety of others. If the guard's action was negligent as to those nearby, it was also negligent as to those outside what might be termed the "danger zone." For Palsgraf (P) to recover, R.R.'s (D) negligence must have been the proximate cause of her injury, a question of fact for the jury.

▶ ANALYSIS

The majority defined the limit of the defendant's liability in terms of the danger that a reasonable person in defendant's situation would have perceived. The dissent argued that the limitation should not be placed on liability, but rather on damages. Judge Andrews suggested that only injuries that would not have happened but for R.R.'s (D) negligence should be compensable. Both the majority and dissent recognized the policy-driven need to limit liability for negligent acts, seeking, in the words of Judge Andrews, to define a framework "that will be practical and in keeping with the general understanding of mankind." The Restatement (Second) of Torts has accepted Judge Cardozo's view.

Quicknotes

FORESEEABILITY A reasonable expectation that change is the probable result of certain acts or omissions.

NEGLIGENCE Conduct falling below the standard of care that a reasonable person would demonstrate under similar conditions.

PROXIMATE CAUSE The natural sequence of events without which an injury would not have been sustained.

Party ID: Quick identification of the relationship between the parties.

Concurrence/Dissent: All concurrences and dissents are briefed whenever they are included by the casebook editor.

Analysis: This last paragraph gives you a broad understanding of where the case "fits in" with other cases in the section of the book and with the entire course. It is a hornbook-style discussion indicating whether the case is a majority or minority opinion and comparing the principal case with other cases in the casebook. It may also provide analysis from restatements, uniform codes, and law review articles. The analysis will prove to be invaluable to classroom discussion.

Issue: The issue is a concise question that brings out the essence of the opinion as it relates to the section of the casebook in which the case appears. Both substantive and procedural issues are included if relevant to the decision.

Holding and Decision: This section offers a clear and in-depth discussion of the rule of the case and the court's rationale. It is written in easy-to-understand language and answers the issue presented by applying the law to the facts of the case. When relevant, it includes a thorough discussion of the exceptions to the case as listed by the court, any major cites to the other cases on point, and the names of the judges who wrote the decisions.

Quicknotes: Conveniently defines legal terms found in the case and summarizes the nature of any statutes, codes, or rules referred to in the text.

Wolters Kluwer Law & Business is proud to offer *Casenote® Legal Briefs*—continuing thirty years of publishing America's best-selling legal briefs.

Casenote® Legal Briefs are designed to help you save time when briefing assigned cases. Organized under convenient headings, they show you how to abstract the basic facts and holdings from the text of the actual opinions handed down by the courts. Used as part of a rigorous study regimen, they can help you spend more time analyzing and critiquing points of law than on copying bits and pieces of judicial opinions into your notebook or outline.

Casenote® Legal Briefs should never be used as a substitute for assigned casebook readings. They work best when read as a follow-up to reviewing the underlying opinions themselves. Students who try to avoid reading and digesting the judicial opinions in their casebooks or online sources will end up shortchanging themselves in the long run. The ability to absorb, critique, and restate the dynamic and complex elements of case law decisions is crucial to your success in law school and beyond. It cannot be developed vicariously.

Casenote® Legal Briefs represents but one of the many offerings in Legal Education's Study Aid Timeline, which includes:

- *Casenote® Legal Briefs*
- *Emanuel® Law Outlines*
- Emanuel® *Law in a Flash* Flash Cards
- Emanuel® *CrunchTime®* Series
- *Siegel's Essay and Multiple-Choice Questions and Answers Series*

Each of these series is designed to provide you with easy-to-understand explanations of complex points of law. Each volume offers guidance on the principles of legal analysis and, consulted regularly, will hone your ability to spot relevant issues. We have titles that will help you prepare for class, prepare for your exams, and enhance your general comprehension of the law along the way.

To find out more about Wolters Kluwer Law & Business' study aid publications, visit us online at *www.wolterskluwerlb.com* or email us at *legaledu@wolterskluwer.com*. We'll be happy to assist you.

A. Decide on a Format and Stick to It

Structure is essential to a good brief. It enables you to arrange systematically the related parts that are scattered throughout most cases, thus making manageable and understandable what might otherwise seem to be an endless and unfathomable sea of information. There are, of course, an unlimited number of formats that can be utilized. However, it is best to find one that suits your needs and stick to it. Consistency breeds both efficiency and the security that when called upon you will know where to look in your brief for the information you are asked to give.

Any format, as long as it presents the essential elements of a case in an organized fashion, can be used. Experience, however, has led *Casenote*® *Legal Briefs* to develop and utilize the following format because of its logical flow and universal applicability.

NATURE OF CASE: This is a brief statement of the legal character and procedural status of the case (e.g., "Appeal of a burglary conviction").

There are many different alternatives open to a litigant dissatisfied with a court ruling. The key to determining which one has been used is to discover *who is asking this court for what.*

This first entry in the brief should be kept as *short as possible.* Use the court's terminology if you understand it. But since jurisdictions vary as to the titles of pleadings, the best entry is the one that addresses who wants what in this proceeding, not the one that sounds most like the court's language.

RULE OF LAW: A statement of the general principle of law that the case illustrates (e.g., "An acceptance that varies any term of the offer is considered a rejection and counteroffer").

Determining the rule of law of a case is a procedure similar to determining the issue of the case. Avoid being fooled by red herrings; there may be a few rules of law mentioned in the case excerpt, but usually only one is *the* rule with which the casebook editor is concerned. The techniques used to locate the issue, described below, may also be utilized to find the rule of law. Generally, your best guide is simply the chapter heading. It is a clue to the point the casebook editor seeks to make and should be kept in mind when reading every case in the respective section.

FACTS: A synopsis of only the essential facts of the case, i.e., those bearing upon or leading up to the issue.

The facts entry should be a short statement of the events and transactions that led one party to initiate legal proceedings against another in the first place. While some cases conveniently state the salient facts at the beginning of the decision, in other instances they will have to be culled from hiding places throughout the text, even from concurring and dissenting opinions. Some of the "facts" will often be in dispute and should be so noted. Conflicting evidence may be briefly pointed up. "Hard" facts must be included. Both must be *relevant* in order to be listed in the facts entry. It is impossible to tell what is relevant until the entire case is read, as the ultimate determination of the rights and liabilities of the parties may turn on something buried deep in the opinion.

Generally, the facts entry should not be longer than three to five *short* sentences.

It is often helpful to identify the role played by a party in a given context. For example, in a construction contract case the identification of a party as the "contractor" or "builder" alleviates the need to tell that that party was the one who was supposed to have built the house.

It is always helpful, and a good general practice, to identify the "plaintiff" and the "defendant." This may seem elementary and uncomplicated, but, especially in view of the creative editing practiced by some casebook editors, it is sometimes a difficult or even impossible task. Bear in mind that the *party presently* seeking something from this court may not be the plaintiff, and that sometimes only the cross-claim of a defendant is treated in the excerpt. Confusing or misaligning the parties can ruin your analysis and understanding of the case.

ISSUE: A statement of the general legal question answered by or illustrated in the case. For clarity, the issue is best put in the form of a question capable of a "yes" or "no" answer. In reality, the issue is simply the Rule of Law put in the form of a question (e.g., "May an offer be accepted by performance?").

The major problem presented in discerning what is *the* issue in the case is that an opinion usually purports to raise and answer several questions. However, except for rare cases, only one such question is really the issue in the case. Collateral issues not necessary to the resolution of the matter in controversy are handled by the court by language known as *"obiter dictum"* or merely *"dictum."* While dicta may be included later in the brief, they have no place under the issue heading.

To find the issue, ask *who wants what* and then go on to ask *why did that party succeed or fail in getting it.* Once this is determined, the "why" should be turned into a question.

The complexity of the issues in the cases will vary, but in all cases a single-sentence question should sum up the issue. *In a few cases,* there will be two, or even more rarely, three issues of equal importance to the resolution of the case. Each should be expressed in a single-sentence question.

Since many issues are resolved by a court in coming to a final disposition of a case, the casebook editor will reproduce the portion of the opinion containing the issue or issues most relevant to the area of law under scrutiny. A noted law professor gave this advice: "Close the book; look at the title on the cover." Chances are, if it is Property, you need not concern yourself with whether, for example, the federal government's treatment of the plaintiff's land really raises a federal question sufficient to support jurisdiction on this ground in federal court.

The same rule applies to chapter headings designating sub-areas within the subjects. They tip you off as to what the text is designed to teach. The cases are arranged in a casebook to show a progression or development of the law, so that the preceding cases may also help.

It is also most important to remember to *read the notes and questions* at the end of a case to determine what the editors wanted you to have gleaned from it.

HOLDING AND DECISION: This section should succinctly explain the rationale of the court in arriving at its decision. In capsulizing the "reasoning" of the court, it should always include an application of the general rule or rules of law to the specific facts of the case. Hidden justifications come to light in this entry: the reasons for the state of the law, the public policies, the biases and prejudices, those considerations that influence the justices' thinking and, ultimately, the outcome of the case. At the end, there should be a short indication of the disposition or procedural resolution of the case (e.g., "Decision of the trial court for Mr. Smith (P) reversed").

The foregoing format is designed to help you "digest" the reams of case material with which you will be faced in your law school career. Once mastered by practice, it will place at your fingertips the information the authors of your casebooks have sought to impart to you in case-by-case illustration and analysis.

B. Be as Economical as Possible in Briefing Cases

Once armed with a format that encourages succinctness, it is as important to be economical with regard to the time spent on the actual reading of the case as it is to be economical in the writing of the brief itself. This does not mean "skimming" a case. Rather, it means reading the case with an "eye" trained to recognize into which "section" of your brief a particular passage or line fits and having a system for quickly and precisely marking the case so that the passages fitting any one particular part of the brief can be easily identified and brought together in a concise and accurate manner when the brief is actually written.

It is of no use to simply repeat everything in the opinion of the court; record only enough information to trigger your recollection of what the court said. Nevertheless, an accurate statement of the "law of the case," i.e., the legal principle applied to the facts, is absolutely essential to class preparation and to learning the law under the case method.

To that end, it is important to develop a "shorthand" that you can use to make marginal notations. These notations will tell you at a glance in which section of the brief you will be placing that particular passage or portion of the opinion.

Some students prefer to underline all the salient portions of the opinion (with a pencil or colored underliner marker), making marginal notations as they go along. Others prefer the color-coded method of underlining, utilizing different colors of markers to underline the salient portions of the case, each separate color being used to represent a different section of the brief. For example, blue underlining could be used for passages relating to the rule of law, yellow for those relating to the issue, and green for those relating to the holding and decision, etc. While it has its advocates, the color-coded method can be confusing and time-consuming (all that time spent on changing colored markers). Furthermore, it can interfere with the continuity and concentration many students deem essential to the reading of a case for maximum comprehension. In the end, however, it is a matter of personal preference and style. Just remember, whatever method you use, underlining must be used sparingly or its value is lost.

If you take the marginal notation route, an efficient and easy method is to go along underlining the key portions of the case and placing in the margin alongside them the following "markers" to indicate where a particular passage or line "belongs" in the brief you will write:

N   (NATURE OF CASE)
RL   (RULE OF LAW)
I   (ISSUE)
HL   (HOLDING AND DECISION, relates to the RULE OF LAW behind the decision)
HR   (HOLDING AND DECISION, gives the RATIONALE or reasoning behind the decision)
HA   (HOLDING AND DECISION, applies the general principle(s) of law to the facts of the case to arrive at the decision)

Remember that a particular passage may well contain information necessary to more than one part of your brief, in which case you simply note that in the margin. If you are using the color-coded underlining method instead of marginal notation, simply make asterisks or checks in the margin next to the passage in question in the colors that indicate the additional sections of the brief where it might be utilized.

The economy of utilizing "shorthand" in marking cases for briefing can be maintained in the actual brief writing process itself by utilizing "law student shorthand" within the brief. There are many commonly used words and phrases for which abbreviations can be substituted in your briefs (and in your class notes also). You can develop abbreviations that are personal to you and which will save you a lot of time. A reference list of briefing abbreviations can be found on page x of this book.

C. Use Both the Briefing Process and the Brief as a Learning Tool

Now that you have a format and the tools for briefing cases efficiently, the most important thing is to make the time spent in briefing profitable to you and to make the most advantageous use of the briefs you create. Of course, the briefs are invaluable for classroom reference when you are called upon to explain or analyze a particular case. However, they are also useful in reviewing for exams. A quick glance at the fact summary should bring the case to mind, and a rereading of the rule of law should enable you to go over the underlying legal concept in your mind, how it was applied in that particular case, and how it might apply in other factual settings.

As to the value to be derived from engaging in the briefing process itself, there is an immediate benefit that arises from being forced to sift through the essential facts and reasoning from the court's opinion and to succinctly express them in your own words in your brief. The process ensures that you understand the case and the point that it illustrates, and that means you will be ready to absorb further analysis and information brought forth in class. It also ensures you will have something to say when called upon in class. The briefing process helps develop a mental agility for getting to the *gist* of a case and for identifying, expounding on, and applying the legal concepts and issues found there. The briefing process is the mental process on which you must rely in taking law school examinations; it is also the mental process upon which a lawyer relies in serving his clients and in making his living.

Abbreviations for Briefs

acceptance	acp	offer	O
affirmed	aff	offeree	OE
answer	ans	offeror	OR
assumption of risk	a/r	ordinance	ord
attorney	atty	pain and suffering	p/s
beyond a reasonable doubt	b/r/d	parol evidence	p/e
bona fide purchaser	BFP	plaintiff	P
breach of contract	br/k	prima facie	p/f
cause of action	c/a	probable cause	p/c
common law	c/l	proximate cause	px/c
Constitution	Con	real property	r/p
constitutional	con	reasonable doubt	r/d
contract	K	reasonable man	r/m
contributory negligence	c/n	rebuttable presumption	rb/p
cross	x	remanded	rem
cross-complaint	x/c	res ipsa loquitur	RIL
cross-examination	x/ex	respondeat superior	r/s
cruel and unusual punishment	c/u/p	Restatement	RS
defendant	D	reversed	rev
dismissed	dis	Rule Against Perpetuities	RAP
double jeopardy	d/j	search and seizure	s/s
due process	d/p	search warrant	s/w
equal protection	e/p	self-defense	s/d
equity	eq	specific performance	s/p
evidence	ev	statute	S
exclude	exc	statute of frauds	S/F
exclusionary rule	exc/r	statute of limitations	S/L
felony	f/n	summary judgment	s/j
freedom of speech	f/s	tenancy at will	t/w
good faith	g/f	tenancy in common	t/c
habeas corpus	h/c	tenant	t
hearsay	hr	third party	TP
husband	H	third party beneficiary	TPB
injunction	inj	transferred intent	TI
in loco parentis	ILP	unconscionable	uncon
inter vivos	I/v	unconstitutional	unconst
joint tenancy	j/t	undue influence	u/e
judgment	judgt	Uniform Commercial Code	UCC
jurisdiction	jur	unilateral	uni
last clear chance	LCC	vendee	VE
long-arm statute	LAS	vendor	VR
majority view	maj	versus	v
meeting of minds	MOM	void for vagueness	VFV
minority view	min	weight of authority	w/a
Miranda rule	Mir/r	weight of the evidence	w/e
Miranda warnings	Mir/w	wife	W
negligence	neg	with	w/
notice	ntc	within	w/i
nuisance	nus	without	w/o
obligation	ob	without prejudice	w/o/p
obscene	obs	wrongful death	wr/d

Table of Cases

CHAPTER 1

Changing Concepts of Marriage and Family

Quick Reference Rules of Law

18. *Zablocki v. Redhail.* When a statutory classification significantly interferes with the right to marry, it is invalid unless there are sufficiently important state interests and it is closely tailored to effectuate only those interests.

City of Ladue v. Horn

City government (P) v. Unmarried cohabitants (D)

Mo. Ct. App., 720 S.W.2d 745 (1986).

NATURE OF CASE: Appeal of injunction enforcing a zoning ordinance.

FACT SUMMARY: A zoning ordinance enacted by the City of Ladue, Missouri (P), limited households to individuals related by blood or marriage.

🏛 RULE OF LAW
A municipality may limit households to individuals related by blood or marriage.

FACTS: The City of Ladue, Missouri (P), enacted a zoning ordinance limiting residential units to persons related by marriage or blood. Horn (D) and Jones (D) were an unmarried couple residing together. The City (P) demanded Horn (D) and Jones (D) vacate the residence and the couple refused. The City (P) then brought an action to enforce the ordinance and Horn (D) and Jones (D) counterclaimed that the ordinance was unconstitutional. The trial court issued an injunction mandating that they cease residing together and dismissed the counterclaim. Horn (D) and Jones (D) appealed the dismissal. Horn (D) and Jones (D) challenged the constitutionality of the ordinance on the basis that it violated their right to associate freely, right to privacy, and that the city did not have a compelling or rational justification for the ordinance.

ISSUE: May a municipality limit households to individuals related by blood or marriage?

HOLDING AND DECISION: (Crandall, J.) Yes. A municipality may limit households to individuals related by blood or marriage. Where a fundamental right is not involved, ordinances regulating civic matters such as health and public welfare are presumptively valid. The Constitution protects the right of families to reside together. However, living together on a long-term basis is not tantamount to marriage. When this sort of arrangement is involved, no fundamental right is implicated, and regulations thereon shall be valid if they rationally achieve their intended effects. Defendants argue that case law has expanded the definition of "family" to include their relationship, but that is not accurate. The ordinance defines family as limited to a relationship by blood or marriage and this court looks to the legislative definition in the ordinance for its definition of "family." The City (P) precisely defined "family" and excluded defendants' relationship from that definition. Here, Horn (D) and Jones (D) were not married, so no heightened standard of review is appropriate. The trial court found the ordinance to be rationally related to the promotion of civic welfare, and no reason for reversal exists. Affirmed.

▶ ANALYSIS

The major case in the constitutional jurisprudence of living arrangements is *Village of Belle Terre v. Boraas*, 416 U.S. 1 (1974). A similar ordinance was there attacked as violative of privacy. The Supreme Court rejected the challenge, holding that a city could legitimately favor the traditional family over alternative living arrangements.

■■■

Marvin v. Marvin (I)

Former live-in girlfriend (P) v. Ex-boyfriend (D)

Cal. Sup. Ct., 18 Cal. 3d 660, 557 P.2d 106 (1976) (en banc).

NATURE OF CASE: Appeal from the denial of enforcement of an oral contract.

FACT SUMMARY: Michelle Marvin (P) attempted to enforce an oral agreement to pool assets when she and Lee Marvin (D) ended their meretricious relationship.

🏛 RULE OF LAW
An oral contract to pool resources during a relationship is valid to the extent that it is not explicitly founded on the rendering of illicit sexual services.

FACTS: Michelle Marvin (P) and Lee Marvin (D) orally agreed to hold themselves out to the public as husband and wife and that she would give him companionship and act as homemaker, cook, and housekeeper. It was further agreed that in consideration for these services and Michelle's (P) giving up a lucrative singing career to devote her full time to these efforts, she and Lee (D) would pool all property acquired during the relationship. Lee (D) was still married at this time to Betty Marvin. Betty obtained a divorce several years later, which included a marital settlement agreement. Lee (D) asked Michelle (P) to leave approximately seven years after the relationship began, and he stopped supporting her. Michelle (P) brought a civil action to enforce the terms of the oral contract granting her a one-half interest in all the property held solely in Lee's (D) name which was acquired during the relationship. The court found, among other factors, that the oral contract was not valid since it was entered into while Lee (D) was still married and dealt with community property between Lee (D) and Betty. Michelle (P) appealed, alleging that to the extent an oral contract to pool resources is not founded on illicit sexual services it is enforceable.

ISSUE: Is an oral contract to pool resources during a relationship valid to the extent that it is not explicitly founded on the rendering of illicit sexual services?

HOLDING AND DECISION: (Tobriner, J.) Yes. An oral contract to pool resources during a relationship is valid to the extent that it is not explicitly founded on the rendering of illicit sexual services. All meretricious relationships are founded in part on sexual behavior, so the contract is unenforceable to the extent that sexual services are an explicit consideration for the agreement. This agreement does not need to satisfy the Statute of Frauds because it is not a marriage contract or prenuptial agreement. In fact, marriage is not contemplated at all. An express contract is not required here. The reasonable expectations of the parties, based on their conduct and the nature of the relationship, allows for an implied contract to pool resources or for a joint venture. An action in quantum meruit for the reasonable value of services rendered is appropriate in cases such as this where no express contract exists. Reversed and remanded.

CONCURRENCE AND DISSENT: (Clark, J.) As the majority states, recovery on the basis of either express or implied agreement is proper. The majority did not, however, need to allow quantum meruit and failed to offer adequate guidelines when it did allow it. An actual spouse could be denied recovery but now an unmarried cohabitant could recover under both equitable principles of contract and quantum meruit. If an express or implied agreement cannot be found, the majority should not impose economic obligations on parties.

▶ ANALYSIS

The major thrust of *Marvin* was that it recognizes that equitable rights and remedies are created in meretricious relationships. Besides illicit sex, if the contract restrains the parties from marrying others, this would be an unlawful consideration. Oral contracts were normally upheld prior to *Marvin* in California. Rarely were implied contracts or quantum meruit recovery allowed. "Property Rights Upon Termination of Unmarried Cohabitation," 90 Harv. L. Rev. 1708 (1977).

■■■

Quicknotes

PRENUPTIAL AGREEMENT An agreement entered into by two individuals in contemplation of marriage, determining their rights and interests in property upon dissolution or death.

QUANTUM MERUIT Equitable doctrine allowing recovery for labor and materials provided by one party, even though no contract was entered into, in order to avoid unjust enrichment by the benefited party.

STATUTE OF FRAUDS A statute that requires specified types of contracts to be in writing in order to be binding.

■■■

Marvin v. Marvin (III)

Former live-in girlfriend (P) v. Ex-boyfriend (D)

Cal. Ct. App., 122 Cal. App. 3d 871, 176 Cal. Reptr. 555 (1981).

NATURE OF CASE: Appeal from that portion of award of damages for economic rehabilitation.

FACT SUMMARY: Lee Marvin (D), who had lived with Michelle Marvin (P) without benefit of marriage, challenged the court's award of $104,000 to her for purposes of "economic rehabilitation" after their relationship ended.

RULE OF LAW
Under appropriate circumstances, an award of support after termination of a nonmarital relationship may be proper, and equitable remedies are available insofar as they would "protect the expectations of the parties" to the nonmarital relationship that has ended.

FACTS: The trial court in which Michelle Marvin (P) instituted her "palimony" action against Lee Marvin (D) found that she had benefited socially and economically from the relationship and had suffered no damage therefrom, even with respect to its termination by Lee Marvin (D). It also found that Lee Marvin (D) never had any agreement with her, implied or in fact, as to her sharing in his property or earnings or being maintained by him. It further found that Lee Marvin (D) had not been unjustly enriched by reason of the relationship or its termination and that he had never acquired anything of value from Michelle Marvin (P) by any wrongful act. Nonetheless, it awarded Michelle Marvin (P) $104,000 for economic rehabilitation after finding that it was unlikely she could resume the singing career she had dropped when she began living with Lee Marvin (D) and that it would probably take two years for her to gain skills and become self-supporting.

ISSUE: Under appropriate circumstances, may an award of support after termination of a nonmarital relationship be proper and are equitable remedies available insofar as they would "protect the expectations of the parties" to the nonmarital relationship that has ended?

HOLDING AND DECISION: (Cobey, J.) Yes. The opinion of the California Supreme Court in the first round of this case made it clear, in two footnotes, that under appropriate circumstances an award of support after termination of a nonmarital relationship was possible and that the evolution of equitable remedies to protect the expectations of the parties to a nonmarital relationship in cases in which existing remedies prove inadequate is proper. The problem here is that the facts in this case and the findings of the trial court give no basis for the use of such remedies. Such relief must be supported by some recognized underlying obligation in law or in equity. No basis in law or equity exists for the challenged rehabilitative award. Affirmed as modified.

ANALYSIS

Much of the criticism of the *Marvin* case was based on the assumption that it weakened the status of marriage. However, a lot of criticism was leveled at the *Marvin* case and its progeny for effectively reviving common law marriage. A number of courts that have followed the *Marvin* decision have expressly stated in their opinions that their decisions should not be so construed.

Quicknotes

EQUITABLE REMEDY A remedy that is based upon principles of fairness as opposed to rules of law; a remedy involving specific performance rather than money damages.

Hofstad v. Christie

Cohabitant who contributed more money (D) v. Cohabitant who did not (P)

Wyo. Sup. Ct., 2010 WY 134, 240 P.3d 816 (2010).

NATURE OF CASE: Appeal from the trial court's decision to partition real property as equal tenants in common.

FACT SUMMARY: Jerald Korwin Hofstad (D) and Cathryn Anne Christie (P) had an unmarried relationship for more than a decade, which resulted in the birth of two children and the purchase of a family home. Upon Christie's (P) suit for partition, the trial court awarded her equal equity as a tenant in common in the real property.

RULE OF LAW
An unmarried cohabitant can establish both a family relationship and donative intent to maintain that co-tenants share equally in property.

FACTS: For more than ten years, Jerald Korwin Hofstad (D) and Cathryn Anne Christie (P) were involved in an intimate relationship, lived together for extended periods of time, and produced two children, but never married. Upon separation, Christie (P) filed suit seeking partition of their home. While Christie (P) contributed little financially to the home's equity, the trial court found that there was a family relationship and donative intent that required a partition as equal tenants in common. Hofstad (D) appealed.

ISSUE: Can an unmarried cohabitant establish both a family relationship and donative intent to maintain that co-tenants share equally in property?

HOLDING AND DECISION: (Hill, J.) Yes. An unmarried cohabitant can establish both a family relationship and donative intent to maintain that co-tenants share equally in property. It is widely accepted that if the instrument does not specify the shares of each co-tenant, then it will be presumed that they take equal, undivided interests. This presumption may be rebutted by parole evidence, such as proof that the co-tenants contributed unequal amounts toward the purchase price of the property, and there is neither a family relationship among the co-tenants nor any evidence of donative intent on the part of those who contributed more than their pro-rata amounts toward the purchase price.

In the instant case, both parties agree that the home was held by them as tenants in common, inasmuch as the warranty deed did not specify a joint tenancy. Having established that Hofstad (D) contributed substantially more money that Christie (P) toward the property, the question is whether there is either a family relationship or evidence of donative intent on the part of Hofstad (D) or a lack thereof.

Although the term "family relationship" is by no means absolute, the parties did share a family relationship, largely by way of their sharing two children. They lived together on and off for approximately ten years, all while sharing an intimate relationship that resulted in the birth of their two children. Hofstad (D) argues there was no donative intent and that he did not gift Christie (P) one-half of the value of the home. Using the rules of co-tenancy, when the conveyance is taken in both names, the parties are presumed to share equally or to share based by donative intent or a family relationship. After reviewing the record, we agree with the district court based on the evidence that Hofstad (D) became engaged to Christie (P), represented to her that he would "change" and engage in counseling, and he furthered that they would be married within three months and that she would become co-owner or equal owner of the home. As conclusive evidence of Hofstad's (D) intent, he put Christie's (P) name on the deed. Affirmed.

▶ ANALYSIS

As common-law marriages do not exist in Wyoming, cohabitants are faced with real dilemmas on how to divide property upon the end of their relationships. In this case, the appellate court upheld the general rules of co-tenancy which presume an equal division of property, despite proof that one party contributed more financially than the other. Upon a showing that either a family relationship or donative intent existed, the court was unwilling to afford one party more equity than the other and upheld the default position of tenants in common. This case is a win for couples who have children and property to divide, where divorce proceedings are not available by virtue of their unmarried relationship.

Quicknotes

DONATIVE INTENT Donor's intent to make a gift.

PARTITION The division of property held by co-owners, granting each sole ownership of his or her share.

PRO RATA In proportion.

TENANTS IN COMMON Two or more people holding an interest in property, each with equal right to its use and possession; interests may be partitioned, sold, conveyed, or devised.

Ralph v. City of New Orleans

Citizens and taxpayers (P) v. City (D)

La. Ct. App., 4 So. 3d 146 (4th Cir. 2009).

NATURE OF CASE: Appeal from the grant of a motion for summary judgment.

FACT SUMMARY: The Plaintiffs (P), citizens and taxpayers in the City of New Orleans, filed suit seeking a declaration that the City and the City Council (D) acted without authority when they established a registry of domestic partnerships and subsequently extended health and other employment benefits to these couples.

🏛 RULE OF LAW
Recognition of domestic partnerships does not violate state law.

FACTS: Plaintiffs (P), citizens and taxpayers in the City of New Orleans, filed suit seeking a declaration that the City and the City Council (D) acted ultra vires and without statutory authority, when they provided for the registry of "Domestic Partnership," and subsequently used this registry as the basis for its extension of health insurance coverage and benefits to the unmarried "domestic partners" of City employees. Plaintiffs (P) sought to enjoin the City (D) from continuing to enforce the ordinances and policies relating to registry of domestic partnership and the extension of benefits to domestic partners of City (D) employees. Plaintiffs (P) and the City and City Council (D) filed cross Motions for Summary Judgment, and Plaintiffs (P) filed a Motion for Default. The trial court denied Plaintiffs' (P) motions and granted the City's (D) Motion for Summary Judgment, which then resulted in an appeal.

ISSUE: Does recognition of domestic partnerships violate state law?

HOLDING AND DECISION: (Armstrong, C.J.) No. Recognition of domestic partnerships does not violate state law. Plaintiffs (D) contend in their petition that the ordinances in question violate Article VI, § 9 of the Louisiana Constitution, which provides in pertinent part: "No local governmental subdivision shall . . . enact an ordinance governing private or civil relationships." Plaintiffs (P) also claim that the City's (D) actions violate a strong Louisiana public policy favoring marriage over unmarried cohabitation. The City (D) argues that the Domestic Partnership Registry does not govern private or civil relationships, that the City (D) is legally allowed to offer healthcare benefits to its employees, and that state has no stated public policy favoring marriage over unmarried cohabitation.

Declaration of domestic partnership is a form provided by the clerk of council whereby two people agree to be jointly responsible for basic living expenses incurred during the domestic partnership, and recites that all the other requirements for domestic partnership are met. Domestic partners are two people who have chosen to share one another's lives in an intimate and committed relationship of mutual caring, who live together and have signed a declaration of domestic partnership in which they have agreed to be jointly responsible for basic living expenses incurred during the domestic partnership, and have established their partnership under the applicable code section. "Live together" means the two people share the same residence. It is not necessary that the right to possess the residence be in both names. Two people may live together even if one or both have an additional separate living residence. Domestic partners do not cease to live together if one leaves the shared living residence but intends to return.

It is clear from the legislative history of the ordinance that it did not create the concept of domestic partnership, and was intended merely to acknowledge the previous and continuing existence of these arrangements, not to give them any particular legal status by setting forth a set of legal rights and obligations that would flow from the already existing relationships. The ordinance does not control the making and administration of domestic partnerships; it merely provides a mechanism whereby persons may register these partnerships in the City (D). The registry ordinance does not control, regulate or direct domestic partnerships. Again, it provides only a means for registering certain domestic partnerships that fit its parameters. Private contracts that might form domestic partnerships are not controlled, regulated or directed by the ordinance.

In the instant case, the right to regulate the private and civil relationships between the domestic partners who may choose to avail themselves of the registry provided for by the ordinance is not affected by the ordinance. Applying this careful scrutiny, the trial court's conclusion is not manifestly erroneous, clearly wrong, or contrary to law. The core issue is whether or not the creation of the registry "governs" private or civil relationships. While it may be argued that the registry ordinance recognizes the de facto existence of such relationships, careful scrutiny does not disclose clear evidence of "governance." The domestic partnership registry does not regulate the creation, maintenance or termination of the partnerships, but provides rules pursuant to which the partnerships may be registered. Applying the strict interpretation does not mean that the registry ordinance rules domestic partnerships by right or authority, exercises a directing or restraining influence over the partnerships, or

Continued on next page.

guides them. Registry is voluntary and confers no legal rights and obligations. The testimony adduced in connection with the consideration of the ordinance indicates that it was intended to be an "acknowledgement of the respect" to which domestic partners as a community are entitled, and an "acknowledgement of a situation that has existed for many years." Since the registry ordinance itself confers no special status, legal benefits or legal responsibilities to the registrants, there is an absence of indicia of governance.

Public policy favors provision of insurance in order to limit the government's exposure to provide public welfare benefits to uninsured persons. This ordinance does not affect the state's definition of marriage. Affirmed.

▶ ANALYSIS

The recognition of domestic partnerships came at a time when civil unions or the right to same sex marriage did not exist. As such, the City (P) sought a workaround solution by establishing the registry and then using it to afford those in domestic partnerships the same benefits given to married couples. Because the ordinance was narrowly tailored and did nothing more than establish the list, it did not violate any other provision of state law. As an end run to gaining recognition and benefits, the court sidestepped the larger political debate Plaintiffs (P) sought.

■═■

Quicknotes

MOTION FOR SUMMARY JUDGMENT Judgment rendered by a court in response to a motion by one of the parties, claiming that the lack of a question of material fact in respect to an issue warrants disposition of the issue without consideration by the jury.

■═■

B.S. v. F.B.

Civil union couple member (P) v. Civil union couple member (D)

N.Y. Sup. Ct., Westchester Cty., 25 Misc. 3d 520, 883 N.Y.S.2d 458 (2009).

NATURE OF CASE: Action for divorce by a same-sex couple which entered into a civil union.

FACT SUMMARY: B.S. (P) and F.B (D) were a same-sex couple who had a religious marriage ceremony in one state, entered into a civil union in another state, and ultimately sought a divorce in another.

🏛 RULE OF LAW
Civil unions are not treated as the same as marriage.

FACTS: B.S. (P) and F.B (D) lived together for over 14 years in a single family home, during which F.B. (D) paid essentially all of household bills. B.S (P) and F.B (D) had participated in a Buddhist "marriage" ceremony in New Mexico and later entered into a "civil union" in Vermont. Upon dissolution of the relationship, B.S. filed for divorce and pendente lite relief in New York. F.B. (D) filed a motion to dismiss, based on lack of subject matter jurisdiction and failure to state a claim.

ISSUE: Do courts hold that civil unions are treated the same as marriage?

HOLDING AND DECISION: (Walker, J.) No. Civil unions are not treated the same as marriage. B.S (P) commenced this action seeking a divorce from F.B. (D) for pendente lite relief. F.B. moved to dismiss the complaint for lack of subject matter jurisdiction and failure to state a valid cause of action. F.B. (D) does not deny the 14-year relationship with B.S. (P), the New Mexico "marriage" ceremony, or civil union in Vermont. F.B. (D) states that New York does not recognize same-sex marriage, and that there is no valid out-of-state marriage entered into by the parties that the state could recognize as a matter of comity.

First, there must be a determination of whether this court has subject matter jurisdiction to entertain the complaint. While New Mexico has a gender-neutral marriage statute, there is no statute or law that permits same-sex persons to marry. No marriage certificate has been offered by B.S. (P) to validate the parties "marriage". This court opines that as the relationship between B.S. (P) and F.B. (D) endured and recognizing the legal infirmities of their New Mexico "marriage ceremony," the parties sought to legitimize their status by entering into a "civil union" in Vermont. Vermont's civil union statute grants spousal legal benefits, protections, and responsibilities.

The question is whether a civil union contracted in Vermont may be dissolved by way of a matrimonial proceeding commenced in New York. First, this court finds that the parties' civil union is valid and properly contracted. F.B.'s

(D) challenge to the language of the statute and its application to the parties is incorrect. Second, the issue is whether there is statutory or legal authority to entertain the dissolution of the parties' union in New York. Migrating same-sex marriages and civil unions are increasingly the subject of litigation given the relatively few states that allow for same-sex marriages or civil unions. The dissolution cases present the classic conflict-of-law problem. Parties from a jurisdiction that offers civil unions are now domiciled in another state and want to dissolve the relationship. The current domicile state does not provide for civil unions, and the question becomes whether the courts of the state will recognize the civil union for the purposes of dissolving it.

New York has not attempted to create any method by which same-sex partners can "legalize" their relationships. In the absence of such a rule, regulation or statute, there is no precedent or authority to use as a standard to address B.S.'s (P) complaint. As a matter of comity, New York courts will generally recognize out-of-court marriages, including common-law marriages, unless barred by positive law (statute) or natural law (incest, polygamy) or where the marriage is otherwise offensive to public policy. While it seems clear from the facts that the parties to this action have a valid Vermont civil union, this court is constrained by precedent and legislative inaction and, therefore, cannot treat the civil union as a marriage. B.S. (P) verified complaint prays for an absolute divorce and for dissolution of the marriage, not for dissolution of the Vermont civil union. Defendant F.B's (D) motion to dismiss is granted without prejudice to plaintiff B.S.'s (P) right to file a verified complaint for dissolution of the Vermont civil union. Motion to dismiss granted.

▶ ANALYSIS

As the court notes, the proliferation of civil unions does not make them the same as marriage. The court's handling of the defendant's motion centered on the specific cause of action sought, namely a "divorce." By not foreclosing the plaintiff's request for relief, the court noted that it would certainly entertain a properly filed motion to dissolve the valid civil union between the parties.

Quicknotes

PENDENTE LITE A matter that is contingent on the disposition of a pending suit.

Continued on next page.

SUBJECT MATTER JURISDICTION The authority of the court to hear and decide actions involving a particular type of issue or subject.

Kerrigan v. Commissioner of Public Health

Eight same-sex couples (P) v. State of Connecticut (D)

Conn. Sup. Ct., 289 Conn. 135, 957 A.2d (2008).

NATURE OF CASE: Appeal from trial court's granting of summary judgment to state.

FACT SUMMARY: Connecticut's (D) legislature passed a civil union law that provided same-sex couples with all legal rights of spouses.

🏛 RULE OF LAW
Connecticut's (D) civil union law constitutes a violation of the state's guarantee of equal protection under the law.

FACTS: Connecticut's legislature passed a civil union law that provided same-sex couples with all legal rights of spouses. Eight same-sex couples (P) applied for marriage licenses in the town of Madison. The town denied the couples licenses and the couples (P) brought suit against the state (D) and the town clerk (D). The trial court granted summary judgment to the defendants and the plaintiffs appealed.

ISSUE: Does Connecticut's civil union law constitute a violation of the state's guarantee of equal protection under the law?

HOLDING AND DECISION: (Palmer, J.) Yes. Connecticut's (D) civil union law constitutes a violation of the state's (D) guarantee of equal protection under the law. We first hold the civil union law confers an inferior status on same-sex couples. This inferior status constitutes a constitutionally cognizable injury. We must now determine if the classification meets the state's (D) constitutional requirements. Sexual orientation is a quasi-suspect classification, based on the long history of purposeful discrimination toward gay persons. Laws impacting gay persons are therefore subject to heightened scrutiny. The state (D) presents two reasons why the legislature has prohibited same-sex marriages. First, the civil union law will promote uniformity with the laws of other jurisdictions. The state (D) has offered no explanation of this alleged governmental interest. The second reason is to preserve the definition of marriage as that of one man and one woman. We must determine if the reasons underlying the traditional definition of marriage satisfy our constitution. Tradition alone and moral disapproval of same-sex marriage are insufficient reasons to deny same-sex couples the right to marry. Moreover, the state's (D) position that the judiciary should refrain from this public policy debate is unavailing. We are presented with a constitutional violation based on the state's (D) civil union law. We are not asked to create a new fundamental right. Instead, we are applying our well established equal protec-

tion jurisprudence to the statute at issue. Here, the state (D) cannot specify any reason to deny same-sex couples the right to marry. The conventional definition of marriage must yield to a more contemporary one. The trial court's judgment is reversed and the case remanded.

▶ ANALYSIS

Connecticut (D) became the fourth state to legalize same-sex marriage with this decision. The legal basis for the decision purports to rest on an equal protection analysis. However, a reading of the decision reveals the court melded equal protection reasoning with a fundamental rights analysis. Rather than analyzing whether any fundamental rights were implicated, the court placed the burden on the state to defend the traditional definition of marriage. The court then returned to an equal protection analysis and concluded the civil union law violates equal protection by denying same-sex couples a right enjoyed by heterosexual couples.

Quicknotes

EQUAL PROTECTION CLAUSE A constitutional provision that each person be guaranteed the same protection of the laws enjoyed by other persons in like circumstances.

FUNDAMENTAL RIGHT A liberty that is either expressly or impliedly provided for in the United States Constitution, the deprivation or burdening of which is subject to a heightened standard of review.

QUASI-SUSPECT CLASS A class of persons who historically have been subjected to discriminatory treatment.

Reynolds v. United States

Bigamist (D) v. Federal government (P)

98 U.S. 145 (1878).

NATURE OF CASE: Appeal from conviction for bigamy.

FACT SUMMARY: Reynolds (D) argued that, as a Mormon, he should not have to comply with federal legislation prohibiting polygamy.

RULE OF LAW
The constitutional guarantee of religious freedom does not protect the practice of polygamy.

FACTS: Reynolds (D), a resident of the Territory of Utah, married another woman while still married to his first wife. The Government (P) prosecuted him for bigamy. At trial, he argued that, as a Mormon, it was his duty to practice polygamy and he had received permission to do so from the authorities in his church. Reynolds (D) also argued that since he was motivated by religious belief, the requisite criminal intent to commit bigamy was lacking. He was convicted, the Supreme Court of the Territory affirmed, and he appealed.

ISSUE: Does the constitutional guarantee of religious freedom protect the practice of polygamy?

HOLDING AND DECISION: (Waite, C.J.) No. The constitutional guarantee of religious freedom does not protect the practice of polygamy. Marriage is a civil contract and usually regulated by law. Historically, under common law, a second marriage was always considered to be void. More recently, Congress has decided that plural marriage will not be permitted. Those who make polygamy a part of their religion are not excepted from the operation of the statute. Otherwise, religious belief would supersede the law of the land, and every citizen would become a law unto himself. In this case, every act necessary to constitute the crime was knowingly done by Reynolds (D). Affirmed.

ANALYSIS

The Supreme Court cited the above case in support of its holding in *Employment Div. v. Smith*, 485 U.S. 660 (1988), that a state could deny unemployment benefits to state workers who used illegal drugs. The protection that the First Amendment provides, stated the Court, did not extend to conduct that a state had validly proscribed. Since *Reynolds* was decided, multiple marriages have come to be treated as criminal or at least voidable in all fifty states. However, small polygamous communities remain in Arizona, Utah, and elsewhere.

Quicknotes

FIRST AMENDMENT Prohibits Congress from enacting any law respecting an establishment of religion, prohibiting the free exercise of religion, abridging freedom of speech or the press, the right of peaceful assembly and the right to petition for a redress of grievances.

POLYGAMY The crime of having many wives or husbands at the same time, or more than one wife or husband at the same time.

Catholic Charities of Sacramento Inc. v. Superior Court

Social service organization (P) v. Trial court (D)

Cal. Sup. Ct., 32 Cal. 4th 527, 85 P.3d 67, *cert. denied*, 125 S. Ct. 53 (2004).

NATURE OF CASE: Appeal from denial of writ of mandate to issue a preliminary injunction.

FACT SUMMARY: California passed legislation requiring health insurance drug benefit plans to include coverage for prescription contraception. Religious employers could exempt themselves from offering such coverage if contraceptives violated the tenets of their faith. Catholic Charities of Sacramento Inc. (P) could not qualify for an exemption and so challenged the constitutionality of the legislation.

RULE OF LAW

Legislation does not offend the Constitution if it relieves its burdens on religious exercise by making accommodations for religious entities.

FACTS: The California Legislature enacted the Women's Contraception Equity Act ("WCEA") in 1999 to address inequalities in the financial burden on women for contraception and prenatal expenses. The WCEA required health insurers offering drug benefits to include prescription contraception drugs in the plan. Employers objecting to contraception in general could purchase drug benefit plans without contraceptive coverage if the organization met the WCEA definition of a "religious employer." This exemption was included primarily at the urging of the Roman Catholic Church because of the Church's historical stance against the use or promotion of contraception. Catholic Charities of Sacramento Inc. (Catholic Charities) (P), a social service organization claiming ties to the Roman Catholic Church, sought to qualify under the WCEA exemption. Catholic Charities (P) argued it could not offer contraception benefits to its employees because it operated under Roman Catholic guidelines although it was an independent corporation from the Roman Catholic Church. Catholic Charities (P) admittedly did not qualify for the exemption because it did not meet any of the four requirements to be considered a "religious employer." Catholic Charities (P) determined it had no choice but to seek a declaratory judgment that the WCEA was an unconstitutional interference with the religion clauses of the federal and state constitutions. Catholic Charities (P) also filed for a preliminary injunction to prevent enforcement of the WCEA. The Superior Court (D) denied the motion for a preliminary injunction and Catholic Charities (P) filed a petition for writ of mandate. The court of appeal denied the writ and Catholic Charities (P) appealed.

ISSUE: Does legislation offend the Constitution if it relieves its burdens on religious exercise by making accommodations for religious entities?

HOLDING AND DECISION: (Werdegar, J.) No. Legislation does not offend the Constitution if it relieves its burdens on religious exercise by making accommodations for religious entities. The WCEA requires a "religious employer" to meet four criteria: (1) the entity's purpose is the inculcation of religious values; (2) employees are primarily of the same religious beliefs; (3) the entity serves persons with primarily the same religious beliefs; and (4) the entity is a nonprofit exempt from filing an annual return with the IRS. Catholic Charities (P) concedes it does not meet any of the four requirements. It is a social services entity rather than a religious entity and is church-backed rather than a church. It employs people with a variety of religious faiths and serves a majority of non-Catholics. Finally, it is a 501(c)(3) but is not exempt from filing an annual return with the IRS. Catholic Charities (P) must therefore refuse to offer prescription drug coverage of any sort or demonstrate the unconstitutionality of the WCEA to avoid its obligations. First, the WCEA does not impermissibly interfere with church property because Catholic Charities (P) is not a church. Next, Catholic Charities (P) argues that the WCEA's religious exemption tenets cannot be defined by the government because the government is prohibited from making distinctions between secular and religious activities. This argument fails because the government is allowed to make such distinctions to relieve burdens upon religious exercise. Catholic Charities (P) argues that the WCEA makes distinctions to burden the Catholic Church by allowing governmental inquiry into an entity's members' and clients' religious beliefs. This might be an appropriate argument if such an entangling inquiry would be made to Catholic Charities (P), but plaintiff openly admits that it does not qualify for the exemption; thus, no inquiry is likely to ensue. The WCEA is facially neutral because it applies to all employers unless the employer qualifies for the exemption. Further, the WCEA does not discriminate in application against the Catholic Church because it specifically allows for any burden upon a religious entity to be relieved under the exemption. Catholic Charities (P) argues that the WCEA was enacted to close a "Catholic gap" in insurance benefits, and the legislation is focused on forcing compliance by Catholic social service agencies and Catholic hospitals. The "gap," referenced in legislative history, is actually the gap between insured Californians with prescription contraceptive coverage and those without. It is not referring to Catholic entities at all. Legislators did consider broadening the exemption to include more Catholic-based entities, but did not do so. It treats Catholic-based entities

Continued on next page.

the same as all other employers and is more favorable to exempt Catholic organizations. This is acceptable and permissible. Finally, Catholic Charities (P) argues that the definition of "religious employer" is arbitrary and thus fails the rational basis test. The exemption itself is rational because it bars government interference with religious entities. A problem does arise with the requirement that a religious entity serve those with the same religious beliefs. This could result in a church soup kitchen only able to serve those sharing its religion instead of all those who are hungry. The legislature should consider this issue. It does not, however, aid Catholic Charities (P) because that entity admittedly does not qualify for the exemption. Affirmed.

▶ ANALYSIS

As the court notes, the legislature had considered broadening the exemption to include Catholic-based charities and hospitals, but in the end did not do so. Many groups filed amicus briefs in support of Catholic Charities based on the belief that the government should not force religious-minded entities to provide a service to employees that the entity considered a religious sin. Catholic Charities itself argued that contraception was today's governmental requirement and payment for abortion services could be tomorrow's. Catholic Charities could have chosen to end prescription drug coverage for its employees in its entirety but it did not want to be forced to choose between that option and its religious beliefs. The many groups filing amicus briefs on behalf of the state argued that equity in insurance coverage was of greater benefit to a greater number of state residents than the slight imposition on a limited number of employers who did not qualify for the exemption. Catholic Charities appealed to the U.S. Supreme Court, but the Court denied certiorari.

■══■

Quicknotes

AMICUS BRIEF A brief submitted by a third party, not a party to the action, that contains information for the court's consideration in conformity with its position.

RATIONAL BASIS REVIEW A test employed by the court to determine the validity of a statute in equal protection actions, whereby the court determines whether the challenged statute is rationally related to the achievement of a legitimate state interest.

■══■

Anastasi v. Anastasi

Ex-girlfriend (P) v. Ex-boyfriend (D)

544 F. Supp. 866 (D.N.J. 1982).

NATURE OF CASE: Action alleging breach of support agreement.

FACT SUMMARY: Mrs. Anastasi (P) had instituted an action alleging that Mr. Anastasi (D), to whom she was not married, had breached an agreement to support her for the rest of her life, and the issue arose as to whether or not the domestic relations exception to federal jurisdiction applied.

🏛 RULE OF LAW
A palimony case applying New Jersey law is a domestic relations case within the domestic relations exception to federal jurisdiction.

FACTS: When Mrs. Anastasi (P) brought a palimony action against Mr. Anastasi (D), she alleged that he breached an agreement whereby he was "to provide plaintiff with all of her financial support and needs for the rest of her life." Mr. Anastasi (D) removed the case to federal court on the basis of diversity of citizenship. On the basis of then-existing New Jersey case law, the judge found that New Jersey law treated the action as one akin to a contract, rather than a domestic relations case. Thus, he ruled that the domestic relations exception to federal jurisdiction did not apply and that remand to the state courts was not required. Subsequently, the New Jersey Supreme Court reversed some of that case law, and the judge reconsidered whether, in light of that change in posture, the case should be remanded to the state court.

ISSUE: Is a palimony case applying New Jersey law a domestic relations case within the domestic relations exception to federal jurisdiction?

HOLDING AND DECISION: (Debevoise, J.) Yes. The most recent decisions of the New Jersey Supreme Court with regard to palimony cases leave no doubt that a palimony case applying New Jersey law is a domestic relations case within the domestic relations exception to federal jurisdiction. These decisions make it clear that New Jersey considers itself to have a significant state interest in the consensual live-in relationship and that protection of this interest requires the trial court in a palimony case to make the same kinds of inquiries that have traditionally brought into play the domestic relations exception to federal jurisdiction. They are the kinds of inquiries and judgments which the state courts are best equipped to handle and which, under the domestic relations exception to federal jurisdiction, may not be made by federal courts. Remanded to the Superior Court of New Jersey.

▶ ANALYSIS

The relative isolation of domestic relations law from federal court scrutiny was, many believe, one of the main reasons that area of the law remained so immune from reform and change until recent years. The domestic relations exception to federal jurisdiction stemmed from dictum in *Barber v. Barber*, 62 U.S. (21 How.) 582 (1858), and is strongly advocated and defended by many commentators.

■══■

Fisher v. Fisher

Married wife (P) v. Unmarried husband (D)

N.Y. Ct. App., 250 N.Y. 313, 165 N.E. 460 (1929).

NATURE OF CASE: Appeal in action for separation.

FACT SUMMARY: In an action for a separation, the primary issue was whether or not Mrs. Fisher (P) and Mr. Fisher (D) had been duly married when the captain of a steamship bound from New York to England performed a marriage ceremony some 40 miles out from the port of New York.

🏛 RULE OF LAW
On board a ship at sea, there is a law of marriage common to all nations that pronounces valid all consensual marriages between a man and a woman who are, in the view of all civilized people, competent to marry.

FACTS: In her action for separation, Mrs. Fisher (P) alleged that she and Mr. Fisher (D) had been duly married on October 24, 1925. Mr. Fisher (D) denied that allegation, claiming that the marriage ceremony was not valid. They had been married by the captain of a steamship bound from New York to England, the ship being some 40 miles out from the port of New York at the time of the ceremony. Mr. Fisher (D), who had been divorced by his previous wife for adultery, was, at the time, precluded by the laws of New York from marrying again as long as the wife who had divorced him for adultery remained alive. Mr. Fisher (D) appealed the decision holding the marriage valid and granting Mrs. Fisher (P) a separation.

ISSUE: Is there a law of marriage on board a ship at sea?

HOLDING AND DECISION: (Kellogg, J.) Yes. There is on board a ship at sea a law of marriage. It is the law common to all nations, the common law of all Christendom, which pronounces valid all consensual marriages between a man and a woman who are, in the view of all civilized people, competent to marry. Thus, the important question here is whether this marriage, although not specifically sanctioned by the law of any state, was condemned by a controlling law of any state. The laws of New York, which would condemn it, did not follow the ship, whose ownership was in an institution domiciled in the District of Columbia. Furthermore, Congress has recognized, in passing various laws, that there is a law of marriage on board a ship at sea, notwithstanding the absence of applicable municipal laws. Thus, the marriage here was valid. Affirmed.

▶ ANALYSIS

In a well publicized case, actress Terry Moore claimed that she had married Howard Hughes in a ceremony performed on a yacht off the coast of California. The Texas court held she was estopped from asserting this as a valid marriage in that no marriage license had been issued and she had subsequently been married to three other men. She eventually settled her claim against the Hughes estate for a substantial sum. *Moore v. Neff*, Tex. Ct. App., 629 S.W.2d 827 (1982).

■▬■

Griswold v. Connecticut

Birth control advisors (D) v. State (P)

381 U.S. 479 (1965).

NATURE OF CASE: Appeal from conviction for making available information and methods of birth control.

FACT SUMMARY: Griswold (D) and Buxton (D) gave information to married couples and prescribed methods of contraception best suited to them, for which they were held in violation of Connecticut (P) law.

RULE OF LAW
Various guarantees of the Bill of Rights create rights of privacy, and marriage is a private right protected by the Constitution.

FACTS: Griswold (D), executive director of Planned Parenthood, and Buxton (D), a Yale Medical School professor and medical director of Planned Parenthood, gave information, instruction, and medical advice to married persons regarding birth-control methods. They were arrested and convicted for violating a state law of Connecticut (P) prohibiting the use of anything that would prevent conception and punishing any person aiding another in such use. Griswold (D) and Buxton (D) argued that the statutes violated the Due Process Clause of the Fourteenth Amendment by interfering with the private relationships between physician and patient and between husband and wife.

ISSUE: Do various guarantees of the Bill of Rights create rights of privacy, and is marriage a private right protected by the Constitution?

HOLDING AND DECISION: (Douglas, J.) Yes. The First Amendment casts a penumbra under which privacy is protected from governmental intrusion as seen in the freedom of association. The Third Amendment, by prohibiting the quartering of soldiers in people's homes, protects privacy. The Fourth Amendment explicitly protects the security of the home and possessions. The Fifth Amendment creates a personal zone of privacy by protecting against self-incrimination. The Ninth Amendment guarantees that rights not specifically mentioned in the Constitution are still to be retained by the people. Under the penumbrae of these amendments, a right of privacy exists. This case deals with a relationship within that zone of privacy. The law in question, by forbidding the use of contraceptives rather than regulating manufacture and sale, has "a maximum destructive impact upon that relationship." When there is a governmental purpose to control or prevent activities constitutionally subject to state regulation, it cannot be done unnecessarily broadly. Reversed.

CONCURRENCE: (Goldberg, J.) Purposes underlying the specific guarantees of the Constitution demonstrate that the rights to marital privacy are fundamental, basic, personal rights retained by the people under the Ninth Amendment.

ANALYSIS

This is the well-known "penumbra" case in which a general right to privacy was first specifically enumerated. Here, marriage was found to be a right of privacy older than the nation itself, "an association that promotes a way of life, not causes; a harmony in living, not political faiths; a bilateral loyalty, not commercial or social projects." In that sense, the idea of police snooping about the marital bedroom for evidence of use of contraceptives is "repulsive to the notions of privacy surrounding the marriage relationship."

Eisenstadt v. Baird

County sheriff (P) v. Lecturer (D)

405 U.S. 438 (1972).

NATURE OF CASE: Appeal from conviction for dispensing contraceptives.

FACT SUMMARY: Baird (D) was arrested when he gave a package of Emko vaginal foam to a young woman attending a lecture he was giving at Boston University.

🏛 RULE OF LAW
A state may not constitutionally discriminate between persons on the basis of their marital status in regulating the distribution of birth control devices.

FACTS: Baird (D) was convicted of exhibiting contraceptives during the course of a lecture he gave at Boston University and for giving a package of Emko vaginal foam to a young woman at the end of the lecture. His conviction for exhibiting contraceptives was unanimously set aside by the Massachusetts Supreme Judicial Court as a violation of the First Amendment, but the conviction for giving away the foam was affirmed. Under Massachusetts law, a person who gave away any contraceptive was liable for a maximum of five years imprisonment with the exception of physicians, who could prescribe contraceptives to married persons, and pharmacists, who could furnish contraceptives to any married person by prescription. The court of appeals ordered Baird (D) discharged. Eisenstadt (P), the sheriff of Suffolk County, appealed.

ISSUE: May a state constitutionally discriminate between persons on the basis of their marital status in regulating the distribution of birth control devices?

HOLDING AND DECISION: (Brennan, J.) No. A state may not constitutionally discriminate between persons on the basis of their marital status in regulating the distribution of birth control devices. For a statutory classification not to be violative of the Equal Protection Clause, it must be reasonable, not arbitrary, and must rest upon some ground of difference having a fair and substantial relation to the object of the legislation, so that all persons similarly circumstanced shall be treated alike. Here, there was no ground of difference that rationally explained the different treatment accorded married and unmarried persons under the Massachusetts law. The statute, viewed as a contraception prohibition per se, violates the rights of single persons under the Equal Protection Clause of the Fourteenth Amendment. The classification is unreasonable and arbitrary. It cannot be said that deterrence of premarital sex may reasonably be regarded as a purpose of this law, when fornication is classified as a misdemeanor with a maximum sentence of three months, and the result may

be the birth of an unwanted child. While married persons receive contraceptives, they are not deterred from engaging in illicit sexual relations with unmarried persons. It is unreasonable to punish an aider and abettor to fornication twenty times as harshly in length of prison term than the fornicator himself. If the purpose of the statute is to protect the health of the community by regulating distribution of harmful articles, the law would be both discriminatory and overbroad. A physician who can prescribe for married persons should be able to do so for single persons. Additionally, not all forms of contraception are harmful to health. Whatever right of access to contraception an individual may have, that right must be the same for the unmarried and the married alike. The right of privacy goes to the individual, married or single, to be free from unwarranted governmental intrusion into matters so fundamentally affecting persons, such as the decision to have children. Affirmed.

▶ ANALYSIS

One concurring opinion indicated that if the contraceptive given away had been birth control pills, it would have been a different question as Emko foam is a widely distributed, nonprescription product. The advent of the "pill" itself has conceived a new area of tort litigation. Causes of action have been sustained where a prescription for the pill was incorrectly filled with tranquilizers, and where the pill was alleged to have caused genetic defects in children born after discontinuance of the pill.

Quicknotes

EQUAL PROTECTION CLAUSE A constitutional provision that each person be guaranteed the same protection of the laws enjoyed by other persons in like circumstances.

FOURTEENTH AMENDMENT Declares that no state shall make or enforce any law that shall abridge the privileges and immunities of citizens of the United States. No state shall deny to any person within its jurisdiction the equal protection of the laws.

Roe v. Wade

Pregnant woman (P) v. District attorney (D)

410 U.S. 113 (1973).

NATURE OF CASE: Appeal from denial of injunctive relief to restrain enforcement of antiabortion statutes.

FACT SUMMARY: Roe (P), a single woman and pregnant, sought to enjoin the enforcement of Texas statutes making it illegal to perform an abortion except to save the life of the mother.

🏛 RULE OF LAW
Antiabortion statutes, which prohibit the abortion procedure except where necessary to save the life of the mother, are vague and violative of the right to privacy.

FACTS: Roe (P) was an unmarried, pregnant woman who wished to terminate her pregnancy by safe, clinical means. However, she was a resident of Texas, where abortions were illegal except to save the life of the mother. Roe (P), unthreatened by her pregnancy, alleged that she could not afford to travel to another state where a safe abortion could be legally obtained. She claimed the Texas statutes were unconstitutionally vague and abridged her right to personal privacy. The district court found the statutes unconstitutional but denied injunctive relief. Both sides appealed, Wade (D) being the Dallas County District Attorney.

ISSUE: Are antiabortion statutes, which prohibit the abortion procedure except where necessary to save the life of the mother, vague and violative of the right to privacy?

HOLDING AND DECISION: (Blackmun, J.) Yes. Antiabortion statutes, which prohibit the abortion procedure except where necessary to save the life of the mother, are vague and violative of the right to privacy. Historically, legislation against abortion is a fairly recent development in the law and reached its most severe point in the late 19th century. There are divergent views on when abortion should be necessary and when life begins. Reasons advanced for abortion laws include discouraging illicit sexual activity, to protect the health of the pregnant woman, and to protect prenatal life. It is not necessary to determine when life begins as where there is at least potential life involved, the state has an interest beyond the protection of the pregnant woman alone. A zone of privacy has been found in the Constitution, but it covers only personal rights that can be deemed "fundamental" or "implicit to a concept of ordered liberty." The right of privacy is invaded when the state would impose upon a pregnant woman a complete denial of her choice to terminate her pregnancy. Children could be distressful to a woman's life physically or psychologically. These factors should be considered by a woman and her physician. Even though there is a right to privacy, there may be appropriate occasions where state regulation in areas protected by that right may be appropriate. Thus, the right of personal privacy includes the abortion decision, but this right is not unqualified and must be considered against important state interests in regulation. Examination of the word "person" in the Constitution does not show it to apply to the unborn. "The unborn have never been recognized in the law as persons in the whole sense." The interests of the woman and the state are separate and distinct, and each grows in substantiality as the pregnant woman approaches term, and, at a point during pregnancy, each becomes compelling. In light of current medical knowledge with respect to the state's important and legitimate interest in the mother's health, the end of the first trimester of pregnancy is the point where that interest arises. It is during that period when the mortality rate from abortion is less than in normal childbirth. But after the first trimester, the state may regulate abortion to the extent it reasonably relates to protection and preservation of the mother's health. Prior to this point, the mother, with her physician, is free to determine without state regulation whether or not to terminate her pregnancy. The state's interest arises at the point of fetal viability, where the fetus can survive outside the mother's womb. The Texas statute is far too broad. There is no distinction between procedures performed early in pregnancy and later on. It limits abortion only to saving the mother's life. Thus, during the first trimester of pregnancy, no abortion regulation is permitted. During the second trimester, reasonable regulation to protect maternal health is allowable. Only in the last trimester may there be a complete ban on abortion except where necessary to protect the mother's health.

▌ ANALYSIS

A companion complaint, filed by John and Mary Doe, a married couple (alleging that Mary, because of health reasons, could not use contraceptive measures nor risk pregnancy, thus facing the need for an abortion), was dismissed for being too speculative. In the companion case of *Doe v. Bolton*, 410 U.S. 179 (1973), three procedural conditions of the Georgia abortion statute were invalidated under the Fourteenth Amendment. The first was that a hospital accredited by the joint committee on accreditation of hospitals was the only place an abortion could be performed; the second that there be advance approval of the hospital medical staff committee where the abortion was to be performed; and the third that two other physi-

Continued on next page.

cians concur in writing to the performing physician's opinion that an abortion should be performed. The Court held there was unreasonable interference with the mother's right to privacy in this scheme.

∎══∎

Quicknotes

FOURTEENTH AMENDMENT Declares that no state shall make or enforce any law that shall abridge the privileges and immunities of citizens of the United States. No state shall deny to any person within its jurisdiction the equal protection of the laws.

RIGHT TO PRIVACY Those personal liberties or relationships that are protected against unwarranted governmental interference.

∎══∎

Gonzales v. Carhart

United States Attorney General (D) v. Physician (P)

550 U.S. 124 (2007).

NATURE OF CASE: Appeal from denial of constitutional challenge to partial-birth abortion legislation.

FACT SUMMARY: Congress enacted the Partial-Birth Abortion Ban Act of 2003 to regulate a particular abortion procedure involving the partial birth of the fetus prior to aborting it. Plaintiffs challenged its constitutionality, arguing the Act was void for vagueness because it proscribed a majority of abortion procedures rather than the specific procedure intended, was overbroad, and was facially invalid.

🏛 RULE OF LAW

Legislation restricting access to a specific abortion method does not have to include a health exception for the mother if reasonable and viable alternatives exist.

FACTS: The vast majority of abortions in the United States occur during the first trimester of pregnancy and involve the vacuum aspiration method of abortion. The majority of the remaining abortions occur in the second trimester of pregnancy and involve the "dilation and evacuation" ("D&E") method of abortion. A variation on the D&E is the "intact D&E" in which the physician "extracts the fetus intact or largely intact" and then crushes the skull, extracts brain matter, or decapitates the fetus to complete the abortion procedure. The intact D&E is sometimes also referred to as partial-birth abortion. In 2003, Congress enacted the Partial-Birth Abortion Ban Act of 2003 (the "Act") in response to the rather "gruesome and medically unnecessary" intact D&E procedure. Plaintiffs challenged the constitutionality of the Act. A similar law had been passed in Nebraska and challenged in *Stenberg v. Carhart*, 530 U.S. 914 (2000). The U.S. Supreme Court held that law was unconstitutional, in part, because it lacked a health exception for the mother. Here, the district court found the Act unconstitutional because it lacked a health exception for the mother and was overbroad in its language including D&E rather than just intact D&E. The Eighth Circuit affirmed on the basis of the missing health exception. Planned Parenthood also challenged the constitutionality of the Act. That district court found the Act unconstitutionally vague, that it imposed an undue burden on a woman's right to terminate her pregnancy, and it lacked a *Stenberg* health exception. The Ninth Circuit affirmed on all grounds. The Supreme Court granted certiorari.

ISSUE: Must legislation restricting access to a specific abortion method include a health exception for the mother if reasonable and viable alternatives exist?

HOLDING AND DECISION: (Kennedy, J.) No. Legislation restricting access to a specific abortion method does not have to include a health exception for the mother if reasonable and viable alternatives exist. The *Planned Parenthood v. Casey* joint opinion, for all of its flaws, laid down the central premise that the state has a "legitimate and substantial interest in preserving and promoting fetal life." *Planned Parenthood of Southeastern Pa. v. Casey*, 505 U.S. 833 (1992). Affirmation here of the courts of appeals would repudiate that rule. This Court must evaluate the Act to determine if it promotes the federal government's legitimate interest in protecting fetal life. The Act is not void for vagueness nor overbroad in its application. It specifically states what abortion method is prohibited and specifically describes what must occur for the abortion method to constitute partial-birth abortion. The Act further requires the physician to knowingly commit an overt act other than delivery that kills the fetus. Physicians are reasonably informed of what act will result in criminal prosecution. If the physician sets out to do a D&E rather than an intact D&E or a method that involves deliberately choosing to remove the fetus in pieces, then the physician will not be prosecuted under this statute. The Act materially departs from *Stenberg* in adding an overt-act requirement. The evidence supports the finding that physicians do not accidentally perform an intact D&E. The vast majority of D&E procedures will remain valid under this Act because a physician must knowingly perform the intact D&E to be in violation of the statute. The Act is a reasonable result of Congress's legitimate interest in respecting life and the emotionally fraught decision to have an abortion. Women often suffer regret and emotional devastation after the choice to abort. Physicians as a result often do not fully explain the process to patients. Such a method is simply not medically necessary, especially where the mother is not able to make a fully informed choice. The next issue is the lack of a health exception for the mother. Medical evidence is divided on the topic of whether an intact D&E is ever medically necessary to preserve the health or life of a mother. The Act survives because Congress can act in the face of medical uncertainty and a D&E is a reasonable, viable alternative that remains to be allowed. Reversed.

CONCURRENCE: (Thomas, J.) The Court's prior abortion precedent has no constitutional basis.

DISSENT: (Ginsburg, J.) The majority's decision demeans *Casey* and *Roe v. Wade*, 410 U.S. 113 (1973). It accepts federal interference in a medical procedure

Continued on next page.

involving a woman's dignity and choice to bear or not bear a child. The state must not unduly subject a woman to a risk to her health or life and this Court previously supported that stance in *Stenberg*. The Act here is no different, recites factual inaccuracies, and Congress found no medical consensus that the procedure is never medically necessary. Congress also made no provisions to require physicians to fully inform their patients so that the patients could make the decision about the procedure. The majority instead relies on the supposed fragility of women and their emotional inability to decide for themselves on medical procedures. Today the Court deprives women of their right to make a choice. It is irrational to say that the Partial-Birth Abortion Act furthers any legitimate government interest.

▶ ANALYSIS

Pro-choice activists decried this decision as opening the doors for greater state intervention in abortion and other medical procedures. Pro-life activities acclaimed the ruling as a potential gateway to overturning *Roe v. Wade*. In its wake, several states have passed, or are in the process of passing, abortion-restriction legislation.

■▬■

Lawrence v. Texas

Homosexual man (D) v. State (P)

539 U.S. 558 (2003).

NATURE OF CASE: Appeal from convictions for deviate sexual intercourse and denial of constitutional challenges.

FACT SUMMARY: Two gay men (D) were arrested while engaging in a sexual act in their private home and charged with having deviate sexual intercourse. They (D) argued that the charging statute was unconstitutional, but the contentions were rejected. The men (D) appealed to the court of appeals. The constitutional arguments were again rejected, and the convictions affirmed. The U.S. Supreme Court then granted certiorari review.

RULE OF LAW
The Equal Protection Clause of the Fourteenth Amendment protects freedom to engage in private conduct among heterosexual and homosexual partners.

FACTS: Lawrence (D) and his homosexual lover, Garner (D), were engaged in sexual acts in the privacy of Lawrence's (D) home. Police officers responded to a reported weapons disturbance and observed Lawrence and Garner in a sexual act. Police arrested both men (D), and they were charged under a Texas statute with deviate sexual intercourse with a member of the same sex. The men (D) argued that the charging statute was a violation of the Equal Protection Clause of the Fourteenth Amendment and the Texas Constitution. They (D) pleaded nolo contendere to the charges. The trial court rejected the constitutional arguments, and Lawrence (D) appealed to the court of appeals. The court rejected the constitutional contentions and affirmed the convictions. Lawrence (D) appealed to the U.S. Supreme Court, which granted certiorari review.

ISSUE: Does the Equal Protection Clause of the Fourteenth Amendment protect freedom to engage in private conduct among heterosexual and homosexual partners?

HOLDING AND DECISION: (Kennedy, J.) Yes. The Equal Protection Clause of the Fourteenth Amendment protects freedom to engage in private conduct among heterosexual and homosexual partners. Consideration of the facts requires a reconsideration of *Bowers v. Hardwick*, 478 U.S. 186 (1986). The primary difference between *Bowers* and the instant case is that the Georgia statute in *Bowers* prohibited the proscribed sexual conduct between any persons, while the Texas statute prohibits the proscribed sexual conduct only between members of the same sex. Homosexual persons have the liberty to define their relationship and experience it within a private home

just as heterosexual persons do, absent injury to the individual or abuse to a legally protected institution. Traditional views of a practice as immoral are insufficient to support continued prohibition, and intimate choices made by married or unmarried persons are protected as a form of liberty. This was Justice Stevens's dissenting view in *Bowers*, and as it should have controlled then, it should control now. The judgment of the court of appeals is reversed, and the case remanded.

CONCURRENCE: (O'Connor, J.) While *Bowers* should not be overruled, the majority is correct in finding the Texas statute here to be unconstitutional. Homosexuals should not be branded as criminals because of moral disapproval when heterosexuals participating in the same conduct are protected. Texas asserts no legitimate state interest here.

DISSENT: (Scalia, J.) Certain sexual behavior can and should be regulated because of moral disapproval. "Liberty" protections do not extend to certain other proscribed activities, such as heroin use and prostitution. Judgments of this kind should be made by the people and not imposed by the courts.

DISSENT: (Thomas, J.) Although the Texas law is a ridiculous waste of legislative resources and should be repealed, a general right of privacy does not exist in the Constitution and petitioners are without recourse here. It is this Court's duty to follow the Constitution, even in the face of a law that regulates private sexual conduct between consenting adults.

▶ ANALYSIS

Legislating morality is always under debate in this country because of a wide variance in the closely held values of American society. The *Lawrence* court held that private behavior among consenting adults should be protected as a liberty interest when the behavior is not harming another, but the court fell short of declaring such behavior a fundamental right. As understanding and acceptance of the gay and lesbian community increases, equal protection will become commonplace and expected, but scholars remain uncertain as to the impact of *Lawrence* on the future expansion of "fundamental" rights.

■━■

Continued on next page.

Quicknotes

EQUAL PROTECTION CLAUSE A constitutional provision that each person be guaranteed the same protection of the laws enjoyed by other persons in like circumstances.

Loving v. Virginia

White man (D) v. State (P)

388 U.S. 1 (1967).

NATURE OF CASE: Appeal from conviction for violation of miscegenation statutes.

FACT SUMMARY: Loving (D), a white man, and Jeter (D), a black woman, both residents of Virginia (P), went to the District of Columbia to marry as marriage between white persons and any other race was prohibited in Virginia.

> 🏛 **RULE OF LAW**
> There is no legitimate overriding purpose independent of invidious racial discrimination that justifies racial classifications for marriage.

FACTS: In 1958, two Virginia residents, Loving (D), a white man, and Jeter (D), a black woman, married in the District of Columbia to evade Virginia's (P) ban on marriages between white persons and those of any other race. They returned to Virginia (P) where they were found guilty of evading the antimiscegenation statutes, and each was sentenced to a year in prison. The sentence was suspended for 25 years on condition that they leave Virginia (P) and not return for that period of time. The Lovings (D) challenged the constitutionality of the Virginia statute on due process and equal protection grounds.

ISSUE: Is there a legitimate overriding purpose independent of invidious racial discrimination that justifies racial classifications for marriage?

HOLDING AND DECISION: (Warren, C.J.) No. There is no legitimate overriding purpose independent of invidious racial discrimination that justifies racial classifications for marriage. Equal protection demands that racial classifications, particularly in criminal statutes, be subjected to the strictest scrutiny. To be upheld, it must be shown to be necessary to the accomplishment of some permissible state objective, independent of racial discrimination, which is sought to be eliminated by the Fourteenth Amendment. Virginia (P) bans only marriages between whites and others. Clearly the state intends only to protect white supremacy. While marriage is left to the states under the Tenth Amendment, their powers to regulate marriage are not unlimited, notwithstanding the Fourteenth Amendment. The law deprives the Lovings (D) of due process as the freedom to marry is one of the vital personal rights essential to the orderly pursuit of happiness by free men. Freedom of choice of marriage cannot be limited by invidious racial discrimination. The freedom to marry a person of another race resides with the individual and cannot be infringed by the state. Convictions are reversed.

▶ *ANALYSIS*

Marriage was first characterized as a fundamental right in a case dealing not with marriage but with sterilization. At least one state declared its antimiscegenation statute unconstitutional 19 years earlier than this Court as a violation of equal protection limiting a fundamental right.

■━■

Zablocki v. Redhail

City clerk (D) v. Deadbeat dad (P)

434 U.S. 374 (1978).

NATURE OF CASE: Appeal from the denial of a marriage license.

FACT SUMMARY: A Wisconsin statute prohibited the issuance of a marriage license to those having minor issue, where there are court-ordered support duties, without obtaining the permission of a judge.

🏛 RULE OF LAW
When a statutory classification significantly interferes with the right to marry, it is invalid unless there are sufficiently important state interests and it is closely tailored to effectuate only those interests.

FACTS: Redhail (P) had been ordered to support a child in a paternity action. Redhail (P) was in arrears on his support, and the child, with or without such support payments, was and would have been on welfare. A Wisconsin statute prohibited the issuance of marriage licenses to all residents who have minor issue, not in their custody, where there have been court-ordered support payments. Permission to marry could be obtained from a judge only if support payments were current and the child was not likely to become a public charge. Redhail (P) applied for a marriage license and was denied by Zablocki (D), a clerk. Redhail (P) filed a class action, alleging that the statute violated the Equal Protection and Due Process Clauses of the Fourteenth Amendment. The court strictly scrutinized the statute since it involved a fundamental right, i.e., marriage. The court found that the state's interests did not justify the statute and it was held to be unconstitutional. The State (D) alleged that the judicial hearing protected the welfare of the minor issue and provided an opportunity for counseling. Redhail (P) argued that the statute was unnecessary to provide for the protection of minor issue and that it was not tailored to accomplish either of the State's (D) announced goals.

ISSUE: Is a statutory classification invalid, when it significantly interferes with the right to marry, unless there are sufficiently important state interests and it is closely tailored to effectuate only those interests?

HOLDING AND DECISION: (Marshall, J.) Yes. When a statutory classification significantly interferes with the right to marry, it is invalid unless there are sufficiently important state interests and it is closely tailored to effectuate only those interests. Here, the State (D) has several other methods available to enforce support payments. The statute merely denies permission to marry. It does not require payment of back-due support. As far as the public charge requirement is concerned, Redhail (P) could not marry, even if he paid his court-ordered support. If the State (D) is concerned about this issue, it should adjust support obligations to eliminate the problem. Moreover, the statute does not even require counseling, the second rationale advanced by the State (D). The statute unconstitutionally infringes on the right to marry. It unnecessarily coerces some people into paying support, would prevent some who are paying support from getting married, and does not accomplish the goals of the State (D). Not all classifications involving the right to marry require strict scrutiny, but where significant barriers to this right are created as herein, strict judicial scrutiny is required. The statute is unconstitutional. Affirmed.

CONCURRENCE IN PART: (Powell, J.) The majority opinion is overbroad in requiring compelling state interest analysis applied to any state regulation "directly and substantially" interfering with a right to marry. Not all bans or restrictions on marriage are unreasonable and the states have long regulated domestic relations within constitutional limits. Traditional due process and equal protection tests should be applied to determine whether the state law is valid. The legislation at issue here simply does not meet constitutional standards. The majority's flat rejection of the "collection device" method, however, may be unreasonable. A restriction on the right to marry conditioned on the payment of support to one's minor issue may be valid in some cases if exceptions are made for those too poor to meet such obligations.

▶ ANALYSIS

In *Boddie v. Connecticut*, 401 U.S. 371 (1971), the Court found that the state's interest in collecting filing fees was insufficient to justify denying access to the courts to indigents seeking a divorce. A person's inability to pay money does not justify deprivation of constitutionally protected liberties. Indirect restraints on marriage, e.g., the termination of welfare benefits, are deemed constitutional, *Califano v. Jobst*, 434 U.S. 47 (1977).

Quicknotes

DUE PROCESS RIGHTS The constitutional mandate requiring the courts to protect and enforce individuals' rights and liberties consistent with prevailing principles of fairness and justice, and prohibiting the federal and state governments from such activities that deprive its citizens of a life, liberty or property interest.

Continued on next page.

EQUAL PROTECTION CLAUSE A constitutional provision that each person be guaranteed the same protection of the laws enjoyed by other persons in like circumstances.

■━━■

Getting Married

Quick Reference Rules of Law

Vigil v. Haber

Former fiancée (P) v. Assaulting fiancé (D)

N.M. Sup. Ct., 119 N.M. 9, 888 P.2d 455 (1994).

NATURE OF CASE: Appeal from denial of motion to return a gift following a temporary order of protection.

FACT SUMMARY: Vigil (P) argued that she should be able to keep the engagement ring that Haber (D) gave her because Haber's (D) misconduct caused her to break off the engagement.

RULE OF LAW
The question of fault or guilt is irrelevant to the breaking of an engagement and to the subsequent duty to return gifts given in anticipation of marriage.

FACTS: After Haber (D) and Vigil (P) exchanged engagement rings, their relationship deteriorated to the point where each accused the other of threats and assaults. After they separated, Vigil (P) petitioned the court for a temporary order of protection. The court granted the order and determined that each side should return the rings they had given to each other. Haber (D) immediately returned his ring, but Vigil (P) refused to give up hers, arguing that she should be allowed to keep the ring because Haber (D), by his misconduct, caused the failure of the condition, i.e., marriage, upon which the gift was based. The district court agreed, and Haber (D) appealed.

ISSUE: Is the question of fault or guilt irrelevant to the breaking of an engagement and to the subsequent duty to return gifts given in anticipation of marriage?

HOLDING AND DECISION: (Franchini, J.) Yes. The question of fault or guilt is irrelevant to the breaking of an engagement and to the subsequent duty to return gifts given in anticipation of marriage. If a wedding is called off, for whatever reason, a gift given on the assumption that the marriage will take place is not capable of becoming a completed gift and must be returned to the donor. In this case, the engagement ring was given to Vigil (P) on condition and in contemplation of marriage. Because the condition failed, Haber (D) is entitled to the return of the ring. Vacated and remanded.

ANALYSIS

The court noted in support of its holding that no-fault divorces were the modern trend. Since the conduct of both spouses contributes to the failure of a marriage, establishing guilt and innocence is not particularly useful. The same approach applies to broken engagements. To permit parties to keep engagement gifts on the fault of another would encourage every disappointed donee to resist the return of engagement gifts by blaming the donor for the breakup of the contemplated marriage, thereby promoting dramatic and time-consuming courtroom accusations and counter-accusations of fault.

Quicknotes

NO-FAULT DIVORCE A basis for terminating a marriage without the need for demonstrating misconduct on the part of either spouse.

Crosson v. Crosson

Common-law wife (P) v. Common-law husband (D)

Ala. Ct. Civ. App., 668 So. 2d 868 (1995).

NATURE OF CASE: Appeal from dismissal of divorce action.

FACT SUMMARY: Mr. Crosson (D) argued that any presumption of the existence of his common-law marriage to Mrs. Crosson (P) was vitiated by their separation and by his subsequent marriage to another woman.

> **RULE OF LAW**
> Once conditions of public recognition and co-habitation have been met, a party cannot legally terminate a common-law marriage by simply changing his mind, if the original understanding was to presently enter into the marriage relationship.

FACTS: The Crossons married in 1982 and divorced in 1993. Two months later, Mr. Crosson (D) invited Mrs. Crosson (P) to move back in with him, stating that he wanted her to come back and be his wife. Mrs. Crosson (P) moved back in the same day. The following year, Mrs. Crosson (P) moved to another state, but the couple continued to visit each other on weekends. During that time, Mrs. Crosson (P) introduced Mr. Crosson (D) as her husband on several occasions, and he did not contradict her. They talked about having a wedding ceremony, but never got around to it. Then, in October of 1994, Mr. Crosson (D) married another woman. Mrs. Crosson (P) immediately sued for divorce, contending that she was his common-law wife and that Mr. Crosson (D) had committed adultery and bigamy. The trial court dismissed the complaint, concluding that Mrs. Crosson (P) had failed to prove the existence of a common-law marriage. Mrs. Crosson (P) appealed.

ISSUE: Can a party legally terminate a marriage by simply changing his mind if the original understanding was to presently enter into the marriage relationship, and conditions of public recognition and cohabitation have been met?

HOLDING AND DECISION: (Crawley, J.) No. A party cannot legally terminate a marriage by simply changing his mind if the original understanding was to presently enter into the marriage relationship, once conditions of public recognition and cohabitation are met. In order for a common-law marriage to exist, the following elements must be present: (1) capacity; (2) present, mutual agreement to permanently enter the marriage relationship to the exclusion of all other relationships; and (3) public recognition of the relationship as a marriage and public assumption of marital duties and cohabitation. In this case, both parties had the capacity to marry. Secondly, the parties' present intent to become married upon their reunification was based on Mr. Crosson's (D) asking Mrs. Crosson (P) to come back and be his wife. Finally, Mr. Crosson's (D) acquiescence to being introduced as her husband manifested a mutual assent to be husband and wife. That there were discussions of a ceremonial marriage between the Crossons that never occurred, that Mr. Crosson (D) dated others, and that he married someone else is not sufficient to rebut the facts suggesting a common-law marriage. Reversed and remanded.

▶ ANALYSIS

Although the vast majority of states no longer recognize common-law marriages as valid, the requisite elements of such marriages have actually been codified in several states. In Utah, for example, an otherwise unsolemnized marriage is considered legal between two consenting adults if they are (a) capable of giving consent; and (b) entering a solemnized marriage; (c) have cohabited; (d) mutually assume marital rights and duties; and (e) hold themselves out as husband and wife. In Texas, couples are permitted to sign a declaration swearing that they have agreed to be married, have lived together as husband and wife, and have represented to others that they were married. The declaration is then considered proof that they are "informally" married.

Carabetta v. Carabetta

[Parties not identified.]

Conn. Sup. Ct., 182 Conn. 344, 438 A.2d 109 (1980).

NATURE OF CASE: Appeal from denial of dissolution for lack of jurisdiction.

FACT SUMMARY: The trial court held the Carabetta marriage was void because it was religiously solemnized yet without a statutorily required marriage license.

RULE OF LAW
An unlicensed ceremonial marriage is not void unless the licensing statute explicitly makes unlicensed marriages invalid.

FACTS: The Carabettas' marriage was religiously observed through a valid ceremony, yet they failed to obtain a marriage license. The Connecticut marriage statute required both a license and religious solemnization, yet did not specifically declare unlicensed marriages void. The trial court granted a motion to dismiss the dissolution action, holding that it lacked subject matter jurisdiction because the marriage was void. The party seeking dissolution appealed.

ISSUE: Is an unlicensed ceremonial marriage valid unless the licensing statute explicitly makes unlicensed marriages invalid?

HOLDING AND DECISION: (Peters, J.) Yes. An unlicensed ceremonial marriage is not void unless the governing licensing statute specifically declares unlicensed marriages to be invalid. It has long been held that a marriage which fails to observe a statutory requirement is dissoluble, yet not void. Where the legislature intended noncompliance to void a marriage, it has specifically so stated. The absence of such specificity evidences grounds for dissolution, but not nullity. Therefore, the marriage here was not void, and the trial court had jurisdiction to dissolve it. Reversed.

► ANALYSIS

It has been argued that although Connecticut does not recognize common law marriage, the holding in this case could be viewed as a revival of such informal entrance into the marriage relationship. Also, under the Uniform Marriage and Divorce Act, a marriage may be solemnized by proxy. This device is used mostly in extraordinary circumstances where the parties are irremediably separated, as during wartime, and cannot marry any other way. In normal circumstances this device is seldom used.

Williams v. Williams

Ex-husband (P) v. Ex-wife (D)

Nev. Sup. Ct., 120 Nev. 559, 97 P.3d 1124 (2004).

NATURE OF CASE: Appeal from judgment for property division and spousal support.

FACT SUMMARY: Richard and Marcie Williams married when Marcie (D), unbeknownst to her, was still married to John Allmaras. Richard (P) sought an annulment years later when he discovered the truth. Marcie (D) sought property division and spousal support pursuant to the putative spouse doctrine.

RULE OF LAW
The putative spouse doctrine allows property division between the couple in annulment proceedings but does not permit spousal support to be awarded.

FACTS: Richard E. Williams married Marcie C. Williams in August 1973. Marcie (D) previously married John Allmaras, but mistakenly believed they were divorced at the time of her marriage to Richard (P). Marcie (D) and Richard (P) lived as a married couple for 27 years, had two children together, and believed they were legally married during that time. In 2000, Richard (P) learned that Marcie (D) and Allmaras were not divorced at the time of Marcie (D) and Richard's (P) wedding. The couple separated in August 2000 and Richard (P) filed for an annulment in February 2001. Marcie (D) sought equitable property division and spousal support as a putative spouse in her counterclaim. At a bench trial in April 2002, Richard (P) testified that Marcie (D) knew or should have known she was still married to Allmaras and that he would not have married her had he known. Marcie (D) testified that Allmaras told her they were divorced and she only learned the truth when Richard (P) filed for an annulment. Marcie (D) was a homemaker and licensed childcare provider during her marriage to Richard (P). At the time of trial, she lived with her daughter because she was financially unable to live on her own. The parties stipulated to the value of their joint property. The trial court granted the annulment, awarded Marcie (D) half of the jointly held property, and awarded her $500 monthly in spousal support for four years from Richard (P) as reimbursement payments for her years as a homemaker. The court did not specify whether its award was based on putative spouse doctrine or quantum meruit. Richard (P) appealed.

ISSUE: Does the putative spouse doctrine allow property division and spousal support between the couple in annulment proceedings to be awarded?

HOLDING AND DECISION: (Per curiam) No. The putative spouse doctrine allows property division between the couple in annulment proceedings but does not permit spousal support to be awarded. The annulment was proper to dissolve the void marriage between Marcie (D) and Richard (P). The marriage was void because of Marcie's (D) ongoing marriage to Allmaras. Richard (P) argues that their void marriage precludes the property division and spousal support awards. The putative spouse doctrine treats the couple in a void marriage as having the rights, the civil effects, of a legally married couple if the couple acted in good faith. The majority of states permit this through case law or statute with variances on the rights granted. This state will follow its sister states in permitting the putative spouse doctrine to grant the civil effects of a valid marriage. The putative spouse doctrine requires a proper marriage ceremony and one or both parties' good faith belief in the validity of the marriage. Good faith is presumed with the objecting party having the burden of proving bad faith. A person's good faith action is a question of fact. A party cannot ignore information that places her on notice that an impediment to a valid marriage may exist. She has a duty to investigate. The district court has the discretion to determine the validity of the parties' testimony. Here, the district court believed that Marcie (D) relied on Allmaras's representations that they were divorced. Marcie (D) therefore entered into her marriage with Richard (P) in good faith and can seek the protections offered by the putative spouse doctrine. Putative spouses in community property states believe that community property principles apply to their property, so no new rules need to be devised for property division. Another approach is to divide the property acquired during the putative marriage under joint tenancy principles, but this court believes that community property division is more appropriate. The majority of states that permit spousal awards do so because of legislation. Nevada does not have such a statute permitting or denying it. In reviewing case law, courts may award alimony in cases of fraud or bad faith even where statutes do not exist to allow it. Here, Nevada has no statute, no fraud or bad faith exists, so alimony is not appropriate. Affirmed as to property division; reversed as to award for spousal support.

ANALYSIS

An annulment is preferred to end an invalid marriage because it is legal recognition that a valid and proper marriage never existed. As the court notes, most states protect the spouse who believed the marriage was valid even if that spouse's innocent conduct is the reason the

Continued on next page.

marriage is invalid. If the party seeking the annulment based on invalidity can show the other party knew or should have known of an impediment, then that party can argue estoppel. Estoppel prevents the person seeking putative spouse status from arguing he or she did not know about the impediment to the marriage.

■━━■

Quicknotes

ANNULMENT To nullify a marriage; to establish that the marital status never existed.

COMMUNITY PROPERTY In community property jurisdictions, refers to all money or property acquired during the term of the marriage in which each spouse has an undivided one-half interest.

ESTOPPEL An equitable doctrine precluding a party from asserting a right to the detriment of another who justifiably relied on the conduct.

PUTATIVE SPOUSE A spouse who has a good faith belief in the existence of a valid marriage, when the marriage is in fact unlawful.

QUANTUM MERUIT Equitable doctrine allowing recovery for labor and materials provided by one party, even though no contract was entered into, in order to avoid unjust enrichment by the benefited party.

SPOUSAL SUPPORT Payments made by one spouse to another in discharge of the spouse's duty pursuant to law, or in accordance with a written divorce or separation decree, in order to provide maintenance for the other spouse.

■━━■

Moe v. Dinkins

Minor wishing to marry (P) v. [Party not identified.]

533 F. Supp. 623 (S.D.N.Y. 1981).

NATURE OF CASE: Motion to intervene and plaintiff's motion for summary judgment in action for declaratory and injunctive relief.

FACT SUMMARY: Moe (P) and others sought declaratory and injunctive relief with regard to New York's law requiring parental consent for the marriage of a minor.

RULE OF LAW
A state law prohibiting a minor from marrying without the consent of his or her then-living parents is constitutional.

FACTS: Moe (P) was among those who, using pseudonyms, sought both declaratory and injunctive relief from those New York statutes that required women between 14 and 16 to obtain judicial approval of any marriage and parental consent thereto, and which also required that all applicants for a marriage license between 14 and 18 had to obtain written consent from their then-living parents. In one case, parental consent was not given, even though the couple had a child and was living together. In another case, the minor girl was eight months pregnant with the prospective groom's child, but parental permission to marry was denied. The allegation was that precluding these parties from marrying because of the aforementioned laws was an unconstitutional denial of the liberty guaranteed by the Due Process Clause of the Fourteenth Amendment.

ISSUE: Is a state law prohibiting a minor from marrying without the consent of his or her then-living parents constitutional?

HOLDING AND DECISION: (Motley, J.) Yes. A state law prohibiting a minor from marrying without the consent of his or her then-living parents is constitutional. Proposed plaintiff-intervenors challenge the same state law. Plaintiffs want this court to grant the motion to intervene because the proposed intervenors are in similar circumstances to the plaintiffs and will present the court with a clearer picture. Proposed intervenor Cristina is now pregnant and could wholly avoid her child's illegitimacy if this state law is found to be unconstitutional. Defendants argue that the proposed intervenors can obtain a marriage license through other means and should also not be permitted to intervene because they refuse to reveal their true identities to the court. Neither objection is valid. The motion to intervene is granted. New York's law, which required that a minor obtain the consent of his or her then-living parents in order to marry, is not an unconstitutional denial of due process. Unlike laws restricting minors' abortion rights or

access to contraceptives, this prohibition on marriage during minority does not involve an irretrievable change in position for the minor. If said minor continues in his or her desire to be married, he or she can marry once majority is reached. The requirement of parental consent is rationally related to the state's legitimate interests in mature decision-making with respect to marriage by minors and preventing unstable marriages, as well as to its legitimate interest in supporting the fundamental privacy right of a parent to act in what that parent perceives to be the best interest of the child free from state court scrutiny. Plaintiff's summary judgment denied and summary judgment granted to defendants.

ANALYSIS

The second circuit upheld Judge Motley's decision in this case, *Moe v. Dinkins*, 669 F.2d 67 (2d Cir. 1982). It specifically approved his use of the rational relation test for determining the constitutionality of New York's statute. Certiorari was subsequently denied by the U.S. Supreme Court, *Moe v. Dinkins*, 103 S. Ct. 61 (1982).

Singh v. Singh

Half-niece (P) v. Uncle (D)

Conn. Sup. Ct., 213 Conn. 637, 569 A.2d 1112 (1990).

NATURE OF CASE: Appeal from denial of motion to open and set aside a judgment of annulment.

FACT SUMMARY: Mrs. Singh argued that, since she was only Mr. Singh's half-niece, their marriage should not be deemed incestuous.

🏛 RULE OF LAW
A marriage between persons related to one another as half-uncle and half-niece is void as incestuous under Connecticut law.

FACTS: Mr. and Mrs. Singh were married in Connecticut in 1983. They sought an annulment a year later when they discovered that they were uncle and niece. They remarried in California in 1988. They then sought to set aside the 1984 Connecticut annulment because they were in fact an uncle and niece of the half-blood (Mrs. Singh's mother was Mr. Singh's half-sister). The trial court denied the motion and both parties appealed.

ISSUE: Is a marriage between persons related to one another as half-uncle and half-niece void as incestuous under Connecticut law?

HOLDING AND DECISION: (Healey, J.) Yes. A marriage between persons related to one another as half-uncle and half-niece is void as incestuous under Connecticut law. The crime of incest is purely statutory. While incest statutes may differ from state to state, they generally define incest as marriage or sexual intercourse between persons too closely related in consanguinity or affinity to be entitled to marry legally. Connecticut's statute prohibits marriages between persons within certain degrees of kinship including that of uncle and niece. It does not contain any language expressly distinguishing between relatives of the whole blood and the half blood. However, when the statute was enacted in 1702, ecclesiastical law as it then existed in England treated both relationships equally as a bar to marriage. Relatedly, Connecticut case law holds that the prohibition against brothers and sisters marrying encompasses half-siblings as well. An interpretation of Connecticut's incest law to include half-uncles and half-nieces does not constitute an unwarranted extension of the incest prohibition that would be contrary to public policy. Affirmed.

▶ ANALYSIS

In instances where adoption has changed blood relations, courts have differing opinions as to whether incest rules should apply. In *State ex rel. Miesner v. Geile*, 747 S.W.2d 757 (Mo. App. 1988), for example, the court permitted marriage between an uncle and an adopted niece. In *Israel v. Allen*, 577 P.2d 762 (Colo. 1978), the court held that the Equal Protection Clause prohibited the application of the sibling marriage restriction to adopted siblings. On the other hand, the Indiana Supreme Court permitted the prosecution of a father for incest notwithstanding his natural daughter's adoption by another man. See *Bohall v. Indiana*, 546 N.E.2d 1214 (Ind. 1989).

■■■

Quicknotes

ANNULMENT To nullify a marriage; to establish that the marital status never existed.

PUBLIC POLICY Policy administered by the state with respect to the health, safety and morals of its people in accordance with common notions of fairness and decency.

■■■

Edmunds v. Edwards

Mentally disabled husband (P) v. Wife (D)

Neb. Sup. Ct., 205 Neb. 255, 287 N.W.2d 420 (1980).

NATURE OF CASE: Appeal in action to annul a marriage.

FACT SUMMARY: Some two years after his ward, Harold Edmunds, married Inez Edwards (D), Renne Edmunds (P) sought to have the marriage annulled on the grounds that his ward was incapable of giving consent to the marriage because of his mental retardation.

🏛 RULE OF LAW
A marriage is valid if the party has sufficient capacity to understand the nature of the contract and the obligations and responsibilities it creates.

FACTS: Harold Edmunds, who was mildly retarded, met Inez Edwards (D) while both were residents at the Beatrice State Home. He lived there for 30 years but eventually was discharged. He obtained employment and lived in an apartment staffed by the Eastern Nebraska Community Office of Retardation. He received promotions and salary increases. When he and Inez (D) decided to marry, they received premarital sex counseling and marriage counseling from the pastor of the church they had been attending. Two years after their marriage, Renne Edmunds (P), a guardian of Harold's estate, brought an action to have the marriage annulled on the grounds that Harold did not have the capacity to consent to marriage due to his mental retardation. After hearing conflicting testimony, the trial court determined that Harold did have the capacity to consent and that his marriage was valid.

ISSUE: Is a marriage valid if the party had sufficient capacity to understand the nature of the contract and the obligations and responsibilities it creates?

HOLDING AND DECISION: (Brodkey, J.) Yes. A marriage is valid if the party has sufficient capacity to understand the nature of the contract and the obligations and responsibilities it creates. Marriages are void when either party, at the time of the marriage, is insane or mentally incompetent to enter into the marriage relationship. There must have been such a want of understanding as to render the party incapable of assenting thereto. Thus, mere weakness or imbecility of mind is not sufficient to render the marriage void unless it prevents the party from comprehending the nature of the contract and the obligations and responsibilities it creates. Since the burden of proof is upon the party seeking annulment and the trial court was in the best position to adjudge the appearance and demeanor of the witnesses, its decision that Harold had the capacity to consent to his marriage was correct. Affirmed.

▶ ANALYSIS

Intoxication, drug use, or other circumstances leading to temporary mental incapacity can render a marriage void. However, subsequent ratification of the marriage after the temporary mental incapacity has abated will validate the marriage. The same ratification concept has been applied in cases where the husband was physically incapable of consummating the marriage at the time it was entered into but in which cohabitation occurred when the disability was later conquered.

Quicknotes

ANNULMENT To nullify a marriage; to establish that the marital status never existed.

Kantaras v. Kantaras

Wife (D) v. Husband (P)

Fla. 29 Fla. L. Weekly D1699 Dist. Ct. App., 884 So. 2d 155 (2004).

NATURE OF CASE: Defendant's appeal from dissolution of marriage.

FACT SUMMARY: Michael Kantaras (P), a female-to-male postoperative transsexual, married Linda Kantaras (D). Michael (P) divorced Linda (D) and Linda (D) appealed on the basis that the marriage was void ab initio because Florida bans same-sex marriage and Michael was biologically female.

RULE OF LAW

Florida law does not permit a postoperative transsexual to marry a member of the person's original gender.

FACTS: Michael Kantaras (P) was born Margo Kantaras, biologically female. As an adult, Margo changed her name to Michael John and underwent gender reassignment surgery, including a total hysterectomy, double mastectomy, and hormone treatment. Michael (P) met Linda (D), then pregnant with another man's child, and the two began a romantic relationship. Linda (D) knew of Michael's (P) surgeries. Linda (D) and Michael (P) applied for a marriage license and Michael (P) represented that he was male. Linda (D) gave birth to a son and the two married in Florida. Michael (P) adopted Linda's (D) son, representing to the court that he was Linda's (D) husband. Linda (D) later gave birth to a daughter using Michael's (P) brother's sperm. Michael (P) filed for divorce from Linda (D) after ten years of marriage and sought primary custody of the two minor children. Linda (D) counterclaimed for divorce and/or annulment on the grounds that their marriage was void ab initio because of Florida's ban on same-sex marriage. Further, Linda (D) claimed that Michael (P) was not the legal or biological parent of her daughter. The trial court found that Michael (P) was male at the time of the marriage, thus the marriage was valid. The court granted the dissolution and awarded Michael primary custody of the two children. Linda (D) appealed.

ISSUE: Does Florida law permit a postoperative transsexual to marry a member of the person's original gender?

HOLDING AND DECISION: (Fulmer, J.) No. Florida law does not permit a postoperative transsexual to marry a member of the person's original gender. The trial court here found that Michael (P) was male based on his self-identity as a male even when biologically female, his gender reassignment surgery, his wife's acceptance of his surgery and status as a male, him holding himself out to society as a male, society's acceptance of him as male, and his diagnosed Gender Identity Dysphoria. Michael (P) and Linda's (D) marriage is only valid if Michael (P) was a male at the time of the marriage. Florida's statutes prohibit same-sex marriage. Other states addressing the issue of postoperative transsexual marriage also prohibit it based on violations of statutes or public policy. Several states have cases that determine that the question of gender can be answered by legislatures in choosing to permit transsexual marriage. The trial court here relied on an Australian case that held a postoperative transsexual is legally the postoperative gender. Michael (P) argues that the Australian approach is correct and follows modern science. This court disagrees, however. The Florida legislature has had opportunities to include transsexuals in statutory language regarding marriage, but has chosen not to do so. The statutory language references the commonly understood definitions of male and female with the immutable traits determined at birth. The changes in modern medical science are a matter for the legislature and not the courts. The trial court's determination that Michael (P) was male at the time of the marriage is error and the marriage is void ab initio. On remand, the trial court must consider the best interests of the children in light of the void marriage. Reversed and remanded.

ANALYSIS

This case caught the interest of the nation and the world. The National Center for Lesbian Rights served as Michael's co-counsel. The Kantarases' three-week trial was aired on Court TV. After this court's opinion was handed down, the couple appeared on the television show "Dr. Phil." The host, Dr. Phil, encouraged Linda and Michael to mediate for the sake of their then-teenaged children. The two agreed and entered into lengthy mediation sessions. Michael retained his parental rights and shares custody with Linda.

■=■

Quicknotes

AB INITIO From its inception or beginning.

ANNULMENT To nullify a marriage; to establish that the marital status never existed.

■=■

Spouses: Changing Roles, Rights, and Duties

Quick Reference Rules of Law

Stuart v. Board of Supervisors of Elections

Married woman (P) v. Election board (D)

Md. Ct. App., 266 Md. 440, 295 A.2d 223 (1972).

NATURE OF CASE: Appeal in action by a woman to retain her maiden name for voter registration.

FACT SUMMARY: Stuart (P) and her husband agreed that she should retain her maiden name during their marriage, but the Board (D) refused to allow her voter registration to be in any name but her married name.

🏛 RULE OF LAW
A person may register to vote using the name he has adopted and chosen in the absence of fraudulent intent or purpose.

FACTS: Stuart (P) married Samuel Austell, and in accordance with their oral antenuptial agreement, Stuart (P) continued to use and be known exclusively by her birth-given name and not by the name of her husband. After explaining to a voter registrar that she was married to Austell but consistently and nonfraudulently retained her maiden name, she registered to vote under the name "Stuart." The Board (D) notified Stuart (P) that unless she changed her registration to her husband's surname, her registration would be stricken from the rolls. When she failed to change the name, her registration was canceled. The trial court held that the Board (D) could require Stuart (P) to register under her married name as the most expedient way to prevent voter fraud.

ISSUE: May a person register to vote using the name he has adopted and chosen in the absence of fraudulent intent or purpose?

HOLDING AND DECISION: (Murphy, C.J.) Yes. A person may register to vote using the name he has adopted and chosen in the absence of fraudulent intent or purpose. There is a common law right, absent a statute to the contrary, for a person to adopt any name by which he may become known and by which he may transact business, execute contracts, or sue and be sued. A person may lawfully change his name without resorting to legal proceedings and by general usage or habit acquire another. Thus, the law manifestly permits a married woman to retain her birth-given name by the same procedure of consistent, nonfraudulent use following her marriage. There is no statutory requirement that a woman adopt her husband's surname. While "the vast majority of women adopt . . . their husband's surnames as their own—the mere fact of the marriage does not, as a matter of law, operate to establish the custody and tradition of the majority as a rule of law binding upon all." Reversed.

▶ ANALYSIS

The dissent which was omitted believed that in order for a woman to retain her maiden name, she would have to legally change it back to that name after marriage. The issue has naturally assumed greater importance with the rise of the women's rights movement. Even so, there appear to be jurisdictions which permit any person to adopt any name if it is to be used consistently and nonfraudulently without use of legal process.

■■■

Henne v. Wright

Mother (P) v. Department of Health director (D)

904 F.2d 1208 (8th Cir. 1990), *cert. denied*, 498 U.S. 1032 (1991).

NATURE OF CASE: Appeal from invalidation of a health statute.

FACT SUMMARY: Wright (D) and the Dept. of Health (D) appealed from a decision ruling that a state statute which restricts the choice of surnames that can be recorded on a newborn child's birth certificate was unconstitutional in that it impermissibly infringed upon the parent's fundamental right to choose a surname for their daughters.

> ## 🏛 RULE OF LAW
> There is no constitutionally protected, fundamental right of privacy which covers the right of a parent to give a child a surname to which the child has no legally recognized parental connection.

FACTS: When Henne's (P) daughter was born, she wished to give her daughter the surname Brinton, the surname of the girl's acknowledged father. Spindell (P) wished to name her daughter McKenzie, simply because her other children were surnamed McKenzie. They were informed by their respective hospitals that those surnames could not be entered on the newborn birth certificates because a statute restricted the surnames that could be entered on birth certificates. Wright (D) headed the Dept. of Health (D), which denied the requests by Spindell (P) and Henne (P). Henne (P) brought suit claiming the actions taken by the Dept. of Health (D) violated her constitutional right of privacy to name her child as she wished, and Spindell (P) intervened. The trial court held in their favor, and from that decision, the Dept. of Health (D) appealed.

ISSUE: Is there a constitutionally protected, fundamental right of privacy which covers the right of a parent to give a surname to which the child has no legally recognized parental connection?

HOLDING AND DECISION: (Bright, J.) No. There is no constitutionally protected, fundamental right to privacy which covers the right of a parent to give a child a surname to which the child has no legally recognized parental connection. The statute in question does not prevent either Henne (P) or Spindell (P) from ever giving their children the surnames they have selected. The parents (P) argue, and the district court agreed, that the constitutional right to privacy extends to include the parents' ability to select their child's surname at birth. To determine whether a "fundamental" right is implicated, the court looks to whether the right is "deeply rooted in the Nation's history and tradition." There is no American tradition which supports an extension of the right of privacy to cover the right to name

their children as asserted by Henne (P) and Spindell (P) herein. Since a fundamental right is not involved, the statute is analyzed under the highly deferential rational standard of review. Here, the law rationally furthers the state's interest in promoting the welfare of children, preventing appropriation of citizens' names for improper purposes, and cost-effective recordkeeping. Reversed.

CONCURRENCE AND DISSENT: (Arnold, J.) Family matters come within the reach of fundamental rights. The right to name children is clearly within the principles of prior cases. The court's analysis of "history and tradition" is unpersuasive.

▶ ANALYSIS

Problems regarding a child's surname often come up in divorce proceedings. The husband often places in custody and visitation documents a limitation on the mother's right to rename the child, even if the mother has remarried. Some states have abolished the common-law notion that a father has a primary right or protectable interest in having the minor children of the marriage bear his surname. See *Marriage of Schiffman*, 169 Cal. Rptr. 918 (1980).

■=■

Quicknotes

RIGHT TO PRIVACY Those personal liberties or relationships that are protected against unwarranted governmental interference.

■=■

McGuire v. McGuire

Wife (P) v. Husband (D)

Neb. Sup. Ct., 157 Neb. 226, 59 N.W.2d 336 (1953).

NATURE OF CASE: Appeal in action for support and attorney fees.

FACT SUMMARY: Mr. McGuire (D) was very tight with his money and refused to give his wife any funds other than to pay for groceries, though they continued to live together.

RULE OF LAW
No support payments can be granted where the parties continue to live together as husband and wife.

FACTS: Mr. McGuire (D) was exceedingly miserly with his money. He refused to give Mrs. McGuire (P) any money of her own. His sole contribution to the family's support was to pay for groceries and to keep a roof over their heads. Mr. McGuire (D) refused her any and all additional comforts. He refused to repair the car, replace the old furniture, fix the heating, buy her clothes, etc. He had more than sufficient funds to substantially raise the level of the family's lifestyle but refused to do so. The parties had lived like this for approximately 33 years. The trial court awarded the wife support, a new car, new furniture, and funds to visit her daughters yearly. Mrs. McGuire (P) continued to live with her husband.

ISSUE: May support payments be granted to one party where the parties continue to live together as husband and wife?

HOLDING AND DECISION: (Messmore, J.) No. Support payments may not be granted to one party where the parties continue to live together as husband and wife. The living standards of a family are the concern of the household, not the courts. As long as the parties remain together as husband and wife, it may be said that the husband is legally supporting the wife and the purpose of the marriage relationship is being carried out. Public policy requires that the courts not interfere in such a situation. Mrs. McGuire's (P) only alternative would be to leave her husband and then to bring suit for support. The decision of the trial court awarding support is reversed.

DISSENT: (Yeager, J.) A husband has the responsibility of furnishing the necessities of life to his family. There is a justification for excluding this protection to women who remain married. The $50 monthly support award was appropriate but the trial court lacked the jurisdiction to award furniture and a car.

▶ ANALYSIS

In *Miller v. Miller*, 320 Mich. 43 (1948), the court affirmed support payments to the wife, even though the parties resided together in the same house. Mr. Miller took his meals alone and lived in a separate room. It was found that they had separated just as certainly as if he had moved out. This decision is, however, rare. For another example of a case denying support see *Commonwealth v. George*, 358 Pa. 118 (1948). The wife there charged that they were separated due to the husband's occasional lengthy drunken sprees. The court held that this was insufficient since the marital relationship was continuing and denied support for the reasons mentioned in *McGuire*.

Quicknotes

DUTY TO SUPPORT FAMILY Duty imposed by statute requiring a spouse to provide for the sustenance of his or her spouse and children.

PUBLIC POLICY Policy administered by the state with respect to the health, safety, and morals of its people in accordance with common notions of fairness and decency.

Trammel v. United States

Convicted heroin importer (D) v. Federal government (P)

445 U.S. 40 (1980).

NATURE OF CASE: Appeal from a conviction for importing heroin and conspiracy to import.

FACT SUMMARY: Trammel (D) sought a reversal of his criminal convictions on the ground that his wife had been allowed to give voluntary adverse testimony against him despite his protests.

🏛 RULE OF LAW
The privilege against adverse spousal testimony belongs to the witness spouse alone, so that the accused spouse may not invoke the privilege to exclude the voluntary testimony of the witness spouse.

FACTS: Trammel (D) and his wife were involved in a heroin ring, and she agreed to testify against him in return for use immunity. The trial court ruled she could testify as to anything except confidential communications between herself and Trammel (D), which were held to be privileged and inadmissible. Trammel (D) appealed the resulting convictions for importing heroin and conspiracy to import heroin, alleging that he had the right to invoke the privilege against adverse spousal testimony so as to exclude the voluntary testimony of his wife in toto. The court of appeals rejected this contention and affirmed the convictions.

ISSUE: Does the privilege against adverse spousal testimony belong to the witness spouse alone, so that the accused spouse may not invoke the privilege to exclude the voluntary testimony of the witness spouse?

HOLDING AND DECISION: (Burger, C.J.) Yes. The accused spouse cannot invoke the privilege against adverse spousal testimony to exclude the voluntary testimony of the witness spouse, inasmuch as the privilege belongs only to the witness spouse. The 1958 *Hawkins v. United States* case, 358 U.S. 74, left the federal privilege for adverse spousal testimony where it found it, continuing "a rule which bars the testimony of one spouse against the other unless both consent." However, since then, support for the privilege has been eroded further, and criticism of the *Hawkins* rule has continued unabated. The consensus of state law as well as the various model statute codes is that the privilege should belong only to the witness spouse. The accused spouse must rely on his ability to preclude testimony as to confidential communications only, as applies with regard to communications with his lawyer, doctor, or priest under a similar privilege for confidential communications. That is precisely this court's holding. Thus, Trammel (D) had no right to prevent the voluntary testimony of his wife. Affirmed.

▶ ANALYSIS

This common law privilege was based on two notions. The first was that one cannot testify in his own behalf, and the second was that husband and wife were one. Despite the abandonment of these concepts, it was not until 1933 that a defendant's spouse was allowed to testify even on behalf of the defendant spouse. *Frank v. United States*, 290 U.S. 371.

■≣■

Warren v. State

Convicted rapist (D) v. State (P)

Ga. Sup. Ct., 255 Ga. 151, 336 S.E.2d 221 (1985).

NATURE OF CASE: Appeal from denial of motion to dismiss criminal indictment.

FACT SUMMARY: Warren (D) contended he could not be charged with rape for having forced sexual intercourse with his wife.

RULE OF LAW
A husband may be convicted of raping his wife or committing sodomy with her.

FACTS: Warren (D) was indicted for rape and sodomy. He moved to dismiss by demurring to the indictment on the basis that he, as the victim's husband, could not be convicted of either crime. The court denied the motion, and Warren (D) obtained a certificate of immediate review and filed an interlocutory appeal.

ISSUE: Can a husband be convicted of raping or committing sodomy on his wife?

HOLDING AND DECISION: (Smith, J.) Yes. A husband may be convicted of raping or committing sodomy on his wife. The common law treatment of women as chattel or as having attenuated rights is no longer valid. The marriage relationship carries no implied consent to criminal conduct. Thus, a husband may be convicted, and the demurrer was properly overruled. Affirmed.

ANALYSIS

A third common law theory discussed by the court that previously served to preclude application of rape statutes to husbands is the unity of person theory. This theory, long since rejected, holds that upon marriage the two persons unite in the eyes of the law to form a single person. This person was the husband, and the wife ceased to have a legal existence. The opinion in this case reflects a drastic evolution of the rights of women since the common law.

Quicknotes

RAPE Unlawful sexual intercourse by means of fear or force and without consent.

Cladd v. State

Convicted burglar (D) v. State (P)

Fla. Sup. Ct., 398 So. 2d 442 (1981).

NATURE OF CASE: Appeal from criminal burglary conviction.

FACT SUMMARY: Cladd (D) argued that he could not be guilty of burglary in entering the premises where his wife lived while separated from him in that he was licensed or invited to enter her premises as a matter of law since he was her husband.

🏛 RULE OF LAW
A spouse who is physically but not legally separated from the other spouse can be guilty of burglary for breaking into the other spouse's premises without consent and with the intent to commit an offense therein.

FACTS: At a time when he was separated physically but not legally from his wife, Cladd (D) entered her premises without her consent, struck her, and attempted to throw her over the second floor stair railing. The State (P) charged him with burglary, but Cladd (D) insisted that his status as husband gave him license or invitation to enter his wife's apartment as a matter of law. The trial court dismissed the charges, but the appellate court held his right to his spouse's company did not include the right to break and enter her apartment with intent to commit an offense therein.

ISSUE: Can a spouse who is physically but not legally separated from the other spouse be guilty of burglary for breaking into the other spouse's premises without consent and with the intent to commit an offense therein?

HOLDING AND DECISION: (Alderman, J.) Yes. A spouse who is physically but not legally separated from the other spouse can be guilty of burglary for breaking into the other spouse's premises without consent and with the intent to commit an offense therein. A husband's right of consortium permits him to enjoy the company of his wife, but it does not preclude him from being charged with and found guilty of burglary if, while they are physically but not legally separated, he enters her premises with the intent to commit an offense therein. Cladd's (D) consortium rights did not immunize him from burglary where he had no right to be on the premises possessed solely by his wife independent of an asserted right to consortium. Affirmed.

DISSENT: (Boyd, J.) The right to consortium between spouses should not be disturbed absent clear direction from the legislature. The legislature should specifically reconcile the right to consortium with criminal laws, particularly where life imprisonment is a risk. The legislature has to date failed to provide appropriate direction.

DISSENT: (England, J.) The wife here occupies a separate marital residence from her husband, but that does not automatically determine the ownership of the property contained therein. This case does not involve assault, already divorced or legally separated spouses, or definitively separate property. This is no different from other households where one spouse has a temporary residence and the other spouse enters. Prosecuting attorneys are now involved in marital disputes.

▶ ANALYSIS

A spouse can be found guilty of the larceny of the other spouse's separate property. "It is no defense that a theft was from the actor's spouse, except that misappropriation of household and personal effects, or other property normally accessible to both spouses, is theft only if it occurs after the parties have ceased living together." § 233.1(4), A.L.I. Model Penal Code.

Quicknotes

BURGLARY Unlawful entry of a building at night with the intent to commit a felony therein.

CONSORTIUM The right of a spouse to enjoy the benefits of association with the other.

State ex rel. Williams v. Marsh

Abused wife (P) v. [Party not identified.]

Mo. Sup. Ct., 626 S.W.2d 223 (1982) (en banc).

NATURE OF CASE: Petition for writ of mandamus.

FACT SUMMARY: Denise Williams (P) sought a writ of mandamus to compel the trial court to issue an order of protection, an order restraining her husband from entering her dwelling, and a temporary order of custody, the court having held the act authorizing such orders unconstitutional.

🏛 RULE OF LAW
Missouri's Adult Abuse Act, which authorizes issuance of orders of protection, orders restraining a spouse from entering the family dwelling, and temporary custody orders pending a hearing, and makes violation of such orders a misdemeanor, is not unconstitutional.

FACTS: Pursuant to Missouri's Adult Abuse Act, Denise Williams (P) petitioned for an ex parte order of protection, an order restraining her husband from entering her dwelling, and a temporary order of custody. After holding the act unconstitutional, the court dismissed her petition. She filed a petition for a writ of mandamus to compel the trial court to issue the orders sought and appealed the dismissal of her petition. After a hearing on her ex parte order, the trial court had found that Ms. Williams's (P) husband, from whom she was physically separated, had beaten her so badly on one occasion as to require her hospitalization for 12 days. In finding the act unconstitutional, the court ruled that it violated the Missouri Constitution by containing more than one subject, i.e., it dealt with issues relating to the support and custody of children, rather than relating exclusively to adults. It also held that the 15 days an ex parte order could be in force prior to a hearing rendered the act unconstitutional.

ISSUE: Is Missouri's Adult Abuse Act unconstitutional?

HOLDING AND DECISION: (Higgins, J.) No. Missouri's Adult Abuse Act is not unconstitutional. The child support and custody provisions therein fairly relate to the subject of adult abuse and promote the purpose of the Act. As to due process guarantees, it meets the applicable standards. The Act contains provisions that are a reasonable means to achieve the state's legitimate goal of preventing domestic violence, and it affords adequate procedural safeguards prior to and after any deprivation occurs. The Act is constitutional.

CONCURRENCE IN PART: (Bardgett, J.) That portion of the opinion upholding the constitutionality of the provision which makes the violation of an order of protection a crime should not have been written, as a decision on that issue should await a criminal case based on such a charge.

DISSENT: (Welliver, J.) The Act is going to create new evils. "Adult Abuse" now includes Chapter 452 child custody, support, and maintenance. Adult abuse orders can be entered without notice or hearing. Crime elements will be determined on a case-by-case basis. These evils violate the requirement that penal statutes be strictly construed against the state and the rule that bills must contain only one subject.

▌ANALYSIS

Efforts to abate spousal abuse are diverse. It has even been suggested that a reporting statute, such as the ones requiring health officials and others to report suspected child abuse, would be effective. However, there has been very little support for that idea.

■═■

Quicknotes

EX PARTE A proceeding commenced by one party.

PROTECTIVE ORDER Court order protecting a party against potential abusive treatment through use of the legal process.

WRIT OF MANDAMUS A court order issued commanding a public or private entity, or an official thereof, to perform a duty required by law.

■═■

Bozman v. Bozman

Ex-husband (P) v. Ex-wife (D)

Md. Ct. App., 376 Md. 461, 830 A.2d 450 (2003).

NATURE OF CASE: Cross-appeals in malicious prosecution action.

FACT SUMMARY: Embroiled in a divorce battle, Nancy Bozman (D) filed criminal charges against William Bozman (P) for violating a Protective Order. The charges were later dismissed against William (P) and he filed counts against Nancy (D) for malicious prosecution. Nancy (D) argued that the doctrine of interspousal tort immunity barred the complaint and William (P) argued that the tort of malicious prosecution was outrageous enough to fall within an exception to the immunity.

🏛 RULE OF LAW
Interspousal tort immunity does not bar a spouse's complaint of intentional tort.

FACTS: William (P) and Nancy (D) Bozman were married for 31 years when William (P) filed for divorce on grounds of adultery. Nancy (D) proceeded to file criminal stalking and harassment charges in violation of a Protective Order against William (P) on three separate occasions. Two months before the divorce was final, William (P) filed a claim of malicious prosecution against Nancy (D), claiming that her criminal charges were baseless and retaliatory for the divorce. Nancy (D) moved to dismiss, arguing that the complaint was barred by interspousal tort immunity. The trial court granted her motion but allowed William (P) to amend his complaint. He did so and Nancy (D) again moved to dismiss based on interspousal tort immunity. William (P) claimed the defense was barred because of *Lusby v. Lusby*, 390 A.2d 77 (1978) where the doctrine was not a defense if the spouse's tortious conduct was sufficiently "outrageous and intentional." William (P) argued that Nancy's (D) conduct fell within *Lusby* because it resulted in multiple incarcerations and house arrest for him. On the date of the motion hearing, William (P) filed a second Amended Complaint in which he added a second count of malicious prosecution. He claimed that Nancy (D) filed another criminal charge, which was ultimately dismissed, in retaliation for the first malicious prosecution action. The dismissal of those charges occurred post-divorce, and William (P) thus argued that interspousal tort immunity did not apply. Nancy (D) filed another motion to dismiss, which the trial court granted. On appeal, the appellate court noted the outdated doctrine of interspousal immunity that was still the law of Maryland. It also addressed whether malicious prosecution was a sufficiently outrageous tort to come within *Lusby*. The appellate court determined it did not, because while embarrassing, the consequences did not involve extreme violence. The appellate court held that malicious prosecution did not

fall within the exception to interspousal tort immunity and affirmed the dismissal of the first count of the second Amended Complaint. William (P) and Nancy (D) cross-appealed.

ISSUE: Does interspousal tort immunity bar a spouse's complaint of intentional tort?

HOLDING AND DECISION: (Bell, C.J.) No. Interspousal tort immunity does not bar a spouse's complaint of intentional tort. Maryland's common law embraced interspousal tort immunity because of the single legal identity of a husband and his wife. A wife could not file a tort claim against her husband for a negligent or tortious act. This is an antiquated doctrine and the courts began its abrogation in *Lusby*. In that case, the husband raped his wife in the presence of two of his friends and threatened her life. The court held that his actions were sufficiently outrageous and intentional to support the wife's tort claim for damages. The court further abrogated the doctrine in a later case when it permitted a wife's negligence claim for personal injuries sustained due to her husband's negligence one year prior to their marriage. The court completed an exhaustive review of the history of interspousal tort immunity and the actions in sister states. The majority of states had moved away from the doctrine and it then only remained for intentional torts in Maryland. This court now fully abrogates the doctrine pursuant to the overwhelming weight of authority. Abrogation shall apply to the case at hand. Reversed and remanded.

▌*ANALYSIS*

Interspousal tort immunity historically affected women far more than it did men. States often permitted married women to file tort claims against spouses when it related to property, but not personal torts. The courts did not want to become involved in "marital relations" such as domestic violence, negligence, or personal injury. Nearly all states have now abrogated the doctrine as antiquated and inequitable for women.

■━■

Quicknotes

ADULTERY Sexual intercourse between a married person and another who is not that person's spouse, or between a person and another who is married.

Continued on next page.

INTENTIONAL TORT A legal wrong resulting in a breach of duty, which is intentionally or purposefully committed by the wrongdoer.

INTERSPOUSAL IMMUNITY A common law doctrine precluding spouses from commencing actions against one another. Some states have abolished the doctrine.

MALICIOUS PROSECUTION The unlawful civil or criminal prosecution of a party without probable cause.

PROTECTIVE ORDER Court order protecting a party against potential abusive treatment through use of the legal process.

CHAPTER 4

Matrimonial Breakdown: Grounds and Jurisdiction for Dissolution

Quick Reference Rules of Law

50-53

Brady v. Brady

Husband (P) v. Wife (D)

N.Y. Ct. App., 64 N.Y.2d 339, 476 N.E.2d 290 (1985).

NATURE OF CASE: Appeal from an order granting divorce.

FACT SUMMARY: The court of appeals reversed the trial court's holding that incompatibility on the part of Mrs. Brady (D) constituted cruel and inhuman treatment of Mr. Brady (P) and supported grounds for divorce.

🏛 RULE OF LAW
The duration of the marriage is a significant factor in determining whether conduct on the part of one marital partner constitutes cruel and inhuman treatment such as to justify the granting of divorce.

FACTS: The Bradys were married in 1956 and had four children between 1957 and 1966. For a period of two years in 1977 through 1979, Mr. Brady (P) infrequently lived in the marital residence and had not lived there since October of 1979. He filed for divorce in 1981, citing cruel and inhuman treatment by Mrs. Brady (D). The evidence presented at trial indicated that Mrs. Brady (D) struck Mr. Brady (P) with objects, threatened him with a knife, attempted to choke him, and frequently berated him. The trial court granted divorce and granted custody of the infant child to Mrs. Brady (D). Mrs. Brady (D) appealed, contending that mere incompatibility within the context of a long-term marriage does not establish cruel and inhuman conduct such as to support a decree of divorce. The court of appeals reversed, and Mr. Brady (P) appealed.

ISSUE: Is the duration of the marriage a significant factor to be considered in determining whether or not conduct is cruel and inhuman so as to grant a decree of divorce?

HOLDING AND DECISION: (Wachtler, C.J.) Yes. The duration of a marriage is a significant factor to be considered in determining whether or not conduct is cruel and inhuman to the extent that it justifies the entering of a divorce decree. In a short-term marriage, conduct which could be considered cruel and inhuman could be considered merely a period of discord in a long-term marriage. The trial court, in this case, concluded, based upon facts which could only lead to the conclusion of incompatibility, that cruel and inhuman treatment had occurred. Without taking into consideration the duration of the marriage, the trial court's holding was erroneous and must be reversed. Affirmed.

▶ ANALYSIS

The court in this case reaffirmed its decision in *Hessen v. Hessen*, 33 N.Y.2d 406. In that case, it was first determined

that mere incompatibility would not be the basis for cruel and inhuman treatment such as to support a divorce decree. In the current case, the court expands upon this by labeling the duration of the marriage a significant factor in determining what is cruel and inhuman treatment. Prior to the enactment of a New York statute allowing for divorce to be granted upon cruel and inhuman treatment, the only basis for divorce was adultery. Many states currently have no-fault divorce statutes, wherein irreconcilable differences are sufficient grounds for a dissolution.

◾■◾

Quicknotes

CRUEL AND ABUSIVE TREATMENT Conduct that is harmful to an individual's mental or physical health.

NO-FAULT DIVORCE A basis for terminating a marriage without the need for demonstrating misconduct on the part of either spouse.

◾■◾

In re Dube

Arsonist wife (D) v. Adulterous husband (P)

N.H. Sup. Ct., 44 A.3d 556, 163 N.H. 575 (2012).

NATURE OF CASE: Appeal from a finding of fault in a final divorce action.

FACT SUMMARY: Upon learning of Eric Dube's (P) adultery, his wife Jeannie Dube (D) attempted to destroy the family home by arson. Eric's (P) petition for divorce was amended from irreconcilable grounds to fault based on Jeannie's (D) conviction for attempted arson.

 RULE OF LAW
Condonation is a defense to fault-based divorce.

FACTS: Jeannie Dube (D) and Eric Dube (P) were married for approximately 15 years, when they became estranged. Shortly after learning that Eric (P) committed adultery, Jeannie (D) stated during a phone conversation that she intended to kill their child, Eric's (P) child from a previous marriage, and Eric's (P) parents who lived with them, and burn down the marital residence. While attempting to destroy the home with an ax, Jeannie (P) chased Eric's (P) parents with the same weapon. Eric (P) filed for divorce based on irreconcilable differences, and later amended his petition to the fault-based grounds of incarceration over one year when Jeannie (D) was convicted of attempted arson among other things. The trial court granted a divorce in Eric's (P) favor and Jeannie (D) subsequently argued Eric's (P) adultery precluded her fault.

ISSUE: Is condonation a defense to fault-based divorce?

HOLDING AND DECISION: (Conboy, J.) Yes. Condonation is a defense to fault-based divorce based on adultery. The first thing to address is Jeannie's (D) contention that the trial court erred in granting Eric (P) a fault-based divorce on the grounds of her conviction and subsequent imprisonment. She asserts Eric (P) is not an "innocent party" because he committed adultery, and, therefore, is precluded from obtaining fault-based divorce. Eric (P) does not dispute his infidelity; yet, he contends that he is still an "innocent party" because Jeannie's (D) conduct was the primary cause of the martial breakdown. His argument that the parties agreed to "work through" the affair constituted Jeannie's (D) condonation of his adultery, thus restoring his status as an "innocent party" is not borne from the facts. Under the condonation doctrine, if either party to a marriage thinks it is proper to forgive the infidelity of the other, it cannot afterwards be set up as a ground for divorce. The record, however, does not support Eric's (P) assertion that Jeanne (D) condoned his infidelity and, as such, he cannot claim the status of an "innocent party." Though it is concluded that Eric (P) is not entitled to a fault-based divorce, the trial court's decision dissolving the marriage through divorce is affirmed, based on irreconcilable differences. Affirmed in part and reversed in part.

ANALYSIS

Timing is the proper focus of this opinion, where Eric Dube (P) filed for divorce based on the fault-based grounds of incarceration for more than one year while still having been subject to Jeannie Dube's (D) allegations of adultery. A finding that Jeannie (D) condoned or forgave his adultery would have permitted the finding of her own fault for trying to burn down the house among other things. The court was not going to lose sight of the facts in this case that Jeannie's (D) actions, while reprehensible, were subsequent to Eric's (P) infidelity which did not give him shelter from his own fault.

Quicknotes

ADULTERY Sexual intercourse between a married person and another who is not that person's spouse, or between a person and another who is married.

CONDONATION In divorce law, forgiveness of a prior matrimonial offense on condition that it will not be repeated; the offense may not later be used as a ground of divorce without evidence of further injury.

IRRECONCILABLE DIFFERENCES A ground for no-fault divorce.

NO-FAULT DIVORCE A basis for terminating a marriage without the need for demonstrating misconduct on the part of either spouse.

Husband W. v. Wife W.

Abused husband (P) v. Abused wife (D)

Del. Sup. Ct., 297 A.2d 39 (1972).

NATURE OF CASE: Appeal from the denial of a divorce petition.

FACT SUMMARY: The trial court held that Mr. W. (P) failed to meet his burden of proving there was no reasonable possibility of reconciliation, and on that basis denied the divorce.

🏛 **RULE OF LAW**
A divorce may be granted for incompatibility where it is shown that no reasonable possibility of reconciliation exists.

FACTS: Mr. W. (P) and Mrs. W. (D) separated in 1970. They constantly had violent quarrels, which often involved the police and the family court. Mrs. W. (D) put lye in Mr. W.'s (P) food, she tried to stab him, and she threw a brick through a window on separate occasions. Mr. W. (P) hit her over the head with a chair, kicked her, threatened her physically, and threatened to burn the house down. Subsequently, Mr. W. (P) sued for divorce on the grounds of incompatibility. At trial, neither party disputed these incidents occurred, and both testified that reconciliation was unlikely. The family court denied the divorce, holding Mr. W. (P) had failed to meet his burden of showing no reasonable possibility of reconciliation. He appealed.

ISSUE: May a divorce be granted for incompatibility where it is shown that no reasonable possibility exists for reconciliation?

HOLDING AND DECISION: (Per curiam) Yes. A divorce may be granted for incompatibility where it is shown that no reasonable possibility of reconciliation exists. In this case, the violence of the parties toward each other and the frequency of the altercations clearly showed that no reasonable possibility existed for reconciliation. As a result, Mr. W. (P) clearly met his burden, and the family court's finding in this regard was clearly erroneous. Reversed and remanded.

▌ *ANALYSIS*

One of the first no-fault grounds for divorce was incompatibility. Because it was not easy to define legislatively, it did not become a vehicle for legislative expansion of the concept of divorce. It is such a wide ground that the formulation of guidelines is virtually impossible.

■■■

Quicknotes

NO-FAULT DIVORCE A basis for terminating a marriage without the need for demonstrating misconduct on the part of either spouse.

■■■

Williams v. North Carolina (I)

Alleged bigamists (D) v. State (P)

317 U.S. 287 (1942).

NATURE OF CASE: Appeal from a conviction.

FACT SUMMARY: Williams (D) and Hendrix (D) were married to others in North Carolina before they decided to leave their spouses, travel to Nevada, obtain respective divorce decrees and marry each other. The State of North Carolina (P) brought charges against them for bigamous cohabitation, which resulted in their conviction.

🏛 RULE OF LAW
The order of a court with proper jurisdiction is subject to full faith and credit.

FACTS: North Carolina residents Williams (D) and Hendrix (D) decided to end their marriages to other individuals and traveled to Nevada to obtain divorce decrees. Their (D) spouses were not served with process in Nevada and their spouses did not enter appearances in Nevada. Once divorced, Williams (D) and Hendrix (D) satisfied the Nevada residency requirement and were married before returning to North Carolina. Later, Williams (D) and Hendrix (D) were charged with bigamous cohabitation. The State (P) argued successfully that the Nevada decrees should not be recognized in North Carolina. Upon conviction, both Williams (D) and Hendrix (D) appealed.

ISSUE: Is the order of a court with proper jurisdiction subject to full faith and credit?

HOLDING AND DECISION: (Douglas, J.) Yes. The order of a court with proper jurisdiction is subject to full faith and credit. The trial court held that North Carolina was not required to recognize the Nevada decrees under the full faith and credit clause of the Constitution (Art. IV, § 1) by reason of *Haddock v. Haddock*, 201 U.S. 562 (1906). The *Haddock* case involved a suit for separation and alimony brought in New York by the wife on personal service of the husband. The husband pleaded in defense a divorce decree obtained by him in Connecticut where he had established a separate domicile. The Court held that New York, the matrimonial domicile where the wife still resided, need not give full faith and credit to the Connecticut decree, since the Connecticut decree was obtained by the husband who wrongfully left his wife in the matrimonial domicile, service on her having been obtained by publication and she not having entered an appearance in the action. But we do not agree with the theory of the *Haddock* case that a decree of divorce granted under such circumstances by one state need not be given full faith and credit in another.

Article IV, § 1 of the Constitution not only directs that "Full Faith and Credit shall be given in each State to the public Acts, Records, and judicial Proceedings of every other State" but also provides that "Congress may by general laws prescribe the Manner in which such Acts, Records and Proceedings shall be proved, and the Effect thereof." Thus, even though the cause of action could not be entertained in the state of the forum, either because it had been barred by the local statute of limitations or contravened local policy, a judgment obtained in a sister state is entitled to full faith and credit.

Each state as a sovereign has a rightful and legitimate concern in the marital status of persons domiciled within its borders. The marriage relation creates problems of large social importance. Protection of offspring, property interests, and the enforcement of marital responsibilities are but a few of commanding problems in the field of domestic relations with which the state must deal. Thus it is plain that each state, by virtue of its command over its domiciliaries and its large interest in the institution of marriage, can alter within its own borders the marriage status of the spouse domiciled there, even though the other spouse is absent.

But if one is lawfully divorced and remarried in Nevada and still married to the first spouse in North Carolina, an even more complicated and serious condition would be realized. Under the circumstances of this case, a man would have two wives, a wife two husbands. Each would be a bigamist for living in one state with the only one with whom the other state would permit him lawfully to live. Children of the second marriage would be bastards in one state but legitimate in the other. And all that would flow from the legalistic notion that where one spouse is wrongfully deserted he retains power over the matrimonial domicile so that the domicile of the other spouse follows him wherever he may go, while, if he is to blame, he retains no such power.

It is assumed that Williams (D) and Hendrix (D) had a bona fide domicile in Nevada, not that the Nevada domicile was a sham. Within the limits of her political power the State (P) may, of course, enforce her own policy regarding the marriage relation—an institution more basic in our civilization than any other. But society also has an interest in the avoidance of polygamous marriages and in the protection of innocent offspring of marriages deemed legitimate in other jurisdictions. And other states have an equally legitimate concern in the status of persons domiciled there as respects the institution of marriage. So, when a court of one state acting in accord with the requirements of procedural due process alters the marital status of one

Continued on next page.

domiciled in that state by granting him a divorce from his absent spouse, the Court cannot say its decree should be excepted from the full faith and credit clause merely because its enforcement or recognition in another state would conflict with the policy of the latter. *Haddock v. Haddock* is therefore overruled, and the judgment is reversed and the cause is remanded to the Supreme Court of North Carolina for proceedings not inconsistent with this opinion. Reversed.

▶ *ANALYSIS*

If a court has proper jurisdiction, its decisions are generally subject to the constitutional guarantees of full faith and credit. As the decision in this case showed, public policy favoring finality weighed against any uncertainty as to an individual's marital status caused by a contest between differing states and the states' requirements for divorce. The Court hinted that if a court does not have proper jurisdiction over a divorce action, another state does not have to honor it. On remand, the State (P) of North Carolina questioned Williams's (D) and Hendrix's (D) divorces based on their failure to satisfy the Nevada residency requirement.

■══■

Quicknotes

BIGAMY The criminal offense of willfully and knowingly marrying a second time while knowing that the first marriage is still undissolved.

DOMICILE A person's permanent home or principal establishment to which he has an intention of returning when he is absent therefrom.

■══■

Williams v. North Carolina (II)

Alleged bigamists (D) v. State (P)

325 U.S. 226 (1945).

NATURE OF CASE: Appeal from the affirmation of a conviction after remand from the Supreme Court.

FACT SUMMARY: Williams (D) and Hendrix (D) lived in North Carolina and were married to others. They left their spouses, traveled to Nevada, obtained divorce decrees and then married each other. The State of North Carolina (P) brought charges against them for bigamous cohabitation, which resulted in their conviction. Upon remand from the Supreme Court, the convictions were affirmed.

RULE OF LAW
The decision of a court without proper jurisdiction is not subject to full faith and credit.

FACTS: North Carolina residents Williams (D) and Hendrix (D) decided to end their marriages to other individuals and traveled to Nevada to obtain divorce decrees. Their spouses were not served with process in Nevada and they were not present during the divorce hearing. Once divorced, Williams (D) and Hendrix (D) satisfied the Nevada residency requirement and were married before they returned to North Carolina. Later, both were charged with bigamous cohabitation. The State (P) argued successfully that the Nevada decrees should not be recognized in North Carolina. Upon conviction, both Williams (D) and Hendrix (D) appealed. The U.S. Supreme Court ordered a remand, and the convictions were upheld based on a finding that Williams (D) and Hendrix (D) did not satisfy the residency requirement to permit Nevada to have proper jurisdiction to issue the divorce decree. This decision was then appealed.

ISSUE: Is the decision of a court without proper jurisdiction subject to full faith and credit?

HOLDING AND DECISION: (Frankfurter, J.) No. The decision of a court without proper jurisdiction is not subject to full faith and credit. The implications of the Full Faith and Credit Clause, Article IV, § 1 of the Constitution are clear in this case. Under our system of law, judicial power to grant a divorce—jurisdiction, strictly speaking—is founded on domicile. Domicile implies a nexus between person and place of such permanence as to control the creation of legal relations and responsibilities of the utmost significance. Divorce, like marriage, is of concern not merely to the immediate parties. It affects personal rights of the deepest significance. It also touches basic interests of society. Since divorce, like marriage, creates a new status, every consideration of policy makes it

desirable that the effect should be the same wherever the question arises.

The state of domiciliary origin should not be bound by an unfounded, even if not collusive, recital in the record of a court of another state. As to the truth or existence of a fact, like that of domicile, upon which depends the power to exert judicial authority, a state not a party to the exertion of such judicial authority in another state but seriously affected by it has a right, when asserting its own unquestioned authority, to ascertain the truth or existence of that crucial fact. In short, the decree of divorce is a conclusive adjudication of everything except the jurisdictional facts upon which it is founded, and domicile is a jurisdictional fact. To permit the necessary finding of domicile by one state to foreclose all states in the protection of their social institutions would be intolerable.

What is immediately before us is the conclusion of the State of North Carolina (P) in its finding that Williams (D) and Hendrix (D), who obtained Nevada decrees, were not domiciled there. The fact that the Nevada court found that they were domiciled there is entitled to respect. However, the record may be fairly summarized by saying that Williams (D) and Hendrix (D) left North Carolina for the purpose of getting divorces from their respective spouses in Nevada, and as soon as each had done so, they married one another, and they left Nevada and returned to North Carolina to live there together as man and wife. It would be highly unreasonable to assert that a jury could not reasonably find that the evidence demonstrated that petitioners went to Nevada solely for the purpose of obtaining a divorce and intended all along to return to North Carolina. Such an intention, the trial court properly charged, would preclude acquisition of domiciles in Nevada.

Williams (D) and Hendrix (D) assumed the risk that this Court would find that North Carolina (P) justifiably concluded that they had not been domiciled in Nevada. Since the divorces which they sought and received in Nevada had no legal validity in North Carolina and their North Carolina spouses were still alive, they subjected themselves to prosecution for bigamous cohabitation under North Carolina law. Affirmed.

ANALYSIS

Williams's (D) and Hendrix's (D) origination convictions were based on North Carolina's (P) refusal to generally recognize their Nevada divorces. The Supreme Court held that such a general prohibition was wrong, and that the

Continued on next page.

decision of a court with proper jurisdiction was entitled to full faith and credit. What "proper jurisdiction" meant was litigated by the State (P), centering on the issue of whether or not Williams (D) and Hendrix (D) actually satisfied the domicile requirement of Nevada. Finding that they did not, both were convicted again. What is clear in this decision is that a court's jurisdiction, not necessarily its ultimate decision, is always subject to review and can endanger full faith and credit finality.

■━■

Quicknotes

BIGAMY The criminal offense of willfully and knowingly marrying a second time while knowing that the first marriage is still undissolved.

FULL FAITH AND CREDIT ACT As provided in the U.S. Constitution, Article IV, any state judicial proceedings shall have such faith and credit given them in every court in the United States as they would in their own state

■━■

Sosna v. Iowa

Iowa wife (P) v. State (D)

419 U.S. 393 (1975).

NATURE OF CASE: Appeal from the denial of a divorce decree.

FACT SUMMARY: In Iowa (D) there was a one-year residency requirement for obtaining a divorce.

🏛 RULE OF LAW
A state may validly impose a reasonable residency requirement on divorce actions.

FACTS: Sosna (P) moved back to Iowa (D) and several months later sought a divorce. Sosna's (P) husband made a special appearance to challenge jurisdiction. The court dismissed the action, finding that Sosna (P) had not been a resident of Iowa (D) for one year preceding the filing of the petition. Sosna (P) moved to have the statute declared unconstitutional as an impermissible restriction on the right to travel.

ISSUE: May a state impose a residency requirement on the right to file for a divorce action?

HOLDING AND DECISION: (Rehnquist, J.) Yes. A state may impose a residency requirement on the right to seek a divorce. This can be justified on the grounds of expense, administrative convenience, or avoidance of officious intermeddling in the affairs of another state. Also, because of the importance of the issues involved, a state may reasonably require a showing of close contacts with it before opening its courts to such actions. These valid reasons are sufficient to justify the imposition of a reasonable residency requirement in divorce actions. More than domiciliary intent is required. The one-year waiting period to establish residency is valid. Affirmed.

DISSENT: (Marshall, J.) The majority fails to consider that the residency requirement is a violation of the constitutional right to travel. As such the statute should be strictly scrutinized to see if less onerous restrictions could accomplish the State's (D) end. Domiciliary intent should be sufficient to allow the court to waive the residency requirement.

▌ *ANALYSIS*

By 1977, at least ten states had lowered their residency requirement to three months or less. Residency is justified on the ground that the state must assure itself that the party intends to remain in it due to the importance of the matter. *Williams v. North Carolina*, 325 U.S. 226 (1945). Domicile for granting of a decree may be challenged in other states where there is an attempt to enforce it.

Perrin v. Perrin

Ex-wife (P) v. Ex-husband (D)

408 F.2d 107 (3d Cir. 1969).

NATURE OF CASE: Appeal from dissolution of marriage and custody award.

FACT SUMMARY: Mrs. Perrin (P) attacked the validity of her Mexican divorce from Mr. Perrin (D) which she procured. She was personally present in Mexico and Mr. Perrin (D), who appeared by counsel, filed a consenting answer.

 RULE OF LAW
Bilateral Mexican divorces are valid and recognized.

FACTS: The Perrins are Swiss citizens who wed in New York. Mrs. Perrin (P) filed a petition for a divorce from Mr. Perrin (D) in a Mexican court. She personally appeared in Mexico. Mr. Perrin (D), who appeared by counsel, filed a consenting answer. The Mexican court granted the dissolution and awarded custody of the minor son to Mr. Perrin (D). Mrs. Perrin (P) later filed a second divorce complaint against Mr. Perrin (D) and sought custody of their son. Mr. Perrin (D) moved to dismiss for lack of subject matter jurisdiction because of the prior divorce and lack of personal jurisdiction because Mr. Perrin (D) and his son were then living in St. Thomas. Mrs. Perrin (P) then attacked the validity of the Mexican divorce on the ground that neither she nor Mr. Perrin (D) was domiciled in Mexico at the time it was rendered. The trial court denied the motion to dismiss and Mr. Perrin appealed.

ISSUE: Are bilateral Mexican divorces valid and recognized?

HOLDING AND DECISION: (Maris, J.) Yes. Bilateral Mexican divorces are valid and recognized. If a defendant was personally served or did actually appear in an action for divorce, he is estopped from impeaching the resulting decree, whether the domiciliary jurisdiction was contested by the defendant or admitted by him. Cases so holding involved the Full Faith and Credit Clause. Here, however, we are dealing with a decree of a foreign state to which the principles of comity, rather than full faith and credit, apply. Here a bilateral divorce is involved since Mrs. Perrin (P) was personally present in Mexico and appeared in court and Mr. Perrin (D) appeared by counsel and filed a consenting answer. A balanced public policy now requires that recognition of bilateral Mexican divorces be recognized rather than withheld, and such recognition, as a matter of comity, offends no public policy. This is especially true here where the party who seeks to attack the Mexican divorce is the one who sought and obtained the decree upon her representation that she resided in Mexico. Reversed.

ANALYSIS

Courts in some states, such as New Mexico, Ohio, and New Jersey, have refused to recognize Mexican decrees resulting from proceedings in which both parties participated. In *Rosenbaum v. Rosenbaum*, 42 N.J. 287, however, a New Jersey court recognized a bilateral Mexican divorce when one of the parties apparently seemed to have a valid Mexican domicile. In some jurisdictions, including California, the doctrine of estoppel may serve to effectively uphold a Mexican divorce decree under some circumstances.

Vanderbilt v. Vanderbilt

Spouse (P) v. Spouse (D)

354 U.S. 416 (1957).

NATURE OF CASE: Review of order of court mandating alimony support payments.

FACT SUMMARY: Mr. Vanderbilt (D) obtained a divorce decree in Nevada and Mrs. Vanderbilt (P) later sued in New York for alimony. But Mr. Vanderbilt (D) claimed that New York was compelled to grant full faith and credit to the Nevada decree, which had destroyed any duty of support to Mrs. Vanderbilt (P).

RULE OF LAW
A court cannot adjudicate a personal claim or obligation unless it has jurisdiction over the person of the defendant.

FACTS: The parties had separated when Mrs. Vanderbilt (P) moved to New York. Mr. Vanderbilt (D) then obtained a Nevada divorce decree, which provided that Mr. Vanderbilt's (D) duty to support Mrs. Vanderbilt (P) had ended. When Mrs. Vanderbilt (P) later started proceedings in New York for separation and alimony, Mr. Vanderbilt (D) appeared specially and contended that the Nevada decree was entitled to full faith and credit in New York. The New York court found the divorce decree had validly ended the marriage but ordered Mr. Vanderbilt (D) to make support payments under a New York state statute. Mr. Vanderbilt (D) claimed that the New York statute was unconstitutional as applied because it violated the Full Faith and Credit Clause of the U.S. Constitution. The support order was upheld on appeal, and Mr. Vanderbilt (D) then applied for certiorari to the Supreme Court.

ISSUE: Can a court adjudicate a personal claim or obligation if it does not have jurisdiction over the person of the defendant?

HOLDING AND DECISION: (Black, J.) No. A court cannot adjudicate a personal claim or obligation unless it has jurisdiction over the person of the defendant. The Full Faith and Credit Clause does not obligate New York to recognize the entire Nevada decree since that decree was void to the extent it purported to affect Mrs. Vanderbilt's (P) right to support. The Nevada divorce court had no personal jurisdiction over Mrs. Vanderbilt (P), and therefore it had no power to extinguish any right she had under New York law for financial support from Mr. Vanderbilt (D). Affirmed.

▶ ANALYSIS

In general, ex parte orders regulating marital relationships are given extraterritorial effect, but ex parte orders regulating the financial interests of the parties are not. Other courts have ruled that dower rights are inchoate and therefore are extinguished by a divorce decree predicated upon either substituted or constructive service. The court in the state in which real property is located always has in rem jurisdiction to divide the property, though some states now permit division of property in a different state if the court in the other state validly asserts in personam jurisdiction over both parties.

■■■

Quicknotes

EX PARTE A proceeding commenced by one party without providing any opposing parties with notice or which is uncontested by an adverse party.

FULL FAITH AND CREDIT Doctrine that a judgment by a court of one state shall be given the same effect in another state.

INCHOATE Impartial or incomplete.

IN PERSONAM JURISDICTION The jurisdiction of a court over a person as opposed to his interest in property.

IN REM JURISDICTION A court's authority over a thing so that its judgment is binding in respect to the rights and interests of all parties in that thing.

■■■

Kulko v. Superior Court of California

New York husband (P) v. California court (D)

436 U.S. 84 (1978).

NATURE OF CASE: Action to increase child support.

FACT SUMMARY: Kulko (P) argued that he had insufficient contacts with California to give its court jurisdiction over him in his wife's suit for an increase in child support.

RULE OF LAW
A state court may not exercise in personam jurisdiction over a nonresident, nondomiciliary parent of minor children domiciled in that state unless that nonresident parent has certain "minimum contacts" with the forum state such that the maintenance of the suit does not offend "traditional notions of fair play and substantial justice."

FACTS: Kulko (P) and his wife had been residents of New York throughout their married life, having stopped in California only to get married while Kulko (P) was en route to a tour of duty in Korea. Upon separation, Mrs. Kulko moved to San Francisco, but she flew to New York to sign a separation agreement drawn up there. It provided the children would live with their father in New York, but would stay with her in California during their Christmas, Easter, and summer vacations. It also set $3,000 per year as child support. After procuring a Haitian divorce, Mrs. Kulko returned to California and remarried. When Kulko's (P) daughter expressed her desire to stay on with her mother after Christmas vacation, Kulko (P) gave his permission and bought her a one-way ticket to California. When the son then told his mother he also desired to live with her, she sent him a ticket to California, unbeknownst to Kulko (P). So both children wound up living with their mother. She eventually brought an action to establish the Haitian divorce decree as a California judgment; to modify the judgment to give her full custody of the children; and to increase Kulko's (P) child support obligations. Kulko (P) appeared specially and moved to quash service of the summons on the ground that he was not a resident of California and lacked sufficient "minimum contacts" with California under the *International Shoe* decision to warrant the state's assertion of personal jurisdiction over him. The trial court summarily denied the motion to quash, and the appellate court affirmed. It held that by consenting to his children's living in California, Kulko (P) had "caused an effect in the state" warranting the exercise of jurisdiction over him. The California Supreme Court affirmed, holding the "purposeful act" warranting the exercise of personal jurisdiction to be Kulko's (P) action in "actively and fully consent[ing] to Ilsa living in California for the school

year . . . and . . . send[ing] her to California for that purpose."

ISSUE: When a state court seeks to exercise in personam jurisdiction over a nonresident, nondomiciliary parent of minor children domiciled in that state, must the parent have certain "minimum contacts" with the forum state such that its exercising jurisdiction does not offend "traditional notions of fair play and substantial justice"?

HOLDING AND DECISION: (Marshall, J.) Yes. *International Shoe v. Washington*, 326 U.S. 310 (1945), sets the prerequisite for a state court's exercising in personam jurisdiction over a nonresident, nondomiciliary parent of minor children domiciled in that state: the nonresident parent must have certain "minimum contacts" with the forum state such that maintenance of the suit does not offend "traditional notions of fair play and substantial justice." In this case, the alleged "minimum contact" was Kulko's (P) allowing his daughter to go to live in California during the school year. However, that is not sufficient contact to confer jurisdiction over Kulko (P). A father who agrees, in the interests of family harmony and his children's preferences, to allow them to spend more time in California than was required under a separation agreement can hardly be said to have "purposefully availed" himself of the "benefits and protection" of California's laws. In light of this conclusion that Kulko (P) did not purposefully derive benefit from any activities relating to the state of California, it is apparent that the California Supreme Court's reliance on his having caused an "effect in California" was misplaced. The "effects" test of jurisdiction is found in the Restatement Second of Conflicts and is not binding on this Court. Furthermore, it was intended to reach wrongful activity outside of the state causing injury within the state or commercial activity affecting state residents. Neither situation applies here. Even if it did, the restatement recognizes that there might be circumstances which would render "unreasonable" the assertion of jurisdiction over the nonresident defendant. This is clearly a case where such circumstances exist. Basic considerations of fairness point decisively in favor of Kulko's (P) state of domicile as the proper forum for adjudication of this case. He resided there at all times during this marriage and continues to do so. He did no more than acquiesce to his child's wish to live with her mother, a single act a reasonable parent would not expect to result in the substantial financial and personal strain of litigating a child support suit in a forum 3,000 miles away. To make jurisdiction turn on whether Kulko (P) bought his daughter her ticket or

Continued on next page.

instead unsuccessfully sought to prevent her departure would impose an unreasonable burden on family relations, one wholly unjustified by the "quality and nature" of his activities in or relating to the state of California. Reversed.

▶ *ANALYSIS*

The decision in this case does not leave Mrs. Kulko without remedy or force her to undergo great expense and personal strain in litigating her case 3,000 miles away in New York. The Uniform Reciprocal Enforcement and Support Act, a version of which has been passed in California, would allow her to file a petition in California and have its merits adjudicated in New York without either her or Kulko (P) having to leave their respective states. A similar action to collect any support payments found owing is also possible under this legislation.

■■■

Quicknotes

IN PERSONAM JURISDICTION The power of a court over a person, as opposed to a court's power over a person's interest in property.

■■■

Marital Breakdown: Resolving the Financial Concerns

Quick Reference Rules of Law

Ruggles v. Ruggles

Ex-wife (P) v. Retired ex-husband (D)

N.M. Sup. Ct., 116 N.M. 52, 860 P.2d 182 (1993)

NATURE OF CASE: Appeal from decision that a divorcing nonemployee spouse's community interest in an employer-sponsored retirement plan, when the employee's interest in the plan is vested and matured, should be paid on an "as it comes in" basis.

FACT SUMMARY: Nancy (P) disputed that she should wait until Joseph (D) retired to start receiving her community interest in Joseph's retirement plan, especially since his interest in the plan was already vested and matured.

🏛 RULE OF LAW
A divorcing nonemployee spouse's community interest in an employer-sponsored retirement plan, when the employee's interest in the plan is vested and matured, should be immediately distributed upon dissolution, even where the employee spouse has not retired.

FACTS: Joseph (D) and Nancy (P) Ruggles, who were divorcing, had entered into a comprehensive marital settlement agreement (MSA) that provided that Nancy (P) was entitled to 48 percent of Joseph's (D) retirement plan. At the time of trial, Joseph's (D) interest in the plan, sponsored by Joseph's employer, was fully vested and matured. Joseph (D), at age 50 and after 30 years of work, was eligible to retire, but had decided not to and he was not sure when he would retire. The MSA, however, did not specify when Nancy (P) was to begin receiving her interest in the plan nor the specific dollar amount she was to receive. The trial court found that as of the date of the trial, Joseph (D) would have been entitled to receive $1,570.71 per month under the plan and ordered that he pay Nancy (P) $753.94 (48 percent of the pension) per month until he retired, at which point Nancy could receive this amount directly from the employer pursuant to a Qualified Domestic Relations Order (QDRO). Joseph (D) appealed to the court of appeals, which reversed, ruling that, contrary to the trial court's findings, the MSA unambiguously provided that Nancy (P) would not receive her share of Joseph's (D) benefits until he actually retired, and that to rule otherwise would be contrary to settled law that requires distribution of retirement benefits on a "pay as it comes in" basis. Nancy (P) then appealed to the New Mexico Supreme Court, which granted review.

ISSUE: Should a divorcing nonemployee spouse's community interest in an employer-sponsored retirement plan, when the employee's interest in the plan is vested and matured, be immediately distributed upon dissolution, even where the employee spouse has not retired?

HOLDING AND DECISION: (Montgomery, J.) Yes. A review of cases dealing with the distribution of a community's interest in retirement benefits upon dissolution of a marriage reveals that such benefits are community property to the extent acquired during the marriage, and are subject to division upon dissolution, even if the interest in such benefits has not matured. However, prior case law (*Schweitzer v. Burch*, 711 P.2d 889 (1985)), stated that upon dissolution, unless both parties agree otherwise, community property retirement benefits must be distributed on a "pay as it comes in" basis. Despite this statement, *Schweitzer* did not involve an issue about how a nonemployee spouse's community interest in a retirement plan should be distributed or otherwise dealt with upon divorce. Nevertheless, *Schweitzer* committed the state to the "reserved jurisdiction" method of distributing the community interest in retirement benefits, where the court reserves jurisdiction to distribute benefits when the employee spouse actually receives them, as opposed to the "lump sum" or "cash value" method. Under the lump sum method, retirement plan benefits are awarded to the employee spouse at the time of dissolution and assets of equivalent value are awarded to the nonemployee spouse. Following the rationale of cases from other community property states—e.g., that the nonemployee spouse's interest should not be impaired by the employee spouse's unilateral choice to postpone retirement—the Court agrees that the lump sum method is the preferable one for satisfying the nonemployee spouse's claim to her community interest in her spouse's retirement plan, and that the trial court should have discretion in implementing that method, even if that includes using the reserved jurisdiction method in appropriate cases. Other guiding principles are that each spouse has a present, vested, one-half interest in the spouses' community property, and that a spouse should be granted complete and immediate control over his or her share of the community property (to reduce future strife between the parties). In *Schweitzer*, this Court was concerned with the possibility of the employee spouse bearing all the risk of forfeiture (if one of the spouses died before the benefits were paid out) and desired instead for both parties to bear the risk. The Court in that case ruled that it is preferable for both spouses to bear the risk of forfeiture equally. However, the Court now thinks that it is impossible to devise a system that in all cases will result in both spouses bearing the risk of forfeiture equally. Under the reserved jurisdiction method, the nonemployee spouse risks losing everything if her husband dies before retirement, but the

Continued on next page.

employee spouse is guaranteed a pension if he lives past retirement, and still has the security of being currently employed. Reversed. On remand, if the court determines that the MSA is clear about when and how the benefits were to be paid to Nancy (P), the MSA governs and should be enforced. If the MSA was not clear, the trial court should reinstate its award to Nancy (P). It is acknowledged that this would not comport with the Court's determination that a lump sum distribution through other assets is the preferred method in such cases, but at this point it would be unwise to undo the division of the parties' other assets pursuant to the MSA. As a final note, the trial court may not disturb the MSA to assure fairness: a voluntary property settlement between divorcing spouses is sacrosanct absent fraud, duress, and the like. Court of Appeals decisions reversed and cases remanded.

▶ ANALYSIS

This case emphasizes the principle in community property that states that equal division of the community estate is presumptive and that each spouse should have complete and immediate control over his or her share upon dissolution. The case also makes it equally clear that these presumptions may be voluntarily modified by agreement of the divorcing spouses and that such agreements will be given full effect, absent circumstances that would invalidate any contract. As with any other contract, any ambiguous provisions are subject to construction by the court.

■■■

Quicknotes

COMMUNITY PROPERTY In community property jurisdictions, refers to all money or property acquired during the term of the marriage in which each spouse has an undivided one-half interest.

VESTED INTEREST A present right to property, although the right to the possession of such property may not be enjoyed until a future date.

■■■

Rainwater v. Rainwater

Wife (P) v. Husband (D)

Ariz. Ct. App., 177 Ariz. 500, 869 P.2d 176 (1993).

NATURE OF CASE: Appeal from maintenance award following dissolution of marriage.

FACT SUMMARY: Mr. Rainwater (D) contended that the trial court had erred when it ordered him to pay maintenance to Mrs. Rainwater (P) until her death or remarriage.

🏛 RULE OF LAW
A court may order indefinite maintenance if a wife's reasonably anticipated income would not meet her reasonable needs as determined by reference to the standard of living established during the marriage.

FACTS: Following the dissolution of their 23-year marriage, the court ordered that Mr. Rainwater (D) pay Mrs. Rainwater (P) spousal maintenance until her death or remarriage. Mr. Rainwater (D) argued that the trial court erred because, in the absence of evidence that a wife was permanently unable to become self-sustaining, Arizona public policy permitted only a fixed-term award to assist her in transition to an independent life. Mrs. Rainwater (P), on the other hand, claimed that the law required a case-by-case determination so the court could balance the factors enumerated in the statute.

ISSUE: May a court order indefinite maintenance if a wife's reasonably anticipated income would not meet her reasonable needs as determined by reference to the standard of living established during the marriage?

HOLDING AND DECISION: (Fidel, C.J.) Yes. A court may order indefinite maintenance if a wife's reasonably anticipated income would not meet her reasonable needs as determined by reference to the standard of living established during the marriage. The trial court did not exceed its discretion in awarding indefinite maintenance in this case. Because maintenance awards are modifiable, an award of maintenance until death or remarriage does not lock long-term maintenance irrefutably into place. Rather, it places the burden on the paying spouse to prove a later change in circumstances sufficiently substantial to warrant shortening the duration of the award. A fixed-term award, by contrast, places the burden on the receiving spouse to prove a change in circumstances sufficiently substantial to warrant extending the award. When, as in this case, the finding that one spouse will never be able to independently approximate the standard of living established during marriage and that the other spouse will remain financially able to contribute to the first spouse's support is supported by the evidence, there is no inequity in placing the burden on the paying spouse to later prove that a substantial and continuing change of circumstances has occurred. Trial court's order of spousal maintenance affirmed.

▶ ANALYSIS

The Arizona Supreme Court later denied the husband's petition for review. See *Rainwater v. Rainwater*, 869 P.2d 175 (Ariz. 1994). One judge dissented at that time, claiming that there was no existing authority for the proposition that one spouse "needs" to live forever in the style to which he or she had become accustomed. Justice Martone contended that "the allowance of lifetime maintenance at the standard of living established during marriage turns the institution of marriage into a lifetime annuity."

Quicknotes

DISSOLUTION Annulment or termination of a formal or legal bond, tie or contract.

MAINTENANCE AWARD An order entered by the court requiring one spouse to make payments to the other for sustenance.

Murphy v. Murphy

[Parties not identified.]

Me. Sup. Jud. Ct., 2003 Me. 17, 816 A.2d 814 (2003).

NATURE OF CASE: Cross-appeals in dissolution case.

FACT SUMMARY: Michael Murphy and Stephanie Murphy cohabited for a number of years prior to marrying. The trial court made determinations of what was non-marital property and marital property during the dissolution proceedings. The trial court also considered the financial circumstances and abilities of the parties when making a spousal support award.

🏛 RULE OF LAW
The trial court has great discretion in awarding spousal support, which may be a transitional award and can include medical, educational, and legal expenses.

FACTS: The couple met and moved in together twenty-six years ago in New York. After a few years, Michael Murphy began working for New England Electric and the couple moved to Massachusetts. They purchased a home as joint tenants and later had a son together. They held themselves out as married this entire time. Stephanie Murphy was a homemaker who also home-schooled their son. The family moved to Maine because Michael began a new job, and the couple purchased a new family home with the proceeds from the sale of their Massachusetts home. Stephanie wished to protect herself and her son in the event something happened to Michael, so the Murphys married in 1993. In 1995, Michael started his own business, and Stephanie helped manage it for about one year. She then worked outside of the home as a psychiatric technician at a hospital where she presently works full-time. The Murphys began divorce proceedings in September 2000, sold real estate prior to trial, and Stephanie received the proceeds of $4600. Stephanie lives with her domestic partner in an apartment and their son resides with Michael. The parents share parental rights and obligations and their son sees Stephanie whenever he wishes. Stephanie requested funds for substantial dental work, therapy for depression, and prescription medication for depression. Assets included the marital home, Michael's retirement account from his Massachusetts job that had not been added to since he rolled it over, a joint account funded by an inheritance from Michael's mother and used solely for his mother's estate expenses with Stephanie never accessing the funds, Michael's private account funded by the inheritance from his mother, two cars, and other personal property. The trial court awarded Michael the marital home and the mortgage, the cheaper car, personal property worth $15,000, his retirement account, and his inheritance. The trial court awarded Stephanie the more expensive car, per-

sonal property worth $5,000, and a lump sum of $50,000 from Michael to divide the marital estate equitably. The trial court found that Michael had $355,000 in nonmarital property and Stephanie had nothing. The court considered Stephanie and her partner's combined earning ability, her medical and dental needs, her educational needs, and her attorneys' fees and awarded her $60,000 in transitional spousal support. Both the Murphys appealed.

ISSUE: Does the trial court have great discretion in awarding spousal support, which may be a transitional award and can include medical, educational, and legal expenses?

HOLDING AND DECISION: (Clifford, J.) Yes. The trial court has great discretion in awarding spousal support, which may be a transitional award and can include medical, educational, and legal expenses. Michael argued on appeal that medical and dental expenses are not part of transitional spousal support awards. The court has great discretion in fashioning spousal support and can consider a number of factors, including health and disabilities of the party. Contrary to Michael's argument, Stephanie's health and counseling expenses are transitional. Michael also argued that the amount was excessive, but given the facts of the case, this court disagrees. Stephanie contended on appeal that the trial court erred in its division of marital property. The valuation of the marital home was not erroneous, because it was based on expert testimony. Stephanie argued that the retirement account was marital property. Property is presumed to be marital, unless it falls within a defined exception. Here, the retirement account was acquired prior to the marriage, was not increased during the marriage, and was never in Stephanie's name. It is not marital property. Similarly, the joint account containing a portion of Michael's inheritance is not marital property, because it falls within an exception, was only briefly held jointly and for an express purpose of paying for his mother's estate, and Stephanie never accessed the funds. The trial court properly divided the marital property and awarded Stephanie a sum to ensure equitable division. Finally, the trial court did not err in requiring each party to pay its own attorneys' fees. The court considered Stephanie's attorneys' fees in its transitional support award. Affirmed.

▎ *ANALYSIS*

Permanent, significant alimony is quickly becoming an award of the past in dissolution cases, particularly as

Continued on next page.

more women are better able to provide for themselves after a divorce. Shorter marriages generally end in a limited, transitional amount of spousal support and it is not always the husband that is required to pay the wife. A particularly well-known current case involves a pop star and her unemployed husband (*Spears v. Federline*). In this case the pop star paid her former husband $20,000 monthly transitional support for just a few months.

■══■

Quicknotes

ALIMONY Allowances (usually monetary) which husband or wife by court order pays to the other spouse for maintenance while they are separated, or after they are divorced (permanent alimony), or temporarily, pending a suit for divorce (pendente lite).

DISSOLUTION PROCEEDING AND DECREE A proceeding and resulting decree to terminate a marriage.

SPOUSAL SUPPORT Payments made by one spouse to another in discharge of the spouse's duty pursuant to law, or in accordance with a written divorce or separation decree, in order to provide maintenance for the other spouse.

■══■

Bell v. Bell

Ex-wife (P) v. Ex-husband (D)

Mass. Sup. Jud. Ct., 393 Mass. 20, 468 N.E.2d 859 (1984).

NATURE OF CASE: Appeal from reversal of dismissal of contempt complaint.

FACT SUMMARY: The former Mrs. Bell (P) appealed from a decision reversing the probate court's decision dismissing a contempt complaint against Mr. Bell (D) for his failure to continue support payments allegedly owed under a judgment of divorce.

> 🏛 **RULE OF LAW**
> If a woman cohabits with a man on a regular basis, sharing the same dwelling place and the same bedroom, the parties give the outward appearance of marriage.

FACTS: The former Mrs. Bell (P) and Mr. Bell (D) were divorced in 1975. Their divorce judgment provided that Mr. Bell (D) would pay a substantial amount of alimony for 15 years unless the former Mrs. Bell (P) died, remarried, or cohabited with another man so as to give "the outward appearance of marriage" at any time prior to May 1, 1981. The divorce judgment also contained a noninterference clause, which provided that neither party would interfere with the personal liberty of the other. Mr. Bell (D) stopped alimony payments, claiming that the former Mrs. Bell (P) was living with a man, referred to as J.R., in violation of the non-cohabitation clause. The former Mrs. Bell (P) filed a contempt complaint with the probate court for Mr. Bell's (D) failure to continue support payments. The probate court found that the former Mrs. Bell (P) had been cohabiting with J.R. for three years, during which time they shared the same bedroom. Even though at no time did she hold herself out as married to J.R., the probate court found that the living arrangement gave the outward appearance of marriage and thus justified stopping the support payments under the divorce judgment. The probate court dismissed the contempt complaint, but the appeals court, relying on the noninterference clause, found that the non-cohabitation clause relieved Mr. Bell (D) of his support obligations only if the former Mrs. Bell (P) were to receive substantial support from, or become entitled to receive substantial support from, another man. From this decision, Mr. Bell (D) appealed.

ISSUE: If a woman cohabits with a man on a regular basis, sharing the same dwelling and the same bedroom, do the parties give the outward appearance of marriage?

HOLDING AND DECISION: (O'Connor, J.) Yes. If a woman cohabits with a man on a regular basis, sharing the same dwelling and the same bedroom, the parties give the outward appearance of marriage. The non-cohabitation clause in the present case, by its plain language, entertains the possibility that the wife might enter a living relationship that resembled marriage without the parties being married or claiming or acknowledging that they were married. The clause does not mention support, and the argument that such a provision is invalid in light of the noninterference clause also fails since the prohibition against cohabitation giving the outward appearance of marriage does not restrict the personal freedom of the parties any more than does the prohibition against marriage. [The court declined to hear the unfair discrimination claim of the former Mrs. Bell (P) since these constitutional challenges had not been raised in the courts below.] Judgment of the probate court affirmed.

DISSENT: (Wilkins, J.) The court's opinion gives no effect at all to the noninterference clause and unduly focuses on the living arrangement between the former Mrs. Bell (P) and J.R. Given the fact that they cohabited together and shared the same bedroom is an indication of nothing, given the nature of modern-day living arrangements.

DISSENT: (Abrams, J.) By not taking the appeals court's interpretation of the divorce judgment and alimony conditions, the court today permits husbands to interfere and meddle into the post-divorce lives of their wives and places such spouses, who may rely on the court's supervision that their entitlement to support is not subject to unreasonable conditions, at the mercy of their ex-spouses.

▶ ANALYSIS

The court did not address the constitutional issues raised by the former Mrs. Bell (P) on appeal for the first time. Had they been timely raised, it does not seem likely that the agreement in the present case, negotiated under the supervision of the courts and entered into voluntarily by the parties, would fall afoul of the unfair discrimination clause of the Constitution. The states, however, have different views of what might give the outward appearance of marriage, and the decision in a similar case may turn on the particular inclinations of the justices hearing the case.

■=■

Quicknotes

ALIMONY Allowances (usually monetary) which husband or wife by court order pays to the other spouse for maintenance while they are separated, or after they are divorced (permanent alimony), or temporarily, pending a suit for divorce (pendente lite).

■=■

Naylor v. Naylor

Hairdresser ex-wife (P) v. Surgeon ex-husband (D)

Utah Sup. Ct., 700 P.2d 707 (1985).

NATURE OF CASE: Appeal from an order granting a modification of a divorce decree.

FACT SUMMARY: After eleven and half years of marriage, Mrs. Naylor (P) and Mr. Naylor (D) divorced. Mrs. Naylor (P) was granted alimony and child support. Several years later, Mrs. Naylor (P) sought to increase the amount of both forms of support and to extend the term for alimony.

RULE OF LAW
Alimony and child support can be modified based on a material change in the circumstances of one or both parties.

FACTS: Mrs. Naylor (P) and Mr. Naylor (D) were married for 11½ years. During this time, Mrs. Naylor (P) was employed as a hairdresser and Mr. Naylor (D) studied and ultimately completed his medical training to become a practicing surgeon. Upon the dissolution of their marriage, a divorce was granted that incorporated a written agreement and property settlement agreement which awarded alimony and child support for Mrs. Naylor (P). Several years later Mrs. Naylor (P) filed an action for modification of the original decree. After a hearing, the trial court found a material change in circumstances warranting an increase in both alimony and child support. Mr. Naylor (D) then appealed.

ISSUE: Can alimony and child support be modified based on a material change in the circumstances of one or both parties?

HOLDING AND DECISION: (Durham, J.) Yes. Alimony and child support can be modified based on a material change in the circumstances of one or both parties. Here, the district court found that, at the time of the original divorce, Mrs. Naylor (P) had an expectancy that in the five-year period for which the alimony was awarded she would be able to establish herself as a hairdresser and have an increase in income sufficient to meet her financial needs, which expectancy has not been fulfilled. The court also found that the living expenses of Mrs. Naylor (P) and the party's child had increased from the time of the divorce due to increases in the cost of living and the fact that the child had become a teenager with significantly greater financial needs. Finally, the court found, Mr. Naylor (D) had the ability to pay an increased and extended alimony award and increased support award.

Mr. Naylor's (D) argument that the trial court exceeded its power in modifying the term of temporary alimony awarded in the original divorce decree even if a substantial change in relevant circumstances had occurred is contrary to the legislative mandate to the district courts and to the principles of equity followed by this court. The objective and purpose of the statute is to give the courts power to enforce, after divorce, the duty of support that exists between a husband and wife or parent and child. Legislators who enacted the law were probably aware of a fact, which is a matter of common knowledge to trial courts, that parties to divorce suits frequently enter into agreements relative to alimony or for child support which, if binding upon the courts, would leave children or divorced wives inadequately provided for. It is therefore reasonable to assume that the law was intended to give the courts power to disregard the stipulations or agreement of the parties in the first instance and enter judgment for such alimony or child support as appears reasonable, and to thereafter modify such judgments when a change of circumstances justifies it, regardless of attempts of the parties to control the matter by contract. Thus, the trial court in this case clearly had the power to modify the alimony provision of the decree.

On a petition for a modification of a divorce decree, the threshold requirement for relief is a showing of a substantial change of circumstances occurring since the entry of the decree and not contemplated in the decree itself. The record here amply supports the trial court's finding on the change of circumstances question: Mr. Naylor's (D) net income has more than doubled since the time of the divorce, even without the inclusion of the income being diverted into pension and profit sharing. Mrs. Naylor's income, on the other hand, has remained approximately the same in dollar amounts, thereby actually decreasing in real value, contrary to the parties' expectation that it would increase. The fact that this expectation, which was a predicate for the original support order, has not been fulfilled constitutes a material change in circumstances. The age and cost of supporting the parties' child has also clearly changed substantially since the time of the divorce.

Concerning the equities of the modification ordered by the trial judge, the trial court's findings were that Mrs. Naylor (P) had supported the parties during Mr. Naylor's (D) four-year medical school course and continued to contribute to their support after he began to earn modest amounts as an intern and resident; Mrs. Naylor has a high school degree; she was not employed as a hairdresser during the marriage, but had just completed her training and was beginning a career in that field at the time of the divorce; she agreed to the limited term of alimony because she anticipated that her work would be more remunerative

Continued on next page.

than it has in fact been; and in order to support herself and the parties' child, she has had to borrow over $13,000 since the divorce, in addition to her earnings and the amounts provided by the appellant. In view of the totality of the circumstances of the parties, the modification ordered by the trial judge constituted an abuse of his discretion or was so unfair or inequitable as to be arbitrary and capricious. Affirmed.

▶ *ANALYSIS*

The impact of the ruling in *Naylor* is that finalized divorce decrees with support settlements are subject to modification. Both in terms of the statute and equity, the court found it was reasonable for Mr. Naylor (D) to pay more as the costs of care for his wife and child increased. Looking at both the expenses and his increase in salary, the court had no difficulty in deciding that a modification of the original order was fair and reasonable. The lesson is that divorce settlements are only a snapshot of the current living situations of the parties and are subject to review and recalculation of any awards.

■═■

Quicknotes

ALIMONY Allowances (usually monetary) which husband or wife by court order pays to the other spouse for maintenance while they are separated, or after they are divorced (permanent alimony), or temporarily, pending a suit for divorce (pendente lite).

CHILD SUPPORT Payments made by one parent to another in satisfaction of the non-custodial parent's legal obligation to provide for the sustenance of the child.

CHILD SUPPORT MODIFICATION The alteration of the payment structure pursuant to which one parent provides payments to another in satisfaction of the non-custodial parent's legal obligation to provide for the sustenance of the child.

DIVORCE DECREE A decree terminating a marriage.

PENDENTE LITE A matter that is contingent on the disposition of a pending suit.

■═■

Hardy v. Hardy

Ex-husband (P) v. Ex-wife (D)

S.C. Ct. App., 311 S.C. 433, 429 S.E.2d 811 (1993)

NATURE OF CASE: Appeal from order (1) reserving alimony and (2) requiring each spouse to satisfy debts in his or her name.

FACT SUMMARY: Mr. Hardy (P) and Mrs. Hardy (D) each had debt in their own name prior to their divorce action. Mr. Hardy (P) argued that the trial court erred in (1) reserving alimony for Mrs. Hardy (D) and (2) requiring each of the spouses to satisfy the debt that had been in his or her name.

RULE OF LAW
(1) Alimony may not be reserved when there is no present or foreseeable circumstance that warrants alimony.
(2) There is a rebuttable presumption that debts incurred by spouses prior to a marital action are marital debts.

FACTS: At the time of divorce, Mr. Hardy (P) owed $32,000 in debt, and Mrs. Hardy (D) owed $2,800. The Hardys were close in age and Mrs. Hardy was in good health, receiving a pension, and working part-time. The trial court reserved alimony for Mrs. Hardy (D) and ordered that each spouse be required to satisfy all indebtedness in their respective names. Mr. Hardy (P) appealed on both issues.

ISSUE:
(1) May alimony be reserved when there is no present or foreseeable circumstance that warrants alimony?
(2) Is there a rebuttable presumption that debts incurred by spouses prior to a marital action are marital debts?

HOLDING AND DECISION: (Gardner, J.) No as to issue 1. Yes as to issue 2.
(1) Alimony may be reserved when there are present or foreseeable circumstances that are likely to generate a need for alimony in the reasonably near future. Here, there were no such circumstances because Mrs. Hardy was in good health, was drawing a pension from the state, and was working part-time. Reversed.
(2) The state's statutory law requires that in making apportionment, a court give weight in such proportion as it finds appropriate to debts incurred by the parties to a marriage, or by either of them, during the course of the marriage. This creates a rebuttable presumption that a debt of either spouse incurred prior to a marital action is a marital debt for purposes of equitable distribution, regardless of whether the parties are legally jointly liable for the debt or whether one party is legally individually liable. Thus, the same considerations of fairness and equity that go into distributing marital property must

also go into distributing marital debt. The burden of proving a spouse's debt as non-marital rests on the party making that assertion, and only if the trial judge finds that the debt was made for non-marital purposes, may the court order satisfaction of the debt by the spouse who created the debt. Here, the trial judge failed to make a determination that Mr. Hardy's (P) debts were non-marital. Reversed and remanded.

▶ ANALYSIS

This case arose in an equitable distribution state, and the court emphasized that the trial judge has significant discretion in providing for the payment of marital debts as a consideration in the equitable division of the marital estate. However, even community property states (e.g., California) provide that debts and assets must be divided equally, but where the community debt exceeds community assets, the court may assign the excess debt equitably. Thus, even in community property states, the trial court may have equitable discretion in disposing of marital debt.

■▬■

Quicknotes

ALIMONY Allowances (usually monetary) which husband or wife by court order pays to the other spouse for maintenance while they are separated, or after they are divorced (permanent alimony), or temporarily, pending a suit for divorce (pendente lite).

EQUITABLE DISTRIBUTION The means by which a court distributes all assets acquired during a marriage by the spouses equitably upon dissolution.

NONMARITAL PROPERTY Property that is owned by one spouse prior to the marriage, or any income derived therefrom, and any property that is received by one spouse pursuant to a gift, devise, bequest or descent.

■▬■

Mahoney v. Mahoney

Ex-husband professional (P) v. Ex-wife (D)

N.J. Sup. Ct., 91 N.J. 488, 453 A.2d 527 (1982).

NATURE OF CASE: Appeal from a property division decree.

FACT SUMMARY: Mrs. Mahoney (D) contended that Mr. Mahoney's (P) M.B.A. degree, which he earned during the marriage, was property and therefore subject to equitable distribution upon dissolution of the marriage.

🏛 RULE OF LAW
A professional degree is not property and therefore is not subject to equitable distribution; however, the other spouse is entitled to reimbursement alimony to compensate for the loss of expected income.

FACTS: The Mahoneys were married in 1971. Mrs. Mahoney (D) worked while Mr. Mahoney (P) earned his M.B.A. degree. Subsequently, Mr. Mahoney (P) filed for divorce, and Mrs. Mahoney (D) petitioned for an equitable distribution of the marital property, including the M.B.A. degree. The trial court held that the degree was property and therefore Mrs. Mahoney (D) was entitled to be reimbursed for the contribution she made to Mr. Mahoney's (P) gaining the degree. Mr. Mahoney (P) appealed.

ISSUE: Is a professional degree property and therefore subject to equitable distribution upon divorce?

HOLDING AND DECISION: (Pashman, J.) No. A professional degree is not property and therefore not subject to equitable distribution upon divorce. Although it is an asset, its future monetary value is too uncertain to be quantifiable, and it is not transferable. Therefore, it cannot be considered property. However, the contributing spouse is entitled to some compensation for her contribution to the degree. Therefore, reimbursement alimony will be awarded for this purpose to reimburse for monetary contributions made to the education of the spouse with the degree. Reversed and remanded.

▶ *ANALYSIS*

The main problem in a case such as this is the lack of an adequate formula to value the spouse's contribution to the other spouse's education. One method that has been used is known as the cost value approach, whereby the value of the spouse's monetary contribution is added to the value of the services performed, such as housework and child rearing, which allowed the other spouse to attend school.

Quicknotes

EQUITABLE DISTRIBUTION The means by which a court distributes all assets acquired during a marriage by the spouses equitably upon dissolution.

MARITAL PROPERTY Property accumulated by a married couple during the term of their marriage.

O'Brien v. O'Brien

Physician ex-husband (P) v. Ex-wife (D)

N.Y. Ct. App., 66 N.Y.2d 576, 489 N.E.2d 712, (1985).

NATURE OF CASE: Appeal from modification of award of marital property.

FACT SUMMARY: Mrs. O'Brien (D) appealed from a decision of the appellate court modifying the trial court's judgment granting her a distributive award to accomplish an equitable division of the value of Mr. O'Brien's (P) license to practice medicine, which she contended was marital property.

> **RULE OF LAW**
> The definition of marital property encompasses a license to practice medicine to the extent that the license was acquired during the marriage.

FACTS: Mr. (P) and Mrs. O'Brien (D) were married in April 1971. The trial court determined that nearly all of their nine-year marriage was devoted to the acquisition of Mr. O'Brien's (P) license to practice medicine and that Mrs. O'Brien (D) had made major contributions, supplying full-time employment and nonfinancial contributions in the form of household activities to the marital estate. Mr. O'Brien (P) filed for divorce in 1980, two months after obtaining his license to practice medicine. In the divorce action, Mrs. O'Brien (D) introduced expert testimony as to the present value of Mr. O'Brien's (P) medical license and the present value of her contribution to Mr. O'Brien's (P) education. The trial court determined that the license was marital property and ordered a distributive award to Mrs. O'Brien (D). On appeal, the appellate division reversed, modifying the award and determining that the license did not constitute marital property. From this decision, Mrs. O'Brien (D) appealed.

ISSUE: Does the definition of marital property encompass a license to practice medicine to the extent that the license was acquired during the marriage?

HOLDING AND DECISION: (Simons, J.) Yes. The definition of marital property encompasses a license to practice medicine to the extent that the license was acquired during marriage. The legislature defined marital property without regard to traditional concepts of property. The court determines exactly what will constitute marital property, giving due regard to contributions of all types to the career or career potential of the other spouse. There is no reason to restrict the clear directive of the statute to existing practices. There is no question that the right to practice medicine is a valuable property right, whose value is exhibited in attainment expenditures, lost opportunities, and enhanced earning potential. The legislature has provided for an award in lieu of the actual distribution of the right to practice medicine, which would be impossible. In the present case, it is clear that Mrs. O'Brien (D) made substantial contributions to the attainment of the license to practice medicine. The court's distributive award to her was proper. [The court then determined that absent particular egregious conduct, fault is not a "just and proper" factor for consideration in the equitable distribution of marital property.] Order modified, judgment reinstated.

CONCURRENCE: (Meyer, J.) The type of distributive award made in the present case may serve to lock the spouse against whom the award is entered into a career choice prior to the time that the spouse has established or even experienced that career choice.

> **ANALYSIS**

The shift in many states away from awarding alimony or maintenance payments conditioned on the marital status of the recipient spouse is reflected in the distributive award system utilized in the present case. Such a distributive award is designed not solely to support and maintain, but also to provide, the recipient spouse with the opportunity to obtain financial independence.

■=■

In re Marriage of Brown

Wife (P) v. Husband (D)

Cal. Sup. Ct., 15 Cal. 3d 838, 544 P.2d 561 (1976).

NATURE OF CASE: Appeal from a property division order.

FACT SUMMARY: The trial court held that Mr. Brown's (D) nonvested pension rights were not property and therefore not subject to division upon divorce.

RULE OF LAW
Nonvested pension rights are property and therefore are a divisible community asset.

FACTS: Mr. Brown (D) worked for General Telephone and by 1973, when he and Mrs. Brown (P) separated, he had accumulated 72 of the 78 points needed for his retirement benefits to vest. Mrs. Brown (P) petitioned for an equitable division of the benefits, yet the trial court held that they were a mere expectancy, rather than property, and therefore not subject to division. Mrs. Brown (P) appealed.

ISSUE: Are nonvested pension rights property and therefore a divisible community asset?

HOLDING AND DECISION: (Tobriner, J.) Yes. Nonvested pension rights are property and therefore are a divisible community asset. Pension rights are not gained through the beneficence of the employer. They are part of the consideration earned by the employee. They are a form of deferred compensation for services rendered, and as such they are an enforceable contractual right. A contractual right is a chose in action, not a mere expectancy. Since a chose in action is a form of property, such pension rights are a divisible community asset. Therefore, the trial court erred in failing to include them in the Browns' property division. Reversed and remanded.

ANALYSIS

There is often confusion in the labels applied to pension rights. Pension rights are considered "vested" when the employee has become irrevocably entitled to payment. Such rights are considered to "mature" when the employee gains a right to immediate payment. In this case, the California court defined "vested" as the point where the right to benefits may not be extinguished through termination of employment. It is at this point that the court held that a property interest arises.

■■■■

Quicknotes

COMMUNITY PROPERTY In community property jurisdictions, refers to all money or property acquired during the term of the marriage in which each spouse has an undivided one-half interest.

VESTED INTEREST A present right to property, although the right to the possession of such property may not be enjoyed until a future date.

■■■■

Mansell v. Mansell

Military ex-husband (P) v. Ex-wife (D)

490 U.S. 581 (1989).

NATURE OF CASE: Appeal from a support judgment.

FACT SUMMARY: The trial court held it could treat as community property portions of Mr. Mansell's (P) military retirement benefits, which had been waived to allow him to receive veteran's disability benefits.

🏛 RULE OF LAW
State courts may not treat military retirement pay waived by the retiree to allow him to receive disability benefits as property divisible upon divorce.

FACTS: Mr. Mansell (P), a veteran, waived a portion of his retirement pay in order to receive veteran's disability benefits, which were nontaxable. He and Mrs. Mansell (D) divorced and agreed to a property settlement which required Mr. Mansell (P) to pay one-half of his total military pay, including that portion waived, to Mrs. Mansell (D). Mr. Mansell (P) subsequently moved to strike that portion of the agreement on the grounds that federal law preempted state community property law and rendered the waived benefits not subject to division. The trial and appellate courts held the benefits were divisible under applicable state law. The Supreme Court granted review.

ISSUE: May state courts treat military retirement benefits waived to allow receipt of disability benefits as divisible community property?

HOLDING AND DECISION: (Marshall, J.) No. State courts may not treat military retirement benefits waived to allow receipt of disability benefits as divisible community property. Such is forbidden by the Uniform Services Former Spouses' Protection Act. While divorce is peculiarly an area in which state law traditionally controls, Congress has clearly acted, under the facts of this case, to preempt state community property laws. Thus, the waived portion of the benefits was not divisible property. Reversed and remanded.

DISSENT: (O'Connor, J.) This decision allows veterans to unilaterally deny their ex-spouses a portion of the retirement benefits earned through service during the marriage. This is unjust.

▌ ANALYSIS

Retirement benefits often cause problems in property settlements. Often the value of the contributions will not be realized for years after the divorce, and an evaluation and liquidation of the contribution is difficult and costly. The result is somewhat less harsh in nonmilitary settings.

Quicknotes

COMMUNITY PROPERTY In community property jurisdictions, refers to all money or property acquired during the term of the marriage in which each spouse has an undivided one-half interest.

Boggs v. Boggs

Widow (P) v. Husband's sons (D)

520 U.S. 833 (1997).

NATURE OF CASE: Appeal from summary judgment for the defense in action for declaratory judgment to resolve ownership in pension plan benefits.

FACT SUMMARY: After Isaac Boggs's first wife died, bequeathing her community property interest in Isaac's undistributed pension plan benefits to her sons (D), his second wife, Dorothy Boggs (P), argued that the Employee Retirement Income Security Act of 1974 (ERISA) prohibited such a transfer.

🏛 RULE OF LAW
ERISA preempts any state law that allows a nonparticipant spouse to transfer by testamentary instrument an interest in undistributed pension plan benefits.

FACTS: Isaac Boggs and Dorothy, his first wife, were married from 1949 until Dorothy's death in 1979. They had three sons. Isaac subsequently married Sandra Boggs (P), retired in 1985, then died in 1989. After Isaac's death, two of his sons (D) from his marriage to Dorothy claimed that they were entitled to the percentage of Isaac's retirement benefits that had been bequeathed to them by Dorothy's will. Sandra (P) countered that she should receive the surviving spouse annuity and the other retirement benefits in their entirety. Sandra (P) filed a complaint in federal court, seeking a declaratory judgment. She argued that ERISA's anti-alienation provision preempted the application of Louisiana's community property and succession laws to the extent that such laws recognized the sons' (D) claim to an interest in the disputed retirement benefits. The district court disagreed and granted summary judgment for the sons (D), having found that there was no assignment or alienation in this case because Dorothy's rights in the benefits were acquired by operation of community property law and not by transfer from Isaac. The Fifth Circuit affirmed. Sandra (P) appealed.

ISSUE: Does ERISA preempt any state law that allows a nonparticipant spouse to transfer by testamentary instrument an interest in undistributed pension plan benefits?

HOLDING AND DECISION: (Kennedy, J.) Yes. ERISA preempts any state law that allows a nonparticipant spouse to transfer by testamentary instrument an interest in undistributed pension plan benefits. The annuity at issue here is a qualified joint and survivor annuity mandated by ERISA. The purpose of the annuity provisions is to ensure a stream of income to surviving spouses. The Retirement Equity Act of 1984 (REA) modified ERISA to permit employees to designate a beneficiary for the survivor's annuity other than the spouse, but only with the spouse's consent. Sandra (P), as the surviving spouse, is entitled to a survivor's annuity under these provisions. She has not waived her right to the annuity, let alone consented to having the sons (D) designated as the beneficiaries. The same holds true for the monthly retirement benefits received by Isaac during his retirement. ERISA provides a mechanism (the Qualified Domestic Relations Order or QDRO) whereby divorced and separated spouses and their dependent children are guaranteed a community property interest in the pension plan. Significantly, Congress is silent with respect to the right of a non-employee spouse to control pension plan benefits by testamentary transfer. This is because Congress has chosen to give a divorced spouse more control over her spouse's pension benefits than a predeceasing spouse. ERISA is concerned with providing for the living. The sons' (D) state-law claims are preempted. Reversed.

▶ ANALYSIS

Justice Kennedy's decision provides a nice overview of ERISA, REA, and the critical QDRO provisions, which apply to any dissolution proceedings involving a spouse who is earning or receiving pension benefits. A QDRO is a limited exception to the pension plan anti-alienation provision and allows courts to recognize a spouse's community property interest in a participating spouse's pension plan. It is a type of domestic relations order that, once approved by the pension plan's administrator and the judge, generally becomes part of the divorce decree.

■━■

Quicknotes

COMMUNITY PROPERTY In community property jurisdictions, refers to all money or property acquired during the term of the marriage in which each spouse has an undivided one-half interest.

TESTAMENTARY INSTRUMENT An instrument that takes effect upon the death of the maker.

■━■

Voishan v. Palma

Father (P) v. Mother (D)

Md. Ct. App., 327 Md. 318, 609 A.2d 319 (1992)

NATURE OF CASE: Appeal from order increasing child support.

FACT SUMMARY: The trial court ordered an increase in John's (P) child support obligation pursuant to statutory guidelines based on the Income Shares Model.

RULE OF LAW
A judge does not abuse his discretion by basing a modification of custody support on statutory guidelines that incorporate the policies behind the Income Shares Model where explicit formulae for incomes above a certain level are not included in the guidelines' schedule.

FACTS: John (P) and Margaret (D) Voishan were divorced in 1981, and Margaret (D) was awarded custody of their two daughters. John (P) was ordered to pay $250 per week toward the girls' support. Four years later, an order increased that amount to $1,400 per month. In 1991, the trial court's intercession was again sought, and the trial court modified John's (P) child support obligation, for the one daughter who was still a minor, from $700 to $1,550 per month. John (P) appealed the modification and this court granted certiorari before the appellate court heard the issue.

ISSUE: Does a judge abuse his discretion by basing a modification of custody support on statutory guidelines that incorporate the policies behind the Income Shares Model where explicit formulae for incomes above a certain level are not included in the guidelines' schedule?

HOLDING AND DECISION: (Chasanow, J.) No. A judge does not abuse his discretion by basing a modification of custody support on statutory guidelines that incorporate the policies behind the Income Shares Model where explicit formulae for incomes above a certain level are not included in the guidelines' schedule. Maryland established custody and support guidelines to comply with federal requirements. After reviewing a variety of potential models, Maryland elected to follow the Income Shares Model. This model establishes child support obligations based on estimates of the percentage of income that parents in an intact household typically spend on their children, and the guidelines set forth a schedule of basic child support obligations for any given number of children based on combined parental income. The trial judge determines each parent's monthly "adjusted actual income." After determining each parent's monthly "adjusted actual income," the judge then adds these two amounts together to arrive at the monthly "combined adjusted actual in-

come" of the parents. Having calculated the combined adjusted actual income of the parents, the judge can then determine whether that figure falls within the range of incomes found in the guidelines' schedule. If the figure is within the schedule, the judge then locates the corresponding "basic child support obligation" for the given number of children. Where the monthly income falls between two amounts set forth in the schedule, the statute dictates that the basic child support obligation is the same as the obligation specified for the next highest income level. The judge then divides this basic child support obligation between the parents in proportion to each of their adjusted actual incomes. The amount arrived at is presumptively correct, but may be rebutted. John's (P) threshold argument is that the judge could not modify child support without a finding that there was a material change of circumstances. This preliminary argument is disposed of by the fact that John's trial counsel admitted that such a change had occurred when counsel conceded that Margaret (D) was entitled to an increase, and by the fact that the judge implicitly found a change of circumstances by doubling the amount of support. John's main argument is that the judge abused his discretion in awarding that amount of child support. As to his argument that the support obligation amount ($1040) applicable to monthly incomes of $10,000 also should be the presumptively correct amount for monthly incomes exceeding $10,000, the amount could provide the presumptive minimum basic award for those with combined monthly incomes above $10,000, but this amount was not intended by the legislature as a cap at the upper limits of the schedule. Had the legislature so intended, it would have explicitly said so, and would not have granted judges discretion in fixing those awards. Moreover, John's proposed approach creates an artificial ceiling and defeats the guidelines' policies—the legislature did not intend for children whose parents earn more than $10,000 per month to have the same standard of living as those whose parents earn $10,000 per month. As to John's (P) alternative argument that the judge should have mechanically extrapolated from the guidelines (an increase of $5 in child support for every $100 increase in income), this approach would significantly restrict the judicial discretion granted by the statute. Although the trial judge should consider the underlying policies of the guidelines and strive toward congruous results, the judge here did not abuse his discretion. John (P) also argues that the Income Shares Model assumes that the percentage of income spent on children decreases as parental income increases, and that,

Continued on next page.

therefore, the legislature could not have intended to impose a percentage that exceeds the percentage represented by the schedule's maximum support obligation. The legislative history does not support this argument, and there is no indication that the legislature intended to impose a maximum percentage of income or any similar restraint on the judge's discretion in setting awards. Instead, the legislative history shows that the legislative judgment was that at higher income levels judicial discretion is better suited than a fixed formula to implement the guidelines' underlying principles. However, the general principles from which the schedule was derived should not be ignored by the trial judge; thus, extrapolation may serve as a guide, but the judge may also exercise independent discretion in balancing the best interests of the child with the parents' finances. Therefore, John's (P) argument that the trial judge abused his discretion because he placed too little reliance on John's suggested extrapolation method is rejected, but also rejected is the argument that the judge placed too much reliance on a mechanical application of the guidelines (the relative percentage of parents' income—83 percent for John (P) and 17 percent for Margaret) because at higher income levels, the guidelines are not based on empirical evidence of the actual household expenditures for children, and therefore offer no assistance in calculating the proper amount of child support. Here, the judge acted properly in using this percentage because it was consistent with the principles of the Income Shares Model that parents share responsibility for support in proportion to their resources and because he also looked to the needs of the child when calculating the parents' proportional shares. Essentially, the guidelines do establish a rebuttable presumption that the maximum support award under the schedule is the minimum that should be awarded in cases above the schedule, and in such cases, the trial judge should examine the needs of the child in light of the parents' resources and determine the amount of support necessary to ensure that the child's standard of living is the same as it would have been had the parents not separated. Affirmed.

CONCURRENCE: (McAuliffe, J.) The economic assumptions underlying the Income Shares Model are based on studies examining expenditures on children as a proportion of household consumption, but the trial judge apparently ignored these studies and instead reverted to an earlier practice of attempting to determine the needs of a child based upon the custodial parent's estimated allocation to the child of a portion of fixed expenses of the family. The Income Shares Model provides guidance for fixing child support even when the combined adjusted actual income is above $10,000, while still granting the judge discretion. One of the model's guiding principles is that the percentage of income expended on child support decreases as income increases. Although John's (P) proposed extrapolation method is not consistent with the legislature's intent to provide judges with discretion in higher-income cases, the legislative intent may nevertheless

be carried out by using the schedule to establish presumptive maximum and minimum amounts for basic child support. Here, the amount in the schedule for monthly incomes of $10,000 should be the presumptive floor for awards based on incomes exceeding $10,000. Likewise, the presumptive maximum should be 10.4 percent of combined income, which is the percentage that the maximum scheduled payment bears to the maximum combined income. Because the percentage of income expended on child support decreases as income increases, it would not be inequitable to establish as a maximum the percentage fixed by the schedule for a lesser amount of combined income. Because the trial judge is granted discretion at higher incomes, there is no need to mathematically project from the schedule. Here, the support ordered is very close to the amount arrived at by using the presumptive minimum and maximum amounts noted above, and falls within the range of discretion the legislature intended to grant to judges.

▶ ANALYSIS

As this case demonstrates, in states where child support guidelines do not provide specific formulae for high-income cases, but do provide for judicial discretion in determining an appropriate child support award, it will be difficult to overturn a child support award in a high-income case on abuse-of-discretion grounds. The likelihood of success of such a challenge is further diminished by the numerous valid approaches available to judges, as exemplified by the different approaches taken in this case by the trial court, the majority, and the concurrence.

Quicknotes

CHILD SUPPORT Payments made by one parent to another in satisfaction of the non-custodial parent's legal obligation to provide for the sustenance of the child.

CHILD SUPPORT MODIFICATION The alteration of the payment structure pursuant to which one parent provides payments to another in satisfaction of the non-custodial parent's legal obligation to provide for the sustenance of the child.

Nash v. Mulle

Mother (P) v. Father (D)

Tenn. Sup. Ct., 846 S.W.2d 803 (1993).

NATURE OF CASE: Appeal in action to increase child support payments.

FACT SUMMARY: Nash (P), the mother of Mulle's (D) child, argued that the court should take Mulle's (D) entire monthly income of $14,727 into account when awarding child support and should also order Mulle (D) to pay into a college trust fund.

RULE OF LAW
(1) A trial court retains the discretion to determine the appropriate amount of child support to be paid when an obligor's net income exceeds the $6,250 per month statutory limit, balancing both the child's need and the parents' means.
(2) Yes. Although child support payments may not extend beyond the child's minority, the benefits from such payments can.

FACTS: After Mulle (D) fathered Nash's (P) child as a result of an extramarital affair in 1981, he was ordered to pay child support payments of $200 per month, based on his $30,000 gross annual income. By 1990, however, his annual income had increased to $260,000. Nash (P) therefore requested an increase in support payments. But since Mulle's (D) monthly income was now $14,727, well in excess of the top monthly income of $6,250 listed in the child support guidelines, the court of appeals limited his payments to 21 percent of $6,250. It also disallowed a college trust fund that the juvenile court had ordered Mulle (D) to establish. Nash (P) appealed.

ISSUE:
(1) Does the trial court retain the discretion to determine the appropriate amount of child support to be paid when an obligor's net income exceeds the $6,250 per month statutory limit?
(2) May the benefits from child support payments extend beyond the child's minority?

HOLDING AND DECISION: (Daughtrey, J.)
(1) Yes. A trial court retains the discretion to determine the appropriate amount of child support to be paid when an obligor's net income exceeds the $6,250 per month statutory limit. The statutory schedule for support payments is deemed to be appropriate in most cases but may be adjusted upward or downward as facts dictate. Therefore, in this case, Mulle's (D) income should not automatically be limited to a $6,250 cap. On the other hand, to simply order him to pay 21 percent of his true monthly income would provide far more money than

most parents would allot for the support of one child. Therefore, the trial judge must reconsider his opinion, balancing both the child's need and the parents' means.
(2) Yes. Although child support payments may not extend beyond the child's minority, the benefits from such payments can. The support guidelines explicitly provide for the use of trusts in cases involving high-income parents. Establishing a program of savings for a college education is a proper element of child support because it allows for equitable contributions from each parent while avoiding a windfall to one of them. It also protects the child of an uncaring noncustodial parent, while at the same time advancing a public policy favoring higher learning. Reversed and remanded.

ANALYSIS

Some state courts have approved the funding of a college education by noncustodial parents who can afford such an expense, although their state laws do not explicitly provide for such a duty. In other states, court authority to order such funding is provided by statute. New York's child support statute, for example, permits an award for post-secondary educational expenses when the court deems it appropriate in light of "the circumstances of the case and of the respective parties and the best interests of the child and as justice requires."

Quicknotes

CHILD SUPPORT Payments made by one parent to another in satisfaction of the non-custodial parent's legal obligation to provide for the sustenance of the child.

In re Barrett

Mother (P) v. Father (D)

N.H. Sup. Ct., 150 N.H. 520, 841 A.2d 74 (2004).

NATURE OF CASE: Appeal from order requiring child support payment for secondary school expenses.

FACT SUMMARY: Barrett (P) and Coyne (D) divorced and Barrett (P) had physical custody of their two daughters. One daughter, Kathryn, enrolled in private high school and Barrett (P) moved for an order requiring Coyne (D) to contribute financially.

🏛 RULE OF LAW
An obligor may be ordered to pay for a minor child's private secondary education on a finding of the child's special needs and the obligor's ability to pay.

FACTS: Susan Barrett (P) divorced Coyne (D) and was awarded primary physical custody of their two daughters, Kathryn and Jacqueline, with the parties sharing legal custody. Coyne (D) did not maintain a relationship with the girls but paid child support. Kathryn, a freshman, suffered from attention deficit disorder and emotional difficulties. Her issues led to her failure of her freshman year. Barrett (P) opted to enroll Kathryn in a private school. Coyne (D) submitted financial information upon request to the school. Kathryn did better and passed all grades through her junior year. Barrett (P) was not able to pay for the school in Kathryn's senior year and she requested the money from Coyne (D). He refused and Barrett (P) moved for an order requiring Coyne (D) to contribute financially. The court denied the motion due to Coyne's (D) inability to pay. On Barrett's (P) motion for reconsideration, the trial court considered Coyne's (D) new wife's income and ordered Coyne (D) to pay $8,000 of Kathryn's tuition. The court did not make a finding of "special circumstances" requiring the additional support. Coyne (D) appealed.

ISSUE: May an obligor be ordered to pay for a minor child's private secondary education on a finding of the child's special needs and the obligor's ability to pay?

HOLDING AND DECISION: (Dalianis, J.) Yes. An obligor may be ordered to pay for a minor child's private secondary education on a finding of the child's special needs and the obligor's ability to pay. Two statutes are at issue here. The first requires a court to make a reasonable support order for the benefit and education of minor children. The second, the child support guidelines, only allows for deviation from the guidelines if application would be "unjust or inappropriate." The statutes seem to be inconsistent with each other, so this court must interpret them to ensure compatibility and reasonableness. The first statute intends parents to share financial responsibili-

ties. The guidelines include deviation for "special circumstances" such as "ongoing extraordinary . . . education expenses." An obligor parent may be ordered to pay for private secondary education if special circumstances exist. The special circumstances parameters include the child's "special needs" and the obligor parent's ability to pay. The trial court must make these findings before ordering a deviation from the guidelines. A demonstrated "special need" may be shown by (1) the child's private school enrollment pre-divorce; (2) availability of appropriate public education and special needs education; (3) child's academic performance; (4) family's religious traditions; and (5) child's particular emotional and/or physical needs. Here, the trial court erred in ordering the support without finding "special needs." On remand, the trial court may consider Coyne's (D) new wife's income. The guidelines specifically allow a court to consider a stepparent's ability to pay when considering a deviation from the guidelines. Coyne (D) next argues that Barrett (P) should have considered alternative educational opportunities or informed him to seek such opportunities within applicable statutory time periods. The trial court inferred Coyne (D) knew of Kathryn's enrollment in private school because he completed the financial forms, so he arguably knew within the statutory time. The court will not consider Coyne's (D) inadequately briefed constitutional claims. Vacated and remanded.

▶ ANALYSIS

Support for private secondary education is not typically awarded or contemplated within guideline statutes. The reason given is that adequate public education is free and available to all students. Private education is usually the result of a contractual agreement, enrollment prior to the divorce proceedings, or a consent order. When a child has special needs, however, most family court judges are more willing to consider a support order. Special needs can run the gamut and parents should be ready to explain the true needs of the child in support of a request for financial contribution.

Quicknotes

CHILD SUPPORT Payments made by one parent to another in satisfaction of the non-custodial parent's legal obligation to provide for the sustenance of the child.

M.H.B. v. H.T.B.

Biological mother (P) v. Purported father (D)

N.J. Sup. Ct., 100 N.J. 567, 498 A.2d 775 (1985).

NATURE OF CASE: Appeal from child support decree.

FACT SUMMARY: Henry (D), a stepparent, was held to be equitably estopped from denying continuing child support due to the close parental relationship he had engendered.

RULE OF LAW
A stepparent who voluntarily agrees to provide support is equitably estopped from denying the obligation.

FACTS: Henry (D) and Marilyn (P) were married and had two children. Marilyn (P) became pregnant as a result of an extramarital affair. Henry (D) learned he was not the biological father three months after the child's birth. The marriage broke up, yet Henry (D) continued to provide child support for all the children. He maintained a close parental relationship. He undertook to provide substantial support payments. Henry (D) filed a petition to gain custody of all three children, and Marilyn (P) counterclaimed for an increase in child support. The trial court held Henry (D) had undertaken to support the child at issue and ordered an increase in support. Henry (D) appealed, contending he was not bound to support the child.

ISSUE: Is a stepparent who voluntarily agrees to provide support to the child equitably estopped from denying a continuing support obligation?

HOLDING AND DECISION: (Per curiam) Yes. A stepparent who voluntarily agrees to provide support is equitably estopped from denying the obligation to continue support payments. In this case, Henry (D) was clearly the psychological parent, even if he was not the biological parent. His emotional attachment was reciprocated by the child. Thus, a support obligation was undertaken and cannot be denied. Affirmed.

CONCURRENCE: (Handler, J.) Equitable estoppel is appropriate based on the analysis in *Miller v. Miller*, 478 A.2d 351 (1984). Henry (D) argues that the New Jersey Parentage Act shields him from child support obligations because the biological father is known. The Act, however, differentiates paternity from support. Here, in any event, K.B.'s biological father is suspected but not known. This case must be recognized as exceptional because this court will not ignore a biological father's duty to support his child. Despite being extraordinary, just as in any support case, the stepfather can seek to modify the support award by a showing of changed circumstances that affect K.B.'s best interests.

CONCURRENCE IN PART DISSENT IN PART: (Pollock, J.) The majority's support order is not based on estoppel but on a perceived bond between the stepfather and the minor child. Miller should not have been so expanded. The equitable estoppel doctrine is meant to be applied cautiously and after demonstration of three conditions: a representation of support relied upon by the biological parent or child and a showing that the child will suffer future financial detriment if the representation is not made reality. A close relationship with the child is not one of the factors. Here, the biological father is available and should not be excused from support.

ANALYSIS

The decision in this case was based directly on the New Jersey Supreme Court's previous decision in *Miller v. Miller*, 478 A.2d 351 (1984). That decision held that estoppel would preclude a withdrawal of stepparent support where such support had actively interfered with support from a natural parent. The best interest of the child is also considered.

Quicknotes

CHILD SUPPORT Payments made by one parent to another in satisfaction of the non-custodial parent's legal obligation to provide for the sustenance of the child.

EQUITABLE ESTOPPEL A doctrine that precludes a person from asserting a right to which he or she was entitled due to his or her action, conduct or failing to act, causing another party to justifiably rely on such conduct to his or her detriment.

Kansas v. United States

State (P) v. Federal government (D)

214 F.3d 1196 (10th Cir. 2000)

NATURE OF CASE: Appeal from dismissal of declaratory and injunctive action brought by a state seeking to enjoin enforcement of a federal child support statute as violative of the Constitution's Spending Clause and Tenth Amendment.

FACT SUMMARY: The Personal Responsibility and Work Opportunity Reconciliation Act (PRWORA) effected sweeping changes in child support enforcement policy and required states to abide by federal regulations to be eligible to receive federal block grants for assisting low-income people. Kansas (P) claimed that the federal requirements were too onerous and expensive and encroached on its ability to determine its own laws, and, because of the amount of money at stake, was being coerced into implementing the program in violation of the Constitution's Spending Clause and Tenth Amendment.

🏛 RULE OF LAW
The Personal Responsibility and Work Opportunity Reconciliation Act (PRWORA) does not violate the Constitution's Spending Clause and Tenth Amendment by attaching conditions to its grant of federal funding to the states.

FACTS: The Personal Responsibility and Work Opportunity Reconciliation Act (PRWORA) of 1996, also known as "welfare reform," replaced the Aid to Families with Dependent Children (AFDC) program with the Temporary Assistance to Needy Families (TANF) program. The new program consisted of federal block grants that were distributed to states, which then used the money to provide cash assistance and other supportive services to low-income families within their borders. This funding structure gave the states greater flexibility in designing their own public assistance programs, but they were required to work toward program goals, satisfy a maintenance-of-effort requirement for the expenditure of state funds, and abide by federal regulations. Title III of the PRWORA amended the Child Support Enforcement Program (IV-D), which provides federal money to assist states in collecting child support from absent parents. The PRWORA imposed greater federal oversight and control over the states participating in the IV-D program, and required states to establish certain databases and to adopt certain uniform statutes and laws as a condition of obtaining federal monies. However, the states were not required to participate in the program. A state that elected to receive the federal block grant under the TANF program, however, was obligated to operate a child support enforcement program that met IV-D's requirements. If a state's child support enforce-

ment program failed to conform to the requirements of IV-D, the state risked the denial of both its IV-D child support enforcement funding and its TANF funding. Kansas (P), which had received about $130 million in combined IV-D and TANF funds, challenged the amended program as too onerous and expensive, necessitating too much manpower, encroaching upon its ability to determine its own laws, and, because of the amount of money at stake, coercing the state into implementing the program requirements in violation of the Constitution's Spending Clause and Tenth Amendment. The district court dismissed, and the court of appeals granted review.

ISSUE: Does the Personal Responsibility and Work Opportunity Reconciliation Act (PRWORA) violate the Constitution's Spending Clause and Tenth Amendment by attaching conditions to its grant of federal funding to the states?

HOLDING AND DECISION: (Seymour, C.J.) No. The Personal Responsibility and Work Opportunity Reconciliation Act (PRWORA) does not violate the Constitution's Spending Clause and Tenth Amendment by attaching conditions to its grant of federal funding to the states. Because Kansas's (P) claims are mirror images of each other, the court addresses the issue as arising under the Spending Clause. A. The most instructive case in this area is *South Dakota v. Dole*, 483 U.S. 203 (1987), which recognized four restrictions on Congress's power under the Spending Clause. These are: (1) Congress's objective must be in pursuit of the "general welfare;" (2) any conditions placed on the states' receipt of funds must be unambiguous; (3) the conditions must be related to the federal interest in the particular program; and (4) there can be no independent constitutional bar to the conditions, i.e., Congress may not induce the states to engage in activities that are themselves unconstitutional. Kansas (P) does not assert that the first two restrictions are implicated by the IV-D conditions. As to the third requirement, Kansas (P) asserts that the IV-D conditions are not sufficiently related to the larger TANF program. The TANF program, which assists low-income families, is clearly related to the IV-D program, which assists low-income families to collect child support from absent parents—thus enabling some families to reduce dependence on welfare programs. It is not mere coincidence that these two programs are to be found in the same statutory subchapter, given that they complement each other. Finally, as to the fourth restriction, Kansas (P)

Continued on next page.

makes only a few cursory arguments that it is being required to violate privacy and due process rights of its citizens; these arguments are not developed in the brief and do not seem to have merit. In this case, Kansas (P) bears a heavy burden in seeking to have the PRWORA declared unconstitutional, and there are no relevant instances where the Supreme Court has invalidated funding conditions. Likewise, federal courts of appeal have been reluctant to invalidate funding conditions.

B. Dole articulated a fifth, indistinct limit on Congress's spending power where the financial inducement offered by Congress is so great that it becomes coercive and passes the point at which "pressure turns into compulsion." This is the theory Kansas (P) relies on most heavily, the crux of its argument being that the size of its IV-D and TANF grants, totaling over $130 million, leaves it no choice but to accept the PRWORA's many requirements. However, the Supreme Court has never used this theory to invalidate a funding condition, and the federal courts have been similarly reluctant to use it. If it has been applied, it has been applied negatively, and never in favor of the challenging party. The boundary between incentive and coercion has never been made clear, and courts have found no coercion in situations where similarly large amounts of federal money were at stake, e.g., conditions on Medicaid grants. For these reasons, the conditioning of TANF funding on compliance with IV-D requirements does not present a situation of impermissible coercion. Rejected is Kansas's (P) invitation to expand the concept of "coercion," as it applies to relations between the federal and state governments, to include large federal grants accompanied by a set of conditions on the theory that such grants create powerful incentives for the state to accept them. The bottom line is that a tempting offer is still just an offer, and a difficult choice remains a choice. Ultimately, Kansas (P) is free to reject that offer; its options have been increased, not constrained, by the offer of more federal money. Affirmed.

▶ ANALYSIS

One of the effects of this case is to uphold federal involvement in child support enforcement, and, by "inducing" states to adopt uniform child support laws, such as the Uniform Interstate Family Support Act, the federal government has effectively "federalized" this area and has made it much easier to enforce child support obligations throughout the country.

■═■

Quicknotes

CHILD SUPPORT Payments made by one parent to another in satisfaction of the non-custodial parent's legal obligation to provide for the sustenance of the child.

SPENDING CLAUSE The power delegated to Congress by the Constitution to spend money in providing for the nation's welfare.

TENTH AMENDMENT The Tenth Amendment to the United States Constitution reserves those powers therein, not expressly delegated to the federal government or prohibited to the states, to the states or to the people.

■═■

Blige v. Blige

Ex-wife (P) v. Ex-husband (D)

Ga. Sup. Ct., 283 Ga. 65, 656 S.E.2d 822 (2008).

NATURE OF CASE: Appeal of judgment following trial by jury.

FACT SUMMARY: Meagan Taylor Blige (P) sought to set aside an antenuptial agreement she entered into with her ex-husband, Willie Alonzo Blige (D). The trial court set it aside for nondisclosure.

🏛 RULE OF LAW
A party seeking enforcement of an antenuptial agreement bears the burden of proof to demonstrate that: (1) the antenuptial agreement was not the result of fraud, duress, mistake, misrepresentation, or nondisclosure of material facts; (2) the agreement is not unconscionable; and (3) taking into account all relevant facts and circumstances, including changes beyond the parties' contemplation when the agreement was executed, enforcement of the antenuptial agreement would be neither unfair nor unreasonable.

FACTS: The day before their wedding, Willie Alonzo Blige (D) took Meagan Taylor Blige (P) to a lawyer he hired on her behalf and asked her to sign an antenuptial agreement. The agreement provided that Willie (D) would retain as his sole and separate property 19.5 acres of land he had previously purchased, together with any house or structure that "may be situated upon" it. There was no house on the property when the parties married. Meagan (P) knew Willie (D) made $10 per hour as a delivery truck driver, and had no knowledge that he had hidden away $150,000 in cash that he planned to use to build a home after the wedding. He eventually built it, and at the time of trial, it was worth between $375,000 and $400,000. At the end of the trial, the jury returned a verdict awarding Willie (D) the property and house minus $160,000 to be paid to Meagan (P).

ISSUE: Does a party seeking enforcement of an antenuptial agreement bear the burden of proof to demonstrate that: (1) the antenuptial agreement was not the result of fraud, duress, mistake, misrepresentation, or nondisclosure of material facts; (2) the agreement is not unconscionable; and (3) taking into account all relevant facts and circumstances, including changes beyond the parties' contemplation when the agreement was executed, enforcement of the antenuptial agreement would be neither unfair nor unreasonable?

HOLDING AND DECISION: (Sears, C.J.) Yes. A party seeking enforcement of an antenuptial agreement bears the burden of proof to demonstrate that: (1) the antenuptial agreement was not the result of fraud, duress, mistake, misrepresentation, or nondisclosure of material

facts; (2) the agreement is not unconscionable; and (3) taking into account all relevant facts and circumstances, including changes beyond the parties' contemplation when the agreement was executed, enforcement of the antenuptial agreement would be neither unfair nor unreasonable. The trial court found that Willie (D) failed to show that there was a full and fair disclosure of the assets of the parties prior to the execution of the agreement, and the evidence supports the trial court's conclusion. Willie's (D) argument that the agreement must be enforced under *Mallen v. Mallen*, 280 Ga. 43 (2005), is rejected, because *Mallen* is distinguishable, since in that case, the parties attached financial disclosure statements to the agreement. In addition, Meagan (P) never moved in with Willie (D) even after the marriage, unlike the situation in *Mallen*, and there was nothing in Willie's (D) lifestyle to indicate he had a stash of cash. Willie's (D) argument that the agreement should be enforced based on Meagan's (P) failure to inquire into his financial status is also rejected, because to accept that argument would undermine the requirement of full disclosure. The burden on each is not to inquire, but to inform. Neither *Mallen* nor Meagan's (P) actions or inactions excuse Willie's (D) nondisclosure. Affirmed.

▶ ANALYSIS

Antenuptial agreements are generally enforceable, and not contrary to public policy, in all 50 states and the District of Columbia. Courts tend to be strict with respect to the issues raised in this case, including disclosure, representation of both parties by independent counsel, and voluntariness.

■■■

Quicknotes

ANTENUPTIAL AGREEMENT An agreement entered into by two individuals, in contemplation of their impending marriage, in order to determine their rights and interests in property upon dissolution or death.

NONDISCLOSURE The failure to communicate certain facts to another person.

■■■

Biliouris v. Biliouris

Antenuptial-agreement-signing husband (P) v. Antenuptial-agreement-signing wife (D)

Mass. Ct. App., 67 Mass. App. Ct. 149, 852 N.E.2d 687 (2006).

NATURE OF CASE: Appeal from a divorce decree enforcing an antenuptial agreement.

FACT SUMMARY: After a short period of dating, Mrs. Biliouris (D) discovered she was pregnant. Mr. Biliouris (P) would not marry her unless she signed an antenuptial agreement. After signing the agreement, the couple was married for ten years before an action for divorce was commenced by Mr. Biliouris (P) seeking enforcement of the agreement.

RULE OF LAW
For an antenuptial agreement to be valid, it must be fair, reasonable, and knowingly signed by each party.

FACTS: The couple had been dating for a short period of time when Mrs. Biliouris (D) discovered she was pregnant. Mr. Biliouris (P) refused to marry her unless she signed an antenuptial agreement. The agreement was drafted by Mr. Biliouris' (P) attorney, and Mrs. Biliouris (D) ultimately signed it, despite being advised by her attorney not to do so. After ten years of marriage and producing two children, Mr. Biliouris (P) filed for divorce and sought to enforce the terms of the parties' antenuptial agreement. Mrs. Biliouris (D) counterclaimed, requesting a divorce. The trial court found the antenuptial agreement valid and Mrs. Biliouris (D) appealed.

ISSUE: For an antenuptial agreement to be valid, must it be fair, reasonable, and knowingly signed by each party?

HOLDING AND DECISION: (Smith, J.) Yes. For an antenuptial agreement to be valid, it must be fair, reasonable, and knowingly signed by each party. Mrs. Biliouris (D) argued that she was under duress at the time she executed the antenuptial agreement and was coerced into signing it due to the circumstances in which she found herself. Specifically, Mrs. Biliouris (D) claimed that there was agreement between the parties where, as a "precondition" of the husband's agreeing to marry her, she would have to become pregnant. Continuing, she asserts that the husband's proposal of an additional condition (i.e., the execution of the antenuptial agreement), after she had become pregnant, was coercive in and of itself. The problem with Mrs. Biliouris's (D) argument is that the judge made no finding that any such oral agreement existed between the parties. Indeed, the trial judge denied Mrs. Biliouris's (D) motion to amend findings of fact in which she sought to include findings with respect to the alleged oral agreement.

It is settled that a person who enters into a contract "under the influence of such fear as precludes him from exercising free will and judgment" may avoid the contract on the grounds of duress. Here, there is nothing in the record that would cause us to disturb the judge's finding that Mrs. Biliouris's (D) execution of the antenuptial agreement was not the product of coercion or duress. Even were we to assume that Mrs. Biliouris (D) was presented with a draft of the antenuptial agreement only one week prior to the parties' wedding, she still had sufficient time to review it, and she did in fact seek the advice of independent counsel as to its terms. As was stated, the opinion of Mrs. Biliouris's (D) counsel was that she should not sign the agreement. Mrs. Biliouris (D) also acknowledged at trial that prior to executing the agreement and in response to a question posed by the notary, she informed the notary that her signing of the agreement was her "free act and deed." While the pregnancy coupled with the husband's (P) insistence that there would be no marriage unless she (D) signed the antenuptial agreement presented the wife (D) with a difficult choice, those factors cannot be said, in the circumstances presented here, to have divested the wife (D) of her free will and judgment.

Mrs. Biliouris (D) argued next that under the circumstances known and reasonably to be anticipated by the parties at the time of the execution of the antenuptial agreement, the waiver of alimony provision, as to her, was neither fair nor reasonable when it was made. Antenuptial agreements that waive alimony are not per se against public policy and may be specifically enforced. However, to be enforceable, an agreement must be valid at the time of execution. In order for such an agreement to be valid at the time of execution, the judge must determine whether (1) the agreement contains a fair and reasonable provision as measured at the time of its execution for the party contesting the agreement; (2) the contesting party was fully informed of the other party's worth prior to the agreement's execution, or had, or should have had, independent knowledge of the other party's worth; and (3) a waiver by the contesting party is set forth.

In determining whether an agreement was fair and reasonable at the time of execution, reference may be made to numerous factors, including the parties' respective worth, ages, intelligence, literacy, and business acumen, and prior family ties or commitments. "It is only where the contesting party is essentially stripped of substantially all marital interests," and indeed, the terms of the agreement "essentially vitiate the very status of marriage," that an agreement

Continued on next page.

is not fair and reasonable. *DeMatteo v. DeMatteo*, 436 Mass. 19 (2002).

In the instant case, the judge did not err in concluding that the waiver of alimony provision of the antenuptial agreement was fair and reasonable at the time of its execution. Mrs. Biliouris (D) was an educated professional who had a demonstrated earning capacity at the time she executed the agreement. There is nothing in the record to suggest that the wife would be incapable of working and earning income to support herself in the event of a divorce in the future. Moreover, the agreement provided that the wife's separate premarital property (valued at approximately $100,000), and any appreciation thereon, would remain her property and not be incorporated into the marital estate subject to division. The agreement (in the absence of any limitation or provision to the contrary) also permitted the wife an interest in marital assets accrued by the parties during the marriage. If the terms of the agreement were unsatisfactory to the wife, she was free not to marry. Affirmed.

▶ *ANALYSIS*

While the allegations made by Mrs. Biliouris (D) are indeed troubling, she did not offer any proof of them at trial. As such, absent a showing that her entry into the antenuptial agreement was not fair, reasonable or knowingly made, it will be enforced. The argument that antenuptial agreements are often the product of unequal bargaining power has to be proven, and here Mrs. Biliouris (D) did not take the advice of her attorney, to her peril.

■▬■

Quicknotes

ANTENUPTIAL AGREEMENT An agreement entered into by two individuals, in contemplation of their impending marriage, in order to determine their rights and interests in property upon dissolution or death.

■▬■

Stregack v. Moldofsky

Decedent's daughter (D) v. Widow (P)

Fla. Sup. Ct., 474 So. 2d 206 (1985).

NATURE OF CASE: Appeal from dismissal of action to cancel an antenuptial agreement.

FACT SUMMARY: Moldofsky (P) contended she could challenge an antenuptial agreement which involved fraudulent nondisclosure of assets.

🏛 RULE OF LAW
Nondisclosure in any form cannot invalidate an antenuptial agreement in probate proceedings of a deceased spouse.

FACTS: Moldofsky's (P) husband died; his will referred to an antenuptial agreement and left her nothing. Moldofsky (P) petitioned the probate court for an elective share of the estate. She also filed suit, challenging the validity of the antenuptial agreement on the basis it contained fraudulent nondisclosures of assets. The probate court struck the petition, and the trial court dismissed the action as moot. On appeal, both orders were reversed. The appellate court held that a surviving spouse could challenge an antenuptial agreement for fraudulent nondisclosure by the deceased spouse. Stregack (D), the daughter of the deceased and representative of the estate, appealed.

ISSUE: Can nondisclosure in any form invalidate an antenuptial agreement in probate proceedings of a deceased spouse?

HOLDING AND DECISION: (McDonald, J.) No. Nondisclosure in any form cannot invalidate an antenuptial agreement in probate proceedings of a deceased spouse. Florida statute 732.702(2) provides no disclosure shall be required for an agreement executed before marriage. This clear legislative enactment fully applies in this case. Therefore, the orders must be reversed.

▌ANALYSIS

The court explained that many people, especially older people, wish to marry without fear of a disadvantageous distribution of their property upon death. Thus, no disclosure is required. If no disclosure is required, nondisclosure, even if fraudulent, cannot affect the agreement.

Quicknotes

ANTENUPTIAL AGREEMENT An agreement entered into by two individuals, in contemplation of their impending marriage, in order to determine their rights and interests in property upon dissolution or death.

MOOT Judgment on the particular issue that has previously been decided or settled.

PROBATE The administration of a decedent's estate.

Pacelli v. Pacelli

Husband (P) v. Wife (D)

N.J. Super. Ct. App. Div., 319 N.J. Super. 185, 725 A.2d 56 (1999).

NATURE OF CASE: Divorce proceeding.

FACT SUMMARY: Husband (P) gave wife (D) $500,000 in full satisfaction of his equitable distribution and alimony obligations in the event of divorce, and then brought this divorce proceeding.

🏛 RULE OF LAW
Mid-marriage agreements resolving issues of equitable distribution and alimony in the event of a divorce are enforceable if fair and equitable.

FACTS: The husband (P) and wife (D) were married and had two children. The husband (P) later informed the wife (D) that he would divorce her unless she agreed to certain terms regarding their economic relationship. Husband (P) sought the advice of counsel, Croland, who informed him that any agreement between the parties had to be fair and equitable after full disclosure of all relevant information regarding the parties' assets. Croland also informed husband (P) that wife (D) should obtain counsel. Wife (D) consulted Skoloff and informed him that husband (P) was going to pay her $500,000 in the event of future divorce, in full satisfaction of his equitable distribution and alimony obligations. Skoloff advised her not to accept, but the wife (D) did not listen. Husband (P) subsequently filed for divorce. The trial court determined the agreement was enforceable and the wife (D) appealed.

ISSUE: Are mid-marriage agreements resolving issues of equitable distribution and alimony in the event of a divorce enforceable if fair and equitable?

HOLDING AND DECISION: (D'Annunzio, J.) Yes. Mid-marriage agreements resolving issues of equitable distribution and alimony in the event of a divorce are enforceable if fair and equitable. There is a contextual difference between prenuptial agreements and agreements made at the end of marriage, when the parties are at an adversarial stage in their relationship. The mid-marriage agreement in this case, however, differs from prenuptial agreements and property settlement agreements made at a marriage's termination. However, the context in which the husband (P) made his demand was inherently coercive. While this is an issue of first impression, courts have faced a similar situation with respect to "reconciliation agreements." In *Nicholson v. Nicholson*, this court stated that such agreements are enforceable if "fair and equitable." A prerequisite to enforcement is a requirement that the "marital relationship has deteriorated at least to the brink of an indefinite separation or a suit for divorce." Here the testimony establishes that the husband's (P) pri-

mary interest was financial. Croland testified the husband's (P) purpose was to stay married, but that he was concerned that his wife did not share in his income beyond a certain point. The evidence supports an inference that the marital crisis here was artificial, and created by the plaintiff to take advantage of his wife. The second requirement is that the agreement be fair and equitable. Here the terms were not fair and just. The agreement was unfair when it was signed in 1986. The $540,000 provided in the agreement was 18 percent of the marital estate at that time, where her share upon equitable distribution would have approximated one-third. In addition, the agreement was unfair, inequitable and unenforceable in light of the inherently coercive circumstances leading to its formation. Reversed and remanded.

▶ ANALYSIS

The court concludes here that applying the standard applicable to a prenuptial agreement to a mid-marriage agreement is inappropriate. Likewise, it distinguishes between mid-marriage agreements and property settlement agreements in contemplation of divorce. While the court declines to declare that such agreements are so inherently coercive that they should be absolutely enforceable, they must be closely scrutinized.

Quicknotes

EQUITABLE DISTRIBUTION The means by which a court distributes all assets acquired during a marriage by the spouses equitably upon dissolution.

PRENUPTIAL AGREEMENT An agreement entered into by two individuals, in contemplation of their impending marriage, in order to determine their rights and interests in property upon dissolution or death.

Johnston v. Johnston

Ex-husband (P) v. Ex-wife (D)

Md. Ct. App., 297 Md. 48, 465 A.2d 436 (1983).

NATURE OF CASE: Appeal from denial of petition to set aside a postnuptial agreement.

FACT SUMMARY: Mrs. Johnston (D) contended that because a postnuptial agreement was incorporated in the final divorce decree, Mr. Johnston's (P) action to invalidate it was barred by the concept of res judicata.

🏛 RULE OF LAW
A separation agreement incorporated, but not merged, in a divorce decree may not be collaterally attacked where its validity is conclusively established by the decree which operates as res judicata.

FACTS: The Johnstons entered into an agreement effecting a settlement of property and support rights that stated it was to be incorporated, but not merged, into the final divorce decree. The court decree reflected this desire and incorporated the agreement. Subsequently, Mr. Johnston (P) sued to invalidate the agreement on the basis of his alleged mental incompetence at the time of its execution. Mrs. Johnston (D) moved to strike the complaint, contending it was barred by the divorce decree, which operated as res judicata. The trial court granted the motion, the appellate court affirmed, and Mr. Johnston (P) appealed.

ISSUE: May a separation agreement that is incorporated, but not merged, in a divorce decree be collaterally attacked where its validity is conclusively established by the decree which operates as res judicata?

HOLDING AND DECISION: (Couch, J.) No. A separation agreement incorporated, but not merged, in a divorce decree may not be collaterally attacked where its validity is conclusively established by the decree which operates as res judicata. In this case, the divorce decree expressly approved the agreement. Therefore, the property and support rights were determined in the divorce proceeding. The decree incorporating the agreement accordingly acts as res judicata and bars Mr. Johnston's (P) action. Affirmed.

▶ ANALYSIS

The Uniform Marriage and Divorce Act allows postnuptial agreements to promote the friendly settlement of disputes over support and property rights. Agreements adopted under the Act are binding on the court unless such agreement is found to be unconscionable. It the court finds the agreement unconscionable, it may allow the parties to submit a revised agreement, or it may make orders for the disposition of property, maintenance, and support.

Quicknotes

COLLATERAL ATTACK A proceeding initiated in order to challenge the integrity of a previous judgment.

DIVORCE DECREE A decree terminating a marriage.

PROPERTY RIGHTS A legal right in specified personal or real property.

RES JUDICATA The rule of law that a final judgment by a court precludes subsequent litigation between the parties regarding the same cause of action.

SEPARATION AGREEMENT A written agreement between spouses who are separated and/or seeking a divorce, setting forth terms of support, custody, and property division.

Hicks on Behalf of Feiock v. Feiock

Ex-wife (P) v. Ex-husband (D)

485 U.S. 624 (1988).

NATURE OF CASE: Review of reversal of contempt citation.

FACT SUMMARY: Feiock (D) was sentenced to a definite term of imprisonment and a definite fine as part of a contempt citation.

🏛 RULE OF LAW
A contempt citation is not of a criminal nature if the contemnor can, through his actions, terminate the sanctions.

FACTS: Feiock (D) went into arrears in support payments to his ex-wife (P). He was ordered by a court to resume payments and to pay off the arrearages. For nine months he failed to do so. A court held him in contempt for five of the nine months, months he could not prove inability to pay. He was sentenced to 25 days in jail, sentence suspended, and placed on three years' probation. He was again ordered to meet present and past payments. The order was unclear as to whether a payment of all obligations would nullify the probation. A state appellate court held the proceeding to be criminal in nature and, since Feiock (D) had had the burden of proving inability to pay, constitutionally infirm. The U.S. Supreme Court granted review.

ISSUE: Is a contempt citation of a criminal nature if the contemnor can, through his actions, terminate the sanctions?

HOLDING AND DECISION: (White, J.) No. A contempt citation is not of a criminal nature if the contemnor can, through his actions, terminate the sanctions. Contempt citations fall into two categories, civil and criminal. The purpose of the first type is to compel certain behavior; the purpose of the latter is to punish. The significance of the distinction is that the various constitutional safeguards due the accused in criminal cases are applicable in criminal contempt actions. The accepted distinction between the two is found in the remedy fashioned by the court. If the sanction made by the court can be terminated by the contemnor's conforming his behavior, the citation is civil. If the sanction administered is inflexible, then the punishment is criminal. Suggested alternative analyses, such as looking into the policies being furthered by the citation in issue, would be too difficult and would leave trial courts in doubt as to their powers. Here, Feiock (D) was sentenced to a specific period of incarceration and a specific fine. This reads like a criminal citation. However, it is unclear from the record whether compliance would nullify the sentence. A "purge" clause in an otherwise criminal-type citation may, depending on its terms, make it civil in nature. Therefore, this case must be remanded for a determination of whether Feiock (D) can purge his sentence. Reversed and remanded.

DISSENT: (O'Connor, J.) The linchpin of the criminal/civil dichotomy should be whether the sanction is ultimately being imposed for the benefit of the court or society at large, or for a particular party. Here, the main intended beneficiary was Ms. Feiock (P).

▶ ANALYSIS

The factor that made the issue here significant was that of burden of proof. The California Court of Appeals had decided that ability to pay was an element of the contempt citation; inability to pay was not an affirmative defense. The California legislature had created a presumption of an ability to pay. Since a criminal defendant is entitled to have every element of the crime proved against him beyond a reasonable doubt, the presumption is invalid if the proceedings are to be judged criminal in nature.

■■■

Quicknotes

CONTEMPT OF COURT Conduct that is intended to obstruct the court's effective administration of justice or to otherwise disrespect its authority.

■■■

CHAPTER **6**

Parent and Child: Legal and Biological Relationships

Quick Reference Rules of Law

1. *Reese v. Muret.* The presumption of parentage is not overcome by a requirement for genetic testing in paternity cases.   94

2. *Stanley v. Illinois.* A state may not deny a biological father custody of his illegitimate children without a hearing to determine his parental fitness.   96

3. *Lehr v. Robertson.* Due process does not require that notice be given in all cases to a biological father of the pendency of an adoption proceeding concerning the child.   97

4. *Michael H. v. Gerald D.* A statute precluding all but the husband and wife from contesting the paternity of children born during the marriage is constitutional.   98

5. *Gomez v. Perez.* Once a state posits a judicially enforceable right on behalf of children to needed support from their natural fathers, there is no constitutionally sufficient justification for denying such an essential right to a child simply because its natural father has not married its mother.   99

6. *Cleo A.E. v. Rickie Gene E.* The best interests of the child standard precludes parties to a domestic proceeding from stipulating to bastardize a child born during their marriage.   100

7. *Buzzanca v. Buzzanca.* Just as a husband is deemed to be the lawful father of a child unrelated to him when his wife gives birth after artificial insemination, so should a husband and wife be deemed the lawful parents of a child after a surrogate bears a biologically unrelated child on their behalf.   101

8. *In re M.J.* A state parentage statute requiring a husband's written consent to artificial insemination does not preclude common law claims based on the husband's conduct of consent.   102

9. *J.B. v. M.B. and C.C.* Absent an enforceable contract to the contrary, frozen pre-embryos of a divorced couple must be destroyed where one of the parties so desires and the other disagrees, but is still capable of having children.   104

10. *Woodward v. Commissioner of Social Security.* In limited circumstances, children born after a parent has died can enjoy the inheritance rights of natural children under the law of intestate succession.   106

11. *Matter of Baby M.* A "surrogacy contract" wherein a woman agrees to have a child and surrender it is void.   109

12. *Raftopol v. Ramey.* The law permits an intended parent who is neither the biological nor the adoptive parent of a child to become a legal parent of that child by means of a valid gestational agreement.   111

Reese v Muret

Presumed child (P) v. Deceased father's estate administrator (D)

Kan. Sup. Ct., 283 Kan. 1, 150 P.3d 309 (2007).

NATURE OF CASE: Appeal of the denial to perform genetic testing in both a probate and paternity action.

FACT SUMMARY: Heather S. Reese (formerly Heather S. Waldschmidt) (hereinafter, "Heather" (P)), was born during the marriage of Wade Samuel Waldschmidt, Jr. (Sam) to Deloris Hibbs (Deloris). After Sam and Deloris divorced, Sam married Sandra Woodard. Upon Sam's death, Heather (P) sought to become the administrator of his estate. Sandra objected and requested genetic testing to prove Heather (P) was Sam's child.

🏛 RULE OF LAW
The presumption of parentage is not overcome by a requirement for genetic testing in paternity cases.

FACTS: Wade Samuel Waldschmidt, Jr. (Sam) marriage to Deloris Hibbs (Deloris) produced a daughter named Heather S. Reese (formerly Heather S. Waldschmidt) (hereinafter, "Heather" (P)). Heather's (P) birth certificate named Sam as her father. Deloris and Sam divorced and the pleadings acknowledged Heather (P) as a child of the union. Sam was granted visitation with Heather and ordered to pay child support to Deloris. After a while, Sam successfully sought to terminate his child support payments because Deloris had disappeared with Heather (P). Though Sam saw Heather (P) at Waldschmidt family gatherings, he did not attempt to have a relationship with her.

Sam married Sandra Woodard and told her that Heather (P) was not his child. Sam and Sandra separated, divorced, moved back in together and then separated, and remarried. During this time Sam executed a will leaving everything to his sisters. Sam did inform his attorney about his estate and that he had a daughter. When Sam committed suicide, Heather (P) petitioned to be appointed administrator for Sam's estate. Sandra responded to Heather's (P) petition, denying that Heather (P) was Sam's daughter and requested the court to appoint her as the administrator for Sam's estate. Sandra also filed a petition in the probate action for genetic testing to determine whether Sam was Heather's (P) biological father. In response to Sandra's motion for genetic testing, Heather (P) filed a paternity action, seeking a determination that Sam was her presumed father because she was born during her mother's marriage to Sam, Sam had acknowledged his paternity in the divorce pleadings, and Sam was ordered to pay child support on Heather's (P) behalf. Sandra filed a motion to intervene and a motion for genetic testing. Over Heather's (P) objection, the district court granted Sandra's

motion to intervene. After a hearing, the district court held that it was not in Heather's (P) best interests to conduct genetic testing and denied Sandra's motion, which she then appealed.

ISSUE: Is the presumption of parentage overcome by a requirement for genetic testing in paternity cases?

HOLDING AND DECISION: (Rosen, J.) No. The presumption of parentage is not overcome by a requirement for genetic testing. Sandra argues that the district court improperly applied the ruling of *In re Marriage of Ross*, 245 Kan. 591, 783 P.2d 331 (1989), in determining whether to order genetic testing in a probate action and in a parentage action brought by an adult for the purposes of applying the probate code. As long as Heather's (P) claim to Sam's estate was based on her being Sam's biological child, the genetic connection between Heather (P) and Sam was in issue. Under this scenario, Sandra correctly argued that *Ross* is inapplicable to an intestate claim based on the biological definition of "child" because genetic testing is the only conclusive means of establishing biological parentage. However, state law does not limit the definition of "children" to biological offspring. Rather, the definition of "children" is much broader, requiring the probate court to treat any person as a "child" if such person's parentage is or has been determined under the Kansas Parentage Act (KPA). Once paternity is established in accordance with the KPA, the probate code provides no mechanism for challenging that paternity determination. Because Heather (P) eliminated the issue of biological parentage in the probate action by filing her paternity action and the probate code does not authorize genetic testing to challenge a paternity determination under the KPA, there is no statutory basis for Sandra's motion for genetic testing in the probate case.

Pursuant to the KPA, a man is presumed to be the father of a child born while the man is married to the child's mother. A child or a person on behalf of the child may file an action at any time to establish paternity when there is a presumption of paternity. However, a presumption based on genetic test results must relate to genetic testing that occurs prior to the filing of the paternity action. However, the *Ross* court tempered the statutory requirement of the KPA by requiring the district court to conduct a hearing prior to issuing an order for genetic testing to determine whether genetic testing is in the best interests of the child.

In *Ross*, the child, R.A.R., was born during the marriage of his mother Sylvia to Robert. When Sylvia and Robert divorced, Sylvia alleged that Robert was R.A.R.'s father.

Continued on next page.

Robert was granted joint custody and ordered to pay child support. Two years later, Sylvia filed a petition pursuant to the KPA to establish Charles as R.A.R.'s biological father. To establish Charles as R.A.R.'s biological parent, Sylvia requested an order compelling all of the parties to submit to genetic testing. The district court ordered the genetic testing pursuant to the KPA and admitted the results over Robert's and Charles's objections. Based on the results of the genetic testing, the district court determined that Charles was R.A.R.'s biological father and ordered him to pay child support. Nevertheless, the district court determined that it was in R.A.R.'s best interest to maintain his relationship with Robert, so the court continued the joint custody arrangement between Sylvia and Robert. The *Ross* court reversed the district court's order for genetic testing and the order establishing Charles as R.A.R.'s biological father. Noting that "the ancient presumption of the legitimacy of a child born in wedlock is one of the strongest presumptions known to the law," the *Ross* court held that the district court must conduct a hearing to determine whether it is in the child's best interests to perform genetic testing and determine the child's biological paternity as opposed to his presumptive paternity.

Sandra's argument that *Ross* only applies to minor children is incorrect. Both *Ross* and other case law were concerned with the purpose for determining a child's biological paternity when there was already a presumptive father. The relevance of who is Heather's (P) biological father is questionable given the strong presumption that Sam was her father. The presumption of Sam's paternity existed for many years prior to the filing of this paternity action. The case law supports the protection of presumptive paternity over biological paternity when it is in the child's best interests. This protection extends to both minor and adult children.

Without a *Ross* hearing to determine whether genetic testing is in the child's best interests, genetic testing becomes conclusive on the issue of paternity regardless of whether any other presumptions apply. As a result, denying adult children the protection of a *Ross* hearing is tantamount to rewriting the KPA because it eliminates all of the other paternal presumptions besides genetic testing. If the legislature intended for genetic testing to be conclusive for determining the paternity of an adult child, it could have included language limiting the remaining presumptions to minor children. Extending *Ross* to adult children also furthers the purpose of the KPA by protecting an adult child's right to inherit from his or her presumptive parent. Finally, extending *Ross* to adult children recognizes the public policy that paternity is both broader and deeper than genetics. The recognition of family identity extends beyond the years of a child's minority. Every adult continues to be someone's son or daughter for purposes of family identification, family bonding, and inheritance. The parental relationship continues to exist regardless of whether the bonds are close, strained, or nonexistent. The presumptions of paternity were instituted to protect and maintain the concept of family identity. Intruding upon this concept can cause emotional damage to children of all ages, not only to minors.

This case illustrates the importance of protecting the presumption of paternity. Although the ultimate issue in this case involves the division of a decedent's estate, the resolution of that issue turns on the legal designation of paternity for a child born with a presumptive father. Heather (P) was born during Sam's and Deloris' marriage. Sam's name appears on Heather's (P) birth certificate. Heather (P) was identified with Sam's familial name and included in the membership of Sam's family. Although her relationship with Sam was externally distant, she always believed he was her father. Requiring the district court to conduct genetic testing without determining whether it is in Heather's (P) best interest would allow Sandra to accomplish after Sam's death that which could not be accomplished during Sam's lifetime. There is no reason to subvert the presumption of paternity in favor of biology without requiring a court to consider whether it is in the child's best interests regardless of the child's age. Interpretation of the relevant statutes, controlling precedent, and public policy support the district court's decision to hold a *Ross* hearing in Heather's (P) paternity action. The district court's well-reasoned opinion denying Sandra's motions for genetic testing in both the probate and paternity cases is affirmed.

▶ ANALYSIS

In an interesting twist between dueling probate and paternity interests, the *Ross* court came down conclusively that the well-established presumption that a child born during marriage is the biological offspring of both parents is not to be so casually disturbed. While the consequences of genetic testing may well have proven that Heather (P) was the child of the decedent Sam, the risk that she was not was something that the court found troubling if not in the "best interests of the child" test. This rebuttable presumption sets a high standard to prevent children (regardless of their age) to testing to prove what they already believed to be true (even if it were not).

■▬■

Stanley v. Illinois

Biological father (P) v. State (D)

405 U.S. 645 (1972).

NATURE OF CASE: Appeal in dependency proceeding.

FACT SUMMARY: The State (D) declared that Stanley's (P) three illegitimate children were wards of the State (D).

🏛 RULE OF LAW
A state may not deny a biological father custody of his illegitimate children without a hearing to determine his parental fitness.

FACTS: Stanley (P) lived with a woman off and on for 18 years. They had three children but were never married. The woman died and the children were declared wards of the State (D). Stanley (P) appealed this decision on the grounds that he loved his children and wished to care for them. Stanley (P) alleged that there had been no showing that he was an unfit father who should be denied custody. The State (D) alleged that under a statute an unwed father had no right to the custody of his illegitimate children. Stanley (P) alleged that this violated the Equal Protection Clause because it failed to consider his fitness and only considered his marital status.

ISSUE: May a state deny a biological father custody of his illegitimate children without a hearing to determine his parental fitness?

HOLDING AND DECISION: (White, J.) No. A state may not deny a biological father custody of his illegitimate children without a hearing to determine his parental fitness. A parent may not be absolutely disabled from having custody of his children even though they are illegitimate. Such a classification of parents, those married and those not, is arbitrary and bears no relation to the State's (D) purpose of seeing that the children are adequately cared for. The parent must be granted a hearing to determine fitness for raising children. Denial on such an arbitrary classification violates the Equal Protection Clause. There is no rational basis for the distinction, and the State (D) obtains no benefit from the removal of the children. Rather, it is undertaking an unnecessary expense. It would split up a "family" for no reason. Failure to determine the fitness of the unmarried father renders the classification overbroad and overinclusive. It deprives all members of the class without any consideration of the individual members and deprives them of important parental rights. The statute is unconstitutional. Reversed and remanded.

DISSENT: (Burger, C.J.) No due process challenge was raised in the case below, and it should not be entertained herein. There is also a valid distinction between unwed mothers and fathers and the role they play in the rearing of the child. The mother's role is generally greater, and she is much more easily identified as the parent. There is a rational basis for the distinction employed by the State (D).

▶ ANALYSIS

The hearings provided unwed fathers require the usual procedural guarantees such as notice, service of process, etc. This has had a great effect on adoption practices where the unwed father must be found and heard before the child can be put up for adoption. Unwed fathers who do not promptly respond lose their right to complain at a later date.

■=■

Quicknotes

CUSTODY The granting of care and control of a child or children to a parent pursuant to an action for dissolution or separation.

■=■

Lehr v. Robertson

Biological father (P) v. Mother (D)

463 U.S. 248 (1983).

NATURE OF CASE: Appeal of an adoption order.

FACT SUMMARY: Lehr (P) contended that a New York statute which allowed his biological child to be adopted without his receiving notice was unconstitutional.

🏛 RULE OF LAW
Due process does not require that notice be given in all cases to a biological father of the pendency of an adoption proceeding concerning the child.

FACTS: Lehr (P) petitioned the court to declare him the father of Jessica M., a child born to Lorraine Robertson. After the birth, Robertson (D) married Mr. Robertson, and Lehr (P) never supported the child and rarely saw her. Lehr (P) failed to place his name with the New York State putative father registry, which would have entitled him to notice of any adoption proceeding concerning the child. Before the court ruled on his petition, another court issued an order of adoption in favor of Mr. Robertson. Lehr (P) challenged the order, claiming because he was not notified of the adoption, even though the court was aware of his paternity action, he was denied due process. The New York Court of Appeals upheld the order as constitutional, and Lehr (P) appealed to the U.S. Supreme Court.

ISSUE: Does due process require that in all cases notice be given to a biological father of the pendency of an adoption proceeding?

HOLDING AND DECISION: (Stevens, J.) No. Due process does not require in all cases that notice be given to a biological father of the pendency of an adoption proceeding concerning the child. Only where an unwed father demonstrates a commitment to the responsibilities of parenting by participating in the rearing of the child does his relationship deserve substantial protection under the Due Process Clause. Mere biological relationships do not command the same constitutional protection because standing alone they lack the emotional connection which is the basis of the concept of family. In this case, the only claim to parenthood asserted by Lehr (P) was biological. His right to notice, therefore, is significantly less than it would have been had he established a relationship with the child. His right to due process was adequately protected by the availability of the putative father registry. His failure to register relieved any duty of notice owed him. Therefore, the adoption order was valid. Affirmed.

DISSENT: (White, J.) Any parental relationship, whether solely biological or solely emotional, is constitutionally recognized and protected. The adoption order deprived Lehr (P) of a constitutionally protected interest, and therefore he must be afforded notice and an opportunity to be heard before the order can be granted finality. Further, no legitimate state interest is served by denying him notice and hearing. Therefore, entry of the order denied him due process.

▶ ANALYSIS

It has been argued that the holding in this case disregards probably the most important consideration, that of the child's right or interest in having a relationship with a biological father. It is further argued that the emotional relationship identified as necessary to establish a strong parental relationship cannot be accomplished if the biological parent is shut off from the child by the custodial parent.

Quicknotes

ADOPTION DECREE A court order terminating the parental rights of a child's natural parents and vesting the child with the rights and privileges of a natural child in respect to his adoptive parents.

BIOLOGICAL PARENTS A man and woman who conceive and give birth to a child.

DUE PROCESS CLAUSE Clauses found in the Fifth and Fourteenth Amendments to the United States Constitution providing that no person shall be deprived of "life, liberty, or property, without due process of law."

PUTATIVE FATHER REGISTRY Registry where an unwed father may file to demonstrate intent to claim paternity of child born out of wedlock, and to protect right to notice of any adoption proceeding.

Michael H. v. Gerald D.

Biological father and daughter (P) v. Legal father of daughter (D)

491 U.S. 110 (1989).

NATURE OF CASE: Appeal from denial of visitation rights.

FACT SUMMARY: Michael H. (P) and Victoria (P) contended that they were denied due process and equal protection by a California statute precluding them from adjudicating her paternity.

🏛 RULE OF LAW
A statute precluding all but the husband and wife from contesting the paternity of children born during the marriage is constitutional.

FACTS: Carole D. and Gerald D. (D) were married. Carole had an extramarital affair with Michael (P), and that affair produced Victoria (P). Victoria (P) (through her guardian ad litem) and Michael (P) sought to establish visitation rights, yet those rights were denied on the basis of a California statute that conclusively presumed paternity in favor of the husband in children born during a marriage. Under the statute, only the husband and wife have standing to rebut that presumption. Victoria (P) and Michael (P) appealed, contending that the presumption violated their federal constitutional rights to due process and equal protection. The U.S. Supreme Court granted review.

ISSUE: Is a statute precluding all but the husband and wife from contesting the paternity of children born during the marriage constitutional?

HOLDING AND DECISION: (Scalia, J.) Yes. A statute that precludes all but the husband and wife from contesting paternity of children born during the marriage is constitutional. It is rationally related to a legitimate state interest in promoting the stability of the nuclear family. Substantive parental rights can only exist in one man and one woman at a time. To grant Michael (P) the relief sought would create a dual parenthood inconsistent with this policy. Further, the same disruption of the familial unit would occur if the child is allowed to rebut the presumption. Therefore, the statute must be upheld. Affirmed.

DISSENT: (Brennan, J.) This decision is based upon a misinterpretation of past cases and a baseless presumption of traditional values. A natural parent cannot be denied at least a hearing on such paternity. The principle of paternity is too important to completely foreclose based upon an arbitrary evidentiary preclusion.

▶ ANALYSIS

The statute at issue has been in effect for over a century. Its main purpose is to provide stability to the concept of the

family. The devastating effect on children, especially those of tender years, that a challenge to paternity presents is avoided as much as possible. The wife cannot even rebut the presumption unless the purported natural father files an affidavit accepting paternity.

■=■

Quicknotes

DUE PROCESS The constitutional mandate requiring the courts to protect and enforce individuals' rights and liberties consistent with prevailing principles of fairness and justice and prohibiting the federal and state governments from such activities that deprive its citizens of a life, liberty or property interest.

EQUAL PROTECTION A constitutional guarantee that no person shall be denied the same protection of the laws enjoyed by other persons in life circumstances.

PATERNITY The relationship of a father to his child.

RATIONAL BASIS REVIEW A test employed by the court to determine the validity of a statute in equal protection actions, whereby the court determines whether the challenged statute is rationally related to the achievement of a legitimate state interest.

VISITATION RIGHTS Rights awarded by the court in a divorce or custody proceeding to a parent who does not have custody over the child or children, permitting that parent to visit with the child or children.

■=■

Gomez v. Perez

Minor child (P) v. Father (D)

409 U.S. 535 (1973).

NATURE OF CASE: Appeal from denial of support to the illegitimate child from his natural father.

FACT SUMMARY: Gomez (P), a minor child, sought support from her natural father, but that support was denied her only because she was illegitimate.

🏛 RULE OF LAW
Once a state posits a judicially enforceable right on behalf of children to needed support from their natural fathers, there is no constitutionally sufficient justification for denying such an essential right to a child simply because its natural father has not married its mother.

FACTS: Perez (D) was the natural father of Gomez (P), his illegitimate daughter. Gomez (P) sued for support from Perez (D). It was determined that even though Perez (D) was the biological father of Gomez (P), and Gomez (P) needed the support and maintenance of her father, she was denied that support only because she was illegitimate. Under Texas law, an illegitimate child did not have a right to support from its father, though a legitimate child had such a right.

ISSUE: May a state constitutionally grant legitimate children a judicially enforceable right to support from their natural fathers and at the same time deny that right to illegitimate children?

HOLDING AND DECISION: (Per curiam) No. Once a state posits a judicially enforceable right on behalf of children to needed support from their natural fathers, there is no constitutionally sufficient justification for denying such an essential right to a child simply because its natural father has not married its mother. In Texas, both at common law and by statute, a natural father has no duty to support his illegitimate children. And fathers may set up as a defense to prosecutions for criminal nonsupport the illegitimacy of the child. However, this Court has held that a state may not invidiously discriminate against illegitimate children by denying them substantial benefits accorded children generally. The classification was illogical and unjust and an unconstitutional denial of equal protection. Reversed and remanded.

▌ ANALYSIS

This case follows, once again, the modern trend toward equality of legitimate and illegitimate children. This trend has been adopted by the Uniform Parentage Act, which states that a parent-child relationship exists regardless of the marital status of the parents. The Court had previously ruled that a state could not create a wrongful death action in favor of legitimate children only, *Levy v. Louisiana*, 391 U.S. 68 (1968), and could not prevent illegitimate children from sharing in workers' compensation benefits paid upon the death of a parent, *Weber v. Aetna Casualty & Surety Co.*, 406 U.S. 164 (1972).

Quicknotes

CHILD SUPPORT Payments made by one parent to another in satisfaction of the non-custodial parent's legal obligation to provide for the sustenance of the child.

Cleo A.E. v. Rickie Gene E.

Mother (D) v. Father (D)

W. Va. Sup. Ct. App., 190 W. Va. 543, 438 S.E.2d 886 (1993).

NATURE OF CASE: Review of an amended final order of divorce.

FACT SUMMARY: The Child Advocate Office ("CAO") (P) contested a divorce order in which Cleo (D) and Rickie E. (D) stipulated that Rickie E. (D) was not the father of a child born during their marriage.

🏛 **RULE OF LAW**
The best interests of the child standard precludes parties to a domestic proceeding from stipulating to bastardize a child born during their marriage.

FACTS: Cleo (D) and Rickie E. (D) were married on May 24, 1981. They had two children during their marriage, Sheila and Amber Dawn. Cleo (D) and Rickie E. (D) filed for divorce, and a final order of divorce was entered in West Virginia. In an effort to collect child support, the CAO (P) filed a Uniform Reciprocal Enforcement of Support Act (URESA) petition in West Virginia. The "URESA" petition was heard in Florida, where Rickie E. (D) was located. At the hearing, Rickie E. (D) denied that he was Amber Dawn's father. However, the Florida court held he was the father and ordered him to pay support. The support order was modified by an amended final order of divorce from West Virginia that included a stipulation by both parties that claimed Rickie E. (D) was not Amber Dawn's father. CAO (P) appealed the amended final order of divorce and sought to have it set aside.

ISSUE: Does the best interests of the child standard preclude parties to a domestic proceeding from stipulating to the bastardization of a child born to the parties during their marriage?

HOLDING AND DECISION: (Workman, C.J.) Yes. The best interests of the child standard precludes parties to a domestic proceeding from stipulating to the bastardization of a child born to the parties during their marriage. Many states accept the concept that a child born during the marriage is presumptively legitimate. Because bastardization seriously affects the child's substantial rights and interests, the court plays an active role in determining paternity. In addition, the child needs independent representation to protect its interests and prevent the issue of paternity from being a bargaining chip. Here, the court did not consider the facts in light of Amber Dawn's best interests, nor did it appoint independent counsel to represent her. Reversed and remanded.

▶ **ANALYSIS**

Traditionally, proceedings establishing paternity and support have not required the child to be made a party to the action. As the case above demonstrates, such proceedings will often involve a conflict of interest between parent and child, especially when a parent in a contested divorce action is willing to sacrifice child support in collusion with the other parent. However, most courts will allow subsequent relitigation by the child since he or she was neither party nor privy to the initial September 19, 1996, proceeding.

■▬■

Quicknotes

BEST INTERESTS OF CHILD Standard used by courts when rendering decisions which involve a child or children.

DIVORCE DECREE A decree terminating a marriage.

■▬■

Buzzanca v. Buzzanca

Father (P) v. Mother (D)

Cal. Ct. App., 61 Cal. App. 4th 1410, 72 Cal. Rptr. 2d 280 (1998).

NATURE OF CASE: Appeal from a judgment declaring a child legally parentless.

FACT SUMMARY: When a husband who had agreed to have a child by artificial insemination filed for divorce six days prior to the birth of the child, the lower court stipulated that the couple were not the lawful parents.

🏛 RULE OF LAW
Just as a husband is deemed to be the lawful father of a child unrelated to him when his wife gives birth after artificial insemination, so should a husband and wife be deemed the lawful parents of a child after a surrogate bears a biologically unrelated child on their behalf.

FACTS: Luanne (D) and John Buzzanca (P) agreed to have an embryo genetically unrelated to either of them implanted in a woman—a surrogate—who would carry and give birth to the child for them. When the Buzzancas split up, John (P) disclaimed any responsibility and the surrogate also made it clear she made no claim to the child. Luanne (D) claimed she and her former husband were the lawful parents, but the court decided that the baby, Jaycee, had no lawful parents. Luanne (D) appealed.

ISSUE: Should a husband and wife be deemed the lawful parents of a child after a surrogate bears a biologically unrelated child on their behalf?

HOLDING AND DECISION: (Sills, J.) Yes. Just as a husband is deemed to be the lawful father of a child unrelated to him when his wife gives birth after artificial insemination, so should a husband and wife be deemed the lawful parents of a child after a surrogate bears a biologically unrelated child on their behalf. In each instance, the child is procreated because a medical procedure was initiated and consented to by intended parents. The trial judge erred because he assumed that legal motherhood, under the relevant California statutes, could only be established in one of two ways, either by giving birth or by contributing an egg. There is a compelling state interest in establishing paternity for all children. Reversed and remanded.

▌ANALYSIS
The court remanded the matter with directions to enter a new judgment declaring Luanne the lawful mother and John the lawful father. The birth certificate was also amended to reflect John Buzzanca as the lawful father.

The matter was also remanded to make an appropriate child support order.

■━■

Quicknotes

SURROGATE MOTHER A woman who agrees to be artificially inseminated with the semen of a man who is married to another woman so that she may conceive and give birth to a child, after which she relinquishes her parental rights to the man and his wife.

■━■

In re M.J.

Biological mother (P) v. Ex-boyfriend (D)

Ill. Sup. Ct., 203 Ill. 2d 526, 787 N.E.2d 144 (2003).

NATURE OF CASE: Appeal from dismissal of complaint in paternity action.

FACT SUMMARY: Mitchell (P) underwent artificial insemination and gave birth to twin boys while in a romantic relationship with Banary (D). Banary (D) had promised to provide support if Mitchell (P) became pregnant. When the relationship ended, the support ended and Mitchell (P) sued to declare paternity and establish a support order.

🏛 RULE OF LAW
A state parentage statute requiring a husband's written consent to artificial insemination does not preclude common law claims based on the husband's conduct of consent.

FACTS: Alexis Mitchell (P) met Raymond Banary (D) in 1986 and the two began a romantic relationship. Banary (D) told Mitchell (P) that his name was Jim Richardson and he was single. They discussed marriage and children, but Banary (D) asked Mitchell (P) to wait for marriage until he retired because his community would not accept their mixed-race relationship. The two tried to conceive, but Banary (D) was infertile. He suggested Mitchell (P) try artificial insemination with donor sperm and he orally agreed to be financially responsible for the child. He helped select the donor, paid for and accompanied Mitchell (P) to the doctor, injected Mitchell (P) with fertility drugs, and then named the resulting twin boys and treated them as his children. He supported them, the family took vacations together, and Banary (D) paid for all expenses. In 1996, Mitchell (P) learned that Banary (D) was not named Jim Richardson and he was married. She ended the relationship and Banary (D) ended support payments for the twins. Mitchell (P) sued Banary (D) to establish paternity and obtain a support order. Two of her counts were common law counts of breach of an oral agreement and promissory estoppel. Her third and final count was to declare paternity and establish child support under Illinois Parentage Act. Banary (D) moved to dismiss on grounds that the common law claims violated the Frauds Act and Illinois public policy. He moved to dismiss all three counts arguing Mitchell (P) failed to state a claim under the Illinois Parentage Act. The trial court held that the Illinois Parentage Act required a husband's written consent to paternity in an artificial insemination case so an unmarried couple should not be treated differently. The trial court dismissed Mitchell's (P) claims on that basis. On appeal, the appellate court also held that the Illinois Parentage Act required written consent. The appeals court affirmed the dismissal. Mitchell (P) appealed.

ISSUE: Does a state parentage statute requiring a husband's written consent to artificial insemination preclude common law claims based on the husband's conduct of consent?

HOLDING AND DECISION: (Kilbride, J.) No. A state parentage statute requiring a husband's written consent to artificial insemination does not preclude common law claims based on the husband's conduct of consent. The Illinois Parentage Act (the "Act") requires a husband's written consent to artificial insemination before he is treated as the resulting child's biological father with all attendant rights and obligations. The Act permits a couple to use donor sperm while making the husband the father, protecting against paternity claims from the donor, and protecting the donor from support obligations. This court previously held that the lack of written consent could prohibit a parent-child relationship between the husband and child, but the court has never determined whether the written consent was mandatory to establish the parent-child relationship. The statutory provision may be directory or mandatory depending on the verb used. If the provision merely directs conduct, it is directory. If the provision safeguards rights, it is mandatory. Here, the provision clearly safeguards rights of parents, so it is a mandatory provision. The trial court did not err in holding the lack of written consent precluded a finding of paternity. The Illinois Legislature should address the full spectrum of legal problems arising with assisted reproduction technology. The next issue is whether the Act precludes common law claims. Prior case law held that the husband's "actual consent" to the insemination permitted further inquiry into the circumstances surrounding the decision to use artificial insemination. Another case also noted that a husband's conduct could demonstrate his consent even while written consent was lacking. Further, Illinois public policy supports the right of a child to full support for its needs. A support obligation could be found even in the absence of a legal parent-child relationship. The legislation could have clearly barred common law claims in the Act, but it did not. Other courts have similarly allowed common law claims under parentage acts because of demonstrated conduct indicating assent. Deliberate conduct involving artificial insemination and resulting in an intended birth should bring a legal support obligation just as deliberate sexual conduct resulting in an unintended birth brings a legal support obligation. Mitchell's (P) common law claims may go forward. Affirmed in part, reversed in part, and remanded.

Continued on next page.

▶ *ANALYSIS*

The majority of states acknowledging the myriad of legal problems arising with assisted reproductive techniques have parentage statutes addressing the parent-child relationships. The artificial insemination donor has to be protected from liability for support obligations, the parents have to be protected from the donor seeking to establish paternity, and the husband has to be protected from a wife receiving donor sperm without the husband's consent. While most states statutorily require consent, the child's interests are paramount and courts will find ways to establish a parent-child relationship so that the child's needs are met.

■══■

Quicknotes

BEST INTERESTS OF CHILD Standard used by courts when rendering decisions which involve a child or children.

CHILD SUPPORT Payments made by one parent to another in satisfaction of the non-custodial parent's legal obligation to provide for the sustenance of the child.

ORAL CONTRACT A contract that is not reduced to written form.

PROMISSORY ESTOPPEL A promise that is enforceable if the promisor should reasonably expect that it will induce action or forbearance on the part of the promisee, and does in fact cause such action or forbearance, and it is the only means of avoiding injustice.

PUBLIC POLICY Policy administered by the state with respect to the health, safety and morals of its people in accordance with common notions of fairness and decency.

■══■

J.B. v. M.B. and C.C.

Mother (P) v. Father (D) and IVF Program (D)

N.J. Sup. Ct., 170 N.J. 9, 783 A.2d 707 (2001).

NATURE OF CASE: Appeal from judgment that frozen pre-embryos of a divorced couple must be destroyed where one of the parties so desires and the other disagrees, but is still capable of having children.

FACT SUMMARY: J.B. (P) and M.B. (D), a divorced couple, disagreed about the disposition of frozen pre-embryos they created when they were married. J.B. (P) wanted the pre-embryos destroyed, but M.B. (D) wanted them implanted or donated to infertile couples. They also disagreed about whether they had entered into an agreement, when they were still married, governing the disposition of the pre-embryos.

🏛 RULE OF LAW
Absent an enforceable contract to the contrary, frozen pre-embryos of a divorced couple must be destroyed where one of the parties so desires and the other disagrees, but is still capable of having children.

FACTS: J.B. (P) and M.B. (D) were married. They had difficulty conceiving a child and went through in vitro fertilization (IVF) procedures that produced 11 pre-embryos that were the result of fertilizing J.B.'s (P) eggs with M.B.'s (D) sperm. Four were placed in J.B. (P), who became pregnant, and the remaining seven were cryopreserved—frozen at extremely low temperatures. J.B. (P) and M.B. (D) later divorced, but disagreed on the disposition of the pre-embryos, the only issue not resolved by the divorce. J.B. (P) wanted them destroyed, but M.B. (D) maintained that he and J.B. (P) had agreed that any unused pre-embryos would be used by J.B. (P) or donated to infertile couples. There was no clear evidence of such an agreement. A consent agreement that the couple had signed as part of the IVF program gave control over the pre-embryos to the IVF program (Cooper Center) upon the couple's divorce, unless a court specified otherwise. The trial court granted J.B. (P) summary judgment on the pre-embryo disposition issue, the appellate division affirmed, and the New Jersey Supreme Court granted review.

ISSUE: Absent an enforceable contract to the contrary, must frozen pre-embryos of a divorced couple be destroyed where one of the parties so desires and the other disagrees, but is still capable of having children?

HOLDING AND DECISION: (Poritz, C.J.) Yes. M.B. (D) contended on appeal that judgment of the court below violated his constitutional rights to procreation and the care and companionship of his children, and that his rights outweighed J.B.'s (P) right not to procreate because

her right to bodily integrity was not implicated. He also argued that he and J.B. (P) had a clear agreement to give the pre-embryos a chance at life. J.B. (P) countered that any alleged agreement between the parties to use or donate the pre-embryos would be unenforceable as a matter of public policy, on the ground that individuals should not be bound by agreements requiring them to enter into family relationships or that seek to regulate personal intimate decisions relating to parenthood or family life. She also argued that absent an express contract, the court should not imply such an agreement. Finally, she argued that requiring the use or donation of the pre-embryos would violate her constitutional right not to procreate, but that destroying the pre-embryos would not significantly affect M.B.'s (D) right to procreate because he is fertile and capable of fathering other children.

As to whether there was an agreement between J.B. (P) and M.B. (D) regarding the disposition of the pre-embryos upon their divorce, a starting point is the consent agreement provided to J.B. (P) and M.B. (D) by the Cooper Center. That form does not manifest a clear intent by J.B. (P) and M.B. (D) as to the pre-embryo disposition issue because although it says that ownership of the pre-embryos will be relinquished to the Center if the couple divorces, it also carves out an exception that permits the parties to obtain a court order directing disposition. This conditional language stands in sharp contrast to language in other consents provided by other IVF facilities that have been upheld. In *Kass v. Kass*, 696 N.E.2d 174 (N.Y. 1998), New York's highest court enforced a couple's written decision to donate their pre-embryos for scientific research when they could not agree on disposition. That court found that the parties had signed an unambiguous contract to relinquish control of their pre-embryos to the facility in the event of a dispute. As opposed to the couple in *Kass*, the couple here is seeking another determination from the court. Here, a formal, unambiguous, memorialization of the parties' intentions would be required to confirm their joint determination. Because the lack of such a writing is not contested, the Court holds that J.B. (P) and M.B. (D) never entered into a separate and binding agreement. Ordinarily, because both parties are contributors to the genetic material comprising the pre-embryos, the decision as to disposition is theirs to make. But here, where the parties disagree, the decision is left to the court.

In the absence of legislative guidance, constitutional cases from other states and the federal judiciary, as well as cases in which the Court has recognized the fundamental nature of procreational rights, provide a framework within

Continued on next page.

which disputes over the disposition of pre-embryos can be resolved. A case from the Tennessee Supreme Court, *Davis v. Davis*, 842 S.W.2d 588 (Tenn. 1992), for example, in a situation similar to the one in this case, balanced the right to procreate of the wife, who sought to donate the pre-embryos, against the right of the husband, who sought destruction of the pre-embryos, to not procreate, and concluded that the husband's right would be significantly affected by unwanted parenthood. Against that interest, the court weighed the wife's burden of knowing that the lengthy IVF procedures she underwent were futile. The court found that the wife's interest, although not insignificant, did not outweigh the father's interest. The court held that the scales ordinarily would tip in favor of the right not to procreate if the opposing party could still become a parent through other reasonable means, and this Court agrees with the Tennessee court in this regard. M.B.'s (D) right to procreate is not lost if he is denied an opportunity to use or donate the pre-embryos; he only loses the right to procreate with his former wife's eggs. In contrast, J.B.'s (P) right not to procreate may be lost through attempted use or donation of the pre-embryos, which could have lifelong repercussions. The Court will not force her to become a biological parent against her will. Additionally, the laws of the state evidence a policy against enforcing private contracts to enter into or terminate familial relationships, such as a surrogate mother agreement that required the biological mother to surrender her parental rights. This is consistent with the policy that consent to terminate parental rights is revocable in all but statutorily approved situations. Therefore, enforcement of an agreement that would allow the implantation of pre-embryos at a future date where one party has reconsidered his or her earlier assent raises similar issues—if implantation is successful, the party will have been forced to become a biological parent contrary to his or her will.

There is disagreement among legal commentators and in the case law on the subject, and there are persuasive reasons for enforcing pre-embryo disposition agreements. Also, because IVF is in widespread use and there is a need for agreements between the participants and the IVF clinics, the better rule, and the one the Court adopts, is to enforce agreements entered into at the time IVF is begun, subject to the right of either party to change his or her mind. This rule promotes the public policies that underlie limitations on contracts involving family relationships by permitting either party to object at a later date to provisions that that party no longer subscribes to. In a large number of cases, the agreements will control, so that the clinics may reasonably rely on them, provided they are written in clear language and not signed in blank, and other similar safeguards are provided. If there is disagreement between the parties because one party has changed his or her position, the interest of both parties must be evaluated. Because ordinarily the party choosing not to become a biological parent will prevail, this decision should not result in increased litigation. The seven remaining pre-embryos must be destroyed, unless M.B. wishes to pay any fees coupled with their storage. Affirmed as modified.

CONCURRENCE: (Verniero, J.) An infertile party should be allowed to assert his or her right to use a pre-embryo against the objections of the other party, if such use is the only means of procreation. In that case, the balance arguably would weigh in the infertile party's favor absent other countervailing considerations.

CONCURRENCE: (Zazzali, J.) Decision making in this developing area should follow a careful, compassionate course that is infused with equity.

▶ *ANALYSIS*

Despite the Court's holding in this case that the couple did not enter into a binding contract directing the disposition of their pre-embryos, it nevertheless discusses at great length whether such agreements are enforceable and also discusses the rule that it adopts regarding enforcement of pre-embryo disposition agreements. It would seem, therefore, that much of the Court's discussion is dicta, the main purpose of which is to anticipate and attempt to guide future cases. If there is one thing that all involved in this area seem to agree on is that the advances in reproductive technologies have outstripped the development of legal principles to resolve the inevitable disputes that accompany such reproductive opportunities, and that there is a need for general principles that will guide resolution of such future disputes.

Quicknotes

DICTUM Statement by a judge in a legal opinion that is not necessary for the resolution of the action.

PUBLIC POLICY Policy administered by the state with respect to the health, safety and morals of its people in accordance with common notions of fairness and decency.

Woodward v. Commissioner of Social Security

Mother of posthumously born children (P) v. Government agency (D)

Mass. Sup. Jud. Ct., 760 N.E.2d 257, 425 Mass. 536 (2002).

NATURE OF CASE: Certification of a question of law.

FACT SUMMARY: Two years after the death of her husband, Lauren Woodward (P) was able to conceive two children as the result of artificial insemination of her husband's sperm. The Social Security Administration (D) denied survivor benefits because the children were not known at the time of death of Woodward's (P) husband.

🏛 RULE OF LAW
In limited circumstances, children born after a parent has died can enjoy the inheritance rights of natural children under the law of intestate succession.

FACTS: After approximately three and one-half years of marriage, Lauren Woodward (Woodward) (P) and her husband Warren Woodward were informed that Warren had leukemia. At the time, the couple was childless. Advised that Warren's leukemia treatment might leave him sterile, the Woodwards arranged for a quantity of the Warren's semen to be medically withdrawn and preserved, in a process commonly known as "sperm banking." Within the year, Warren died and Woodward (P) was appointed administratrix of his estate. Two years later Woodward (P) was able to conceive two twin children through artificial insemination. Woodward's (P) claims to the Social Security Administration (SSA) for survivor benefits were rejected on the ground that she had not established that the twins were her husband's "children" within the meaning of the Act. During a series of unsuccessful administrative appeals, Woodward (P) was able to have a state court enter a judgment of paternity and order that both children's birth certificates declared Warren to be the children's father. The judgment of paternity and the amended birth certificates did not persuade the SSA, which upheld its decision to deny benefits. Woodward (P) then filed suit in the federal district court, which certified a question to the appellate court.

ISSUE: Can children born after a parent has died enjoy the inheritance rights of natural children under the law of intestate succession?

HOLDING AND DECISION: (Marshall, J.) Yes. In limited circumstances, children born after a parent has died can enjoy the inheritance rights of natural children under the law of intestate succession. The question is to determine the inheritance rights under Massachusetts law of children conceived from a deceased individual and his or her surviving spouse. This case presents a narrow set of circumstances, yet the issues it raises are far reaching.

Because the law regarding the rights of posthumously conceived children is unsettled, the certified question is understandably broad. Moreover, the parties have articulated extreme positions. The wife's (Lauren Woodward's (P)) principal argument is that, by virtue of their genetic connection with the decedent, posthumously conceived children must always be permitted to enjoy the inheritance rights of the deceased parent's children under our law of intestate succession. The Government's (SSA's (D)) principal argument is that, because posthumously conceived children are not "in being" as of the date of the parent's death, they are always barred from enjoying such inheritance rights. Neither party's position is tenable.

The state's intestacy statute directs that, if a decedent "leaves issue," such "issue" will inherit a fixed portion of his real and personal property, subject to debts and expenses, the rights of the surviving spouse, and other statutory payments not relevant here. To answer the certified question, then, the Court must first determine whether the twins are the "issue" of the husband. The intestacy statute does not define "issue." However, in the context of intestacy the term "issue" means all lineal (genetic) descendants, and now includes both marital and non-marital. The term "descendants" has long been held to mean persons "who by consanguinity trace their lineage to the designated ancestor." (Lockwood v. Adamson, 409 Mass. 325 (1991)

The "posthumous children" provision of the intestacy statute is yet another expression of the legislature's intent to preserve wealth for consanguineous descendants. That section provides that "posthumous children shall be considered as living at the death of their parent. The legislature, however, has left the term "posthumous children" undefined. The Massachusetts intestacy statute thus does not contain an express, affirmative requirement that posthumous children must "be in existence" as of the date of the decedent's death. The legislature could surely have enacted such a provision had it desired to do so. The determination must be made whether, under our intestacy law, there is any reason that children conceived after the decedent's death who are the decedent's direct genetic descendants—that is, children who "by consanguinity trace their lineage to the designated ancestor"—may not enjoy the same succession rights as children conceived before the decedent's death who are the decedent's direct genetic descendants.

Continued on next page.

The question whether posthumously conceived genetic children may enjoy inheritance rights under the intestacy statute implicates three powerful state interests: the best interests of children, the state's interest in the orderly administration of estates, and the reproductive rights of the genetic parent. First and foremost courts consider the overriding legislative concern to promote the best interests of children. The protection of minor children, most especially those who may be stigmatized by their "illegitimate" status has been a hallmark of legislative action and of the jurisprudence of this court. Also considered is that some of the assistive reproductive technologies that make posthumous reproduction possible have been widely known and practiced for several decades. In that time, the legislature has not acted to narrow the broad statutory class of posthumous children to restrict posthumously conceived children from taking in intestacy. Moreover, the legislature has in great measure affirmatively supported the assistive reproductive technologies that are the only means by which these children can come into being.

Posthumously conceived children may not come into the world the way the majority of children do. But they are children nonetheless. The court can assume that the legislature intended that such children be "entitled," in so far as possible, to the same rights and protections of the law as children conceived before death.

However, in the context of the intestacy laws, the best interests of the posthumously conceived child, while of great importance, are not in themselves conclusive. They must be balanced against other important state interests, not the least of which is the protection of children who are alive or conceived before the intestate parent's death. In an era in which serial marriages, serial families, and blended families are not uncommon, according succession rights under our intestacy laws to posthumously conceived children may, in a given case, have the potential to pit child against child and family against family. Any inheritance rights of posthumously conceived children will reduce the intestate share available to children born prior to the decedent's death. Such considerations, among others, lead the court to examine a second important legislative purpose: to provide certainty to heirs and creditors by effecting the orderly, prompt, and accurate administration of intestate estates.

The intestacy statute furthers the legislature's administrative goals in two principal ways: (1) by requiring certainty of filiation between the decedent and his issue, and (2) by establishing limitations periods for the commencement of claims against the intestate estate. In answering the certified question, we must consider each of these requirements of the intestacy statute in turn.

First, the intestacy law mandates that absent the father's acknowledgment of paternity or marriage to the mother, a non-marital child must obtain a judicial determination of paternity as a prerequisite to succeeding to a portion of the father's intestate estate. Both the United States Supreme Court and this court have long recognized that the state's strong interest in preventing fraudulent claims justifies certain disparate classifications among non-marital children based on the relative difficulty of accurately determining a child's direct lineal ancestor.

The court can turn to the second way in which the legislature has met its administrative goals: the establishment of a limitations period for bringing paternity claims against the intestate estate. Both the SSA (D) and the administrative law judge concluded that the wife (P) and the children were not entitled to Social Security survivor benefits because, among other things, the paternity actions were not brought within the one-year period for commencing paternity claims mandated by the intestacy statute. Nevertheless, the limitations question is inextricably tied to consideration of the intestacy statute's administrative goals. In the case of posthumously conceived children, the application of the one-year limitations period is not clear; it may pose significant burdens on the surviving parent, and consequently on the child. It requires, in effect, that the survivor make a decision to bear children while in the freshness of grieving. It also requires that attempts at conception succeed quickly.

Finally, the question certified implicates a third important state interest: to honor the reproductive choices of individuals. This is not to address the wife's (P) argument that her reproductive rights would be infringed by denying succession rights to her children under our intestacy law. Nothing in the record even remotely suggests that she (P) was prevented by the state from choosing to conceive children using her deceased husband's semen. The husband's reproductive rights are a more complicated matter In a previous case, *A.Z. v. B.Z.*, 431 Mass. 150 (2000), the court considered certain issues surrounding the disposition of frozen preembryos. Persuasive, among other factors, was the lack of credible evidence of the husband's true intention regarding the disposition of the frozen preembryos and the changed family circumstance resulting from the couple's divorce. Recognizing that the laws strongly affirm the value of bodily and reproductive integrity, we held that "forced procreation is not an area amenable to judicial enforcement." In short, the Court has recognized that individuals have a protected right to control the use of their gametes

Consonant with the principles in *A.Z. v. B.Z.*, a decedent's silence, or his equivocal indications of a desire to parent posthumously, ought not to be construed as consent. The prospective donor parent must clearly and unequivocally consent not only to posthumous reproduction but also to the support of any resulting child. After the donor-parent's death, the burden rests with the surviving parent, or the posthumously conceived child's other legal representative, to prove the deceased genetic parent's affirmative consent to both requirements for posthumous parentage: posthumous reproduction and the support of any resulting child. Without evidence that the deceased

Continued on next page.

intestate parent affirmatively consented (1) to the posthumous reproduction and (2) to support any resulting child, a court cannot be assured that the intestacy statute's goal of fraud prevention is satisfied

It is undisputed in this case that the husband is the genetic father of the wife's children. However, for the reasons stated above, that fact, in itself, cannot be sufficient to establish that the husband is the children's legal father for purposes of the devolution and distribution of his intestate property. Woodward (P) may come forward with other evidence as to her husband's consent to posthumously conceive children. The conclusion is that limited circumstances may exist, consistent with the mandates of our legislature, in which posthumously conceived children may enjoy the inheritance rights of "issue" under our intestacy law. These limited circumstances exist where, as a threshold matter, the surviving parent or the child's other legal representative demonstrates a genetic relationship between the child and the decedent. The survivor or representative must then establish that the decedent affirmatively consented (1) to posthumous conception and (2) to the support of any resulting child. Even where such circumstances exist, time limitations may preclude commencing a claim for succession rights on behalf of a posthumously conceived child. In any action brought to establish such inheritance rights, notice must be given to all interested parties.

▶ ANALYSIS

In an age where science makes it possible to conceive children after the death of the father, the tension is between the common-sense acknowledgment of the offspring as a product of the deceased parent and the legal ramifications of the ability to receive government benefits or inheritance rights. As the *Woodward* court noted, the ability to conceive after death complicates many aspects of the finality of probate and what are the best interests of the children. In attempting to provide guidance, the court posed the interesting question of what proof is there that the father wanted the offspring in the event of his death. This would seem inconsistent with the fact that the sperm was actually donated for the purpose of conception and add the additional hurdle of intent specifically for the possibility of "posthumous conception."

■◼▬◼■

Matter of Baby M

Biological father (P) v. Surrogate mother (D)

N.J. Sup. Ct., 109 N.J. 396, 537 A.2d 1227 (1988).

NATURE OF CASE: Appeal of order determining parentage and child custody.

FACT SUMMARY: Whitehead (D) reneged on an agreement to provide a baby fathered by Stern (P) and give it up to the Sterns (P).

🏛 RULE OF LAW
A "surrogacy contract" wherein a woman agrees to have a child and surrender it is void.

FACTS: Elizabeth Stern (P) did not wish to give birth due to a possible genetic defect. Nonetheless, the Sterns (P) wanted a baby. They contracted with Whitehead (D) that the latter would be inseminated by William Stern (P), give up the baby, and receive $10,000. Whitehead (D) had the baby, but did not want to give it up. Following a protracted series of maneuverings the Sterns (P) obtained custody. They filed a complaint seeking to have the contract enforced and custody permanently awarded to them. The trial court found the contract valid, awarded custody to the Sterns (P), and cut off Whitehead's (D) parental rights entirely. Whitehead (D) appealed.

ISSUE: Is a "surrogacy contract" wherein a woman agrees to have a child and surrender it void?

HOLDING AND DECISION: (Wilentz, C.J.) Yes. A "surrogacy contract" wherein a woman agrees to have a child and surrender it is void. A contract of this nature conflicts with at least three categories of statutes: (1) laws prohibiting the use of money in connection with adoptions; (2) laws requiring proof of parental unfitness prior to termination of parental rights; and (3) laws that make surrender of custody and consent to adoption revocable. Further, contracts of this type conflict with nonstatutory, but nonetheless accepted, policy considerations governing child placement. First and foremost of these is that the paramount consideration in deciding where a child shall be placed be the best interests of the child. A contract such as that in question gives no weight to that consideration. Also, such contracts, by favoring the natural father over the natural mother, conflict with the policy that natural parents shall receive equal considerations. Further, it is impossible not to conclude that such contracts constitute baby selling, which public policy strongly disfavors. For these reasons, contracts such as those at issue here are void. The trial court terminated Whitehead's (D) parental rights but erred in doing so because no statutory basis for the termination exists. The termination cannot occur without an analysis of the constitutional claims asserted by both natural parents. Stern (P) contends his right to custody of

Baby M flows from his right to procreate, whether through intercourse or artificial insemination. Stern's (P) right to procreate does not, however, trump Whitehead's (D) rights. Whitehead (D) asserts a right to custody based on her constitutional right to her child's companionship. Stern (P) also claims his equal protection rights were violated because he is treated differently than a consenting husband in artificial insemination parentage statutes. That claim, however, is Mrs. Stern's because she is essentially standing in the husband's place as consenting to an artificial insemination technique and seeking to be adjudicated the resulting child's natural parent. The trial court's custody determination was appropriate and in the best interests of Baby M. It should be noted though that it must remain very rare for a child to be taken from the custody of his or her natural mother pendent lite because of the strong bond between mother and child. Here, Baby M was in the temporary custody of Stern (P) pending the outcome and that cannot become standard. Even in the face of risk of flight of the natural mother, as here, courts must treat cautiously in making an erroneous temporary custody determination. The trial court improperly terminated Whitehead's (D) parental rights, so visitation was not decided. Visitation is appropriate here and the trial court must determine the extent and substance. Affirmed in part, reversed in part, and remanded.

▶ ANALYSIS

This was one of the country's most closely watched cases in 1987 and 1988. It was the first major case on the validity of surrogate parenting contracts. What little legislative reaction that had occurred as of the time of this writing tended to codify the court's holding. The court's decision does not prohibit voluntary arrangements performed without consideration (i.e., payment to the natural mother).

■—■—■

Quicknotes

BEST INTERESTS OF CHILD Standard used by courts when rendering decisions which involve a child or children.

CHILD CUSTODY DECREE A court order awarding responsibility for the care and control over a child or children in a dissolution or separation proceeding.

EQUAL PROTECTION CLAUSE A constitutional provision that each person be guaranteed the same protection of the laws enjoyed by other persons in like circumstances.

Continued on next page.

NATURAL PARENTS The biological parents of a child as opposed to those parents whose rights have either been assigned or are otherwise recognized by law.

PENDENTE LITE A matter that is contingent on the disposition of a pending suit.

TERMINATION OF PARENTAL RIGHTS The purposeful cessation of lawfully recognized rights between a child and its parents and of the parent to the child, including physical possession of the child, companionship and support, the right to discipline the child, and control over the child's property.

Raftopol v. Ramey

Biological and intended parent (P) v. Surrogate and state agency (D)

Conn. Sup. Ct., 299 Conn, 681, 12 A.3d 783 (2011).

NATURE OF CASE: Appeal from decision of trial court to grant declaratory judgment.

FACT SUMMARY: The plaintiffs, Anthony Raftopol (P) and his domestic partner Shawn Hargon (P) entered into a gestational (surrogacy) agreement with Karma Ramey (D), in which a third party donor's eggs would be fertilized by Raftopol's (P) sperm. Prior to the expected delivery date, plaintiffs sought a declaratory judgment that they both were the fathers and for the Department of Public Health (D) to signify as such on the children's birth certificate.

🏛 **RULE OF LAW**
The law permits an intended parent who is neither the biological nor the adoptive parent of a child to become a legal parent of that child by means of a valid gestational agreement.

FACTS: The plaintiffs, Anthony Raftopol (P) and his domestic partner Shawn Hargon (P) entered into a written agreement (gestational agreement) with Karma Ramey (D), in which she agreed to act as a gestational carrier [surrogate] for the plaintiffs. Pursuant to the gestational agreement, eggs were recovered from a third party egg donor and fertilized with sperm contributed by Raftopol (P). When Ramey (D) gave birth to two children, DNA testing confirmed that Raftopol (P) was the biological father. Pursuant to the gestational agreement, Ramey (D) had agreed to terminate her parental rights to any children resulting from the procedures and to sign any forms necessary for the issuance of a replacement birth certificate naming the plaintiffs as the parents. Ramey (D) also had agreed to consent to the adoption of any such children by Hargon (P) and to cooperate fully to obtain this goal.

Prior to the expected delivery date, plaintiffs Raftopol (P) and Hargon (P) sought a declaratory judgment that the gestational agreement was valid, that the plaintiffs were both the legal parents of the children, and requested the Department of Public Health (Department) (D) to issue a replacement birth certificate reflecting that they, and not Ramey (D), were parents of the children. The Department (D) responded that the court lacked jurisdiction over the matter because Hargon (P) did not allege that he had conceived the children and because the court lacked jurisdiction to terminate the parental rights of the gestational carrier (Ramey), the egg donor, and any husbands either may have. When the trial court issued a ruling declaring that: (1) the gestational agreement was valid; (2) Raftopol (P) was the genetic and legal father of the children; (3) Hargon (P) was the legal father of the children; and (4)

Ramey (D) was not the genetic or legal mother of the children, the Department (D) appealed.

ISSUE: Does the law permit an intended parent who is neither the biological nor the adoptive parent of a child to become a legal parent of that child by means of a valid gestational agreement?

HOLDING AND DECISION: (McLachlan, J.) Yes. The law permits an intended parent who is neither the biological nor the adoptive parent of a child to become a legal parent of that child by means of a valid gestational agreement. In our view, our laws should provide an answer to the following two basic questions: (1) who are the legal parents of children born as a result of artificial insemination; and (2) what steps must such persons take to clarify their status as legal parents of such children? The first issue is whether the trial court lacked subject matter jurisdiction to declare Hargon (P) a legal parent of the children because he was not biologically related to the children and did not adopt them. Included within this issue is the question of whether the court was required, as a prerequisite to making any determination regarding Hargon's (P) parental status, to terminate Ramey's (D) parental rights, and, if so, whether the court had jurisdiction to terminate those rights. The conclusion is that: (1) because Ramey (D) did not have any parental rights with respect to the children, the termination of those nonexistent rights was not a necessary prerequisite to a determination of Hargon's (P) parental status with respect to the children; and (2) the court had jurisdiction to issue a declaratory ruling regarding Hargon's (P) parental status.

Preliminarily, the Department (D) claimed that the trial court lacked subject matter jurisdiction to declare Hargon (P) a parent because the termination of Ramey's (D) parental rights—over which the trial court would have lacked jurisdiction—was a necessary prerequisite to Hargon's acquiring parental status with respect to the children. Because Ramey (D) had no parental rights to terminate, the trial court was not deprived of jurisdiction. The statutes and case law establish that a gestational carrier who bears no biological relationship to the child she has carried does not have parental rights with respect to that child. The courts have long recognized that there are three ways by which a person may become a parent: conception, adoption or pursuant to the artificial insemination statutes. The legislature provided the third means by which a person may gain parental status. Accordingly, a child born to a married woman and conceived through artificial insemination by an egg or sperm donor is the child of the wife and husband

Continued on next page.

who requested and consented to the use of artificial insemination with the use of donated sperm or eggs from an identified or anonymous donor.

Under any of the three specified ways of acquiring parental status, as set forth both in our statutes and interpretive case law, Ramey (D) is not a parent of the children in the present case. It is undisputed that she is neither the biological nor the adoptive mother to the children. Nor does she fall within the parameters of the artificial insemination statutes. Accordingly, Ramey (D) did not have parental rights that required termination before Hargon (P) could acquire parental status with respect to the children. Affirmed.

▶ *ANALYSIS*

In an elemental approach, the *Raftopol* court reasoned that if the surrogate mother is not in fact the biological mother, then not only is the known biological father a parent, but so is any intended parent who is subject to the gestational (surrogacy) agreement. This logic would apply regardless of the nature of the couples' relationship and is made a fait accompli based on the ability to designate who is a parent (biological or adoptive) in the agreement.

■■■

Raising Children: Competing Interests

Quick Reference Rules of Law

Wisconsin v. Yoder

State (P) v. Amish leader (D)

406 U.S. 205 (1972).

NATURE OF CASE: Appeal from denial of order to compel school attendance.

FACT SUMMARY: The state of Wisconsin (P) sought to compel Yoder (D) and others, who were Amish, to send their children to school until age 16, as required by state law.

🏛 RULE OF LAW
Parents may successfully avoid prosecution under compulsory school attendance laws only by a positive showing that continued public schooling would seriously interfere with their religious beliefs which are inseparably intertwined with their mode of life and that their children will be offered a substantial equivalent to the schooling they will miss.

FACTS: Yoder (D) was the leader of a group of Amish parents who refused to send their children to public schools beyond the eighth grade. Wisconsin (P) had a statute which required all children to attend school until the age of 16. Since most of the Amish children were only 14 or 15 when they finished the eighth grade, Wisconsin (P) sought to prosecute the parents for violating the statute. Yoder (D) and the other parents resisted on the grounds that the statute was an unconstitutional interference with their free exercise of religion.

ISSUE: May parents successfully avoid prosecution under compulsory school attendance laws by a positive showing that continued public schooling would seriously interfere with their religious beliefs which are inseparably intertwined with their mode of life and that their children will be offered a substantial equivalent to the schooling they will miss?

HOLDING AND DECISION: (Burger, C.J.) Yes. Parents may successfully avoid prosecution under compulsory school attendance laws only by a positive showing that continued public schooling would seriously interfere with their religious beliefs which are inseparably intertwined with their mode of life and that their children will be offered a substantial equivalent to the schooling they will miss. In order to withstand this challenge, the state law must be shown not to interfere with the free exercise of religion; or that if interference does occur, that the state interest is so compelling that it overrides the constitutional freedom involved. Yoder (D) demonstrated that the Amish religion and the Amish lifestyle are so intertwined that interference with the lifestyle is interference with the religion. The strong 300-year history of this religion would be severely threatened if these children were to attend high school against the parents' wishes. The State (P) has failed to overcome its burden of showing that its compelling interest should override the exercise of this constitutional freedom. This is particularly so where, as here, the parents have demonstrated that the children will be offered vocational training that is the substantial equivalent of the schooling they will miss. The issue raised by Justice Douglas that the children's opinions were not sought misses the point. It is the parents who are being prosecuted since the parents are held responsible for their children's schooling. Whether the state can properly interfere with the parent-child relationship with respect to religion is not considered nor decided. Affirmed.

DISSENT IN PART: (Douglas, J.) What has been lost sight of in this case is the best interests of the children involved. By denying them higher education, the majority denies them any opportunity to participate in our modern technological society. To do this without consulting them is a denial of their freedoms.

▶ ANALYSIS

Compulsory school attendance laws have been subjected to increasing scrutiny in recent years. Many authorities point out that keeping a child in school until an arbitrary minimum age against his will is at best useless, and at worst, counterproductive. Compulsory attendance laws may, in fact, produce truly antisocial adults.

■═■

Quicknotes

BEST INTERESTS OF CHILD Standard used by courts when rendering decisions which involve a child or children.

FREE EXERCISE OF RELIGION The right to practice one's religious beliefs free from governmental conduct or interference.

■═■

Smith v. Ricci

[Party not identified.] v. State Board of Education (D)

N.J. Sup. Ct., 89 N.J. 514, 446 A.2d 501 (1982).

NATURE OF CASE: Constitutional challenge to a regulation establishing a family life education program.

FACT SUMMARY: Smith (P) contended that a regulation that required local schools to implement a family life education program impinged on the free exercise of religion and constituted an establishment of religion in violation of the First Amendment.

🏛 RULE OF LAW
Where there is an adequate provision of excusal for conscientiously held beliefs, a family life education program does not violate the Free Exercise or Establishment Clauses of the First Amendment.

FACTS: The State Board of Education (D) enacted a regulation requiring local schools to develop and implement a family life education program, which emphasized instruction on human sexuality. The regulation included an "excusal clause" permitting pupils to be excused from any part of the course found to be objectionable to their parent or guardian. Smith (P) sought review in the appellate division on the grounds that the regulation violated the Free Exercise and Establishment Clauses of the First Amendment. Before argument was heard, the state supreme court certified the matter directly in order to review the regulation.

ISSUE: Does a family life education program violate the Free Exercise or Establishment Clauses of the First Amendment if it includes an adequate provision of excusal for conscientiously held beliefs?

HOLDING AND DECISION: (Clifford, J.) No. Where there is an adequate provision of excusal for conscientiously held beliefs, a family life education program does not violate the Free Exercise or Establishment Clauses of the First Amendment. The U.S. Supreme Court upholds neutral laws that are generally applicable even if those laws somehow burden the exercise of religion. Here, the regulation does not compel the inhibition of religious exercise because an adequate provision for excusal is included. Furthermore, if the government refused to offer curricula offensive to certain religions, it would violate the Establishment Clause by adopting that group's view as government policy. Finally, since there is nothing in the regulation that favors a "secular" view of its subject matter over a "religious" one, the current program does not constitute an establishment of religion. The Board's (D) action is affirmed.

▌ *ANALYSIS*

The Supreme Court reached a similar conclusion in *Bowen v. Kendrick*, 487 U.S. 589 (1988), which involved a challenge, under the Religion Clauses of the First Amendment, of the federal Adolescent Family Life Act. The Act provided federal funding to organizations, including religious organizations that provided services designed to combat teenage pregnancy. The Court held that the Act, on its face, did not violate the Establishment Clause, as it had a valid secular purpose, did not advance religion, and did not create an excessive entanglement of church and state.

■=■

Quicknotes

ESTABLISHMENT CLAUSE The constitutional provision prohibiting the government from favoring any one religion over others, or engaging in religious activities or advocacy.

FREE EXERCISE CLAUSE The guarantee of the First Amendment to the United States Constitution prohibiting Congress from enacting laws regarding the establishment of religion or prohibiting the free exercise thereof.

■=■

Arizona Christian School Tuition Organization v. Winn

Tax credit recipient (D) v. Taxpayers (P)

131 S. Ct. 1436, 179 L.Ed.2d 523 (2011).

NATURE OF CASE: Appeal from a decision that the plaintiff had standing.

FACT SUMMARY: A group of state taxpayers (collectively, Plaintiffs) brought suit against the State (D) for providing tax credits (vouchers) for contributions to school tuition organizations (like the Arizona Christian School Tuition Organization) (D). The trial court's decision that the Plaintiffs lack standing was reversed by the state's highest appellate court, only to be appealed to the U.S. Supreme Court.

RULE OF LAW
Taxpayers do not automatically have standing to challenge the state's providing of tax credits for school tuition organizations.

FACTS: Plaintiffs, a group of state taxpayers, brought suit against the State (D) for providing tax credits [vouchers] for contributions to school tuition organizations (STOs) (like the Arizona Christian School Tuition Organization (D)) based on their status as state taxpayers. STOs use these contributions to provide scholarships to students attending private schools, many of which are religious. Plaintiffs claimed the tax credit was a violation of Establishment Clause principles under the First and Fourteenth Amendments. The trial court denied Plaintiffs' claims based on a lack of standing; the decision was overturned on appeal to the state's highest court, and then was subject to a writ of certiorari to the U.S. Supreme Court.

ISSUE: Do taxpayers automatically have standing to challenge the state's providing of tax credits for school tuition organizations?

HOLDING AND DECISION: (Kennedy, J.) No. Taxpayers do not automatically have standing to challenge the state's providing of tax credits for school tuition organizations. To obtain a determination on the merits in federal court, parties seeking relief must show that they have standing under Article III of the Constitution. Standing in Establishment Clause cases may be shown in various ways. Some plaintiffs may demonstrate standing based on the direct harm of what is claimed to be an establishment of religion, such as a mandatory prayer in a public school classroom. Other plaintiffs may demonstrate standing on the ground that they have incurred a cost or been denied a benefit on account of their religion. Those costs and benefits can result from alleged discrimination in the tax code, such as when the availability of a tax exemption is conditioned on religious affiliation. For their part, Plaintiffs contend that they have standing to challenge Arizona's STO tax credit for one and only one

reason: because they are Arizona taxpayers. But the mere fact that a plaintiff is a taxpayer is not generally deemed sufficient to establish standing in federal court. To overcome that rule, Plaintiffs must rely on an exception created in *Flast v. Cohen*, 392 U.S. 83 (1968). For the reasons discussed below, Plaintiffs cannot take advantage of *Flast's* narrow exception to the general rule against taxpayer standing. As a consequence, Plaintiffs lacked standing to commence this action, and their suit must be dismissed for want of jurisdiction.

Taxpayer Plaintiffs challenged provisions of the state code that allows citizens taxpayers to obtain dollar-for-dollar tax credits of up to $500 per person and $1,000 per married couple for contributions to STOs. If the credit exceeds an individual's tax liability, the credit's unused portion can be carried forward up to five years. A charitable organization could be deemed an STO only upon certain conditions. The organization was required to be exempt from federal taxation under § 501(c)(3) of the Internal Revenue Code. The organization could not limit its scholarships to students attending only one school. And it had to allocate "at least ninety per cent of its annual revenue for educational scholarships or tuition grants" to children attending qualified schools. A "qualified school," in turn, was defined in part as a private school that did not discriminate on the basis of race, color, handicap, familial status, or national origin.

Plaintiffs suggest that their status as taxpayers provides them with standing to challenge the STO tax credit. Absent special circumstances, however, standing cannot be based on a plaintiff's mere status as a taxpayer. This Court has rejected the general proposition that an individual who has paid taxes has a continuing, legally cognizable interest in ensuring that those funds are not used by the government in a way that violates the Constitution. This precept has been referred to as the rule against taxpayer standing.

The doctrinal basis for the rule was discussed in *Frothingham v. Mellon*, 262 U.S. 447 (1923). There, a taxpayer-plaintiff had alleged that certain federal expenditures were in excess of congressional authority under the Constitution. The plaintiff argued that she had standing to raise her claim because she had an interest in the government Treasury and because the allegedly unconstitutional expenditure of government funds would affect her personal tax liability. The Court rejected those arguments. The "effect upon future taxation, of any payment out of funds," was too "remote, fluctuating and uncertain" to give rise to a case or controversy. As a consequence, *Frothingham* held that the taxpayer-plaintiff had not presented a "judicial

Continued on next page.

controversy" appropriate for resolution in federal court but rather a "matter of public . . . concern" that could be pursued only through the political process.

In a second pertinent case, *Doremus v. Board of Ed. of Hawthorne,* 342 U.S. 429 (1952), the Court considered *Frothingham*'s prohibition on taxpayer standing in connection with an alleged Establishment Clause violation. A New Jersey statute had provided that public school teachers would read Bible verses to their students at the start of each school day. A plaintiff sought to have the law enjoined, asserting standing based on her status as a taxpayer. The plaintiff in *Doremus* lacked any "direct and particular financial interest" in the suit, and, as a result, a decision on the merits would have been merely "advisory."

In holdings consistent with *Frothingham* and *Doremus,* more recent decisions have explained that claims of taxpayer standing rest on unjustifiable economic and political speculation. When a government expends resources or declines to impose a tax, its budget does not necessarily suffer. The primary contention of Plaintiffs, of course, is that, despite the general rule that taxpayers lack standing to object to expenditures alleged to be unconstitutional, their suit falls within the exception established by *Flast.* It must be noted at the outset that, as this Court has explained, *Flast*'s holding provides a "narrow exception" to "the general rule against taxpayer standing." At issue in *Flast* was the standing of federal taxpayers to object, on First Amendment grounds, to a congressional statute that allowed expenditures of federal funds from the general Treasury to support, among other programs, "instruction in reading, arithmetic, and other subjects in religious schools, and to purchase textbooks and other instructional materials for use in such schools." *Flast* held that taxpayers have standing when two conditions are met.

The first condition is that there must be a "logical link" between the plaintiff's taxpayer status "and the type of legislative enactment attacked." This condition was not satisfied in *Doremus* because the statute challenged in that case—providing for the recitation of Bible passages in public schools—involved at most an "incidental expenditure of tax funds." In *Flast,* by contrast, the allegation was that the federal government violated the Establishment Clause in the exercise of its legislative authority both to collect and spend tax dollars.

The second condition for standing under *Flast* is that there must be "a nexus" between the plaintiff's taxpayer status and "the precise nature of the constitutional infringement alleged." This condition was deemed satisfied in *Flast* based on the allegation that Government funds had been spent on an outlay for religion in contravention of the Establishment Clause. In *Frothingham,* by contrast, the claim was that Congress had exceeded its constitutional authority without regard to any specific prohibition. Confirming that *Flast* turned on the unique features of Establishment Clause violations, this Court has "declined to lower the taxpayer standing bar in suits alleging

violations of any constitutional provision apart from the Establishment Clause."

Plaintiffs contend that these principles demonstrate their standing to challenge the STO tax credit. In their view the tax credit is, for *Flast* purposes, best understood as a governmental expenditure. That is incorrect. It is easy to see that tax credits and governmental expenditures can have similar economic consequences, at least for beneficiaries whose tax liability is sufficiently large to take full advantage of the credit. Yet tax credits and governmental expenditures do not both implicate individual taxpayers in sectarian activities. The distinction between governmental expenditures and tax credits refutes Plaintiffs' assertion of standing. When state taxpayers choose to contribute to STOs, they spend their own money, not money the state has collected from Plaintiffs or from other taxpayers. On the contrary, Plaintiffs and other state taxpayers remain free to pay their own tax bills, without contributing to an STO. Plaintiffs are likewise able to contribute to an STO of their choice, either religious or secular. And Plaintiffs also have the option of contributing to other charitable organizations, in which case Plaintiffs may become eligible for a tax deduction or a different tax credit. The STO tax credit is not tantamount to a religious tax or to a tithe and does not visit the injury identified in *Flast.* It follows that Plaintiffs have neither alleged an injury for standing purposes under general rules nor met the *Flast* exception.

The present suit serves as an illustration of these principles. The fact that Plaintiffs are state taxpayers does not give them standing to challenge the subsidies allegedly provided to religious STOs. To alter the rules of standing or weaken their requisite elements would be inconsistent with the case-or-controversy limitation on federal jurisdiction imposed by Article III. Reversed.

DISSENT: (Kagan, J.) Since its inception, the state private-school-tuition tax credit has cost the state, by its own estimate, nearly $350 million in diverted tax revenue. Taxpayer Plaintiffs who instituted this suit allege that the use of these funds to subsidize STOs breaches the Establishment Clause's promise of religious neutrality. Many of these STOs, Plaintiffs claim, discriminate on the basis of a child's religion when awarding scholarships. For almost half a century, litigants like the Plaintiffs have obtained judicial review of claims that the government has used its taxing and spending power in violation of the Establishment Clause. Beginning in *Flast,* and continuing in case after case for over four decades, this Court and others have exercised jurisdiction to decide taxpayer-initiated challenges not materially different from this one. Not every suit has succeeded on the merits, or should have. But every taxpayer-plaintiff has had her day in court to contest the government's financing of religious activity.

Continued on next page.

Today, the Court breaks from this precedent by refusing to hear taxpayers' claims that the government has unconstitutionally subsidized religion through its tax system. These litigants lack standing, the majority holds, because the funding of religion they challenge comes from a tax credit, rather than an appropriation. A tax credit, the Court asserts, does not injure objecting taxpayers, because it "does not extract and spend their funds in service of an establishment."

This novel distinction in standing law between appropriations and tax expenditures has as little basis in principle as it has in our precedent. Cash grants and targeted tax breaks are means of accomplishing the same government objective—to provide financial support to select individuals or organizations. Taxpayers who oppose state aid of religion have equal reason to protest whether that aid flows from the one form of subsidy or the other. Either way, the government has financed the religious activity. And so either way, taxpayers should be able to challenge the subsidy.

Still worse, the Court's arbitrary distinction threatens to eliminate all occasions for a taxpayer to contest the government's monetary support of religion. Precisely because appropriations and tax breaks can achieve identical objectives, the government can easily substitute one for the other. Today's opinion thus enables the government to end-run *Flast*'s guarantee of access to the judiciary. From now on, the government need follow just one simple rule—subsidize through the tax system—to preclude taxpayer challenges to state funding of religion.

The majority reaches a contrary decision by distinguishing between two methods of financing religion: A taxpayer has standing to challenge state subsidies to religion, the Court announces, when the mechanism used is an appropriation, but not when the mechanism is a targeted tax break, otherwise called a "tax expenditure." In the former case, but not in the latter, the Court declares, the taxpayer suffers cognizable injury.

Our taxpayer standing cases have declined to distinguish between appropriations and tax expenditures. Today's decision devastates taxpayer standing in Establishment Clause cases. The government, after all, often uses tax expenditures to subsidize favored persons and activities. Still more, the government almost always has this option. Appropriations and tax subsidies are readily interchangeable; what is a cash grant today can be a tax break tomorrow. The Court's opinion thus offers a roadmap—more truly, just a one-step instruction—to any government that wishes to insulate its financing of religious activity from legal challenge. Structure the funding as a tax expenditure, and *Flast* will not stand in the way. No taxpayer will have standing to object.

government expenditures. With noting that the damage or harm to the taxpayers in the present matter was speculative because a tax credit is not an expenditure, the Court set forth a tougher test for establishing standing. The far-reaching effect of this case, according to the dissent by Justice Kagan, is that government will simply structure funding as a tax expenditure to avoid review of aid to religious organizations.

▶ ANALYSIS

In this voucher program decision, the U.S. Supreme Court rejected the general proposition that an individual who has paid taxes automatically has standing to bring suit against

L.A.M. v. State

Minor (D) v. State (P)

Alaska Sup. Ct., 547 P.2d 827 (1976).

NATURE OF CASE: Appeal from an institutionalization proceeding.

FACT SUMMARY: L.A.M. (D), a minor, was ordered institutionalized for repeatedly ignoring court orders.

🏛 RULE OF LAW
The state's interest in its citizens and the rights of parents to the custody of their children justify depriving minors of liberty to run away or otherwise conduct themselves free of parental interference.

FACTS: L.A.M. (D), a minor, was a repeated runaway. After numerous incidents, her mother filed a petition to have L.A.M. (D) declared a child in need of supervision. Although placed under court order not to run away, L.A.M. (D) continued to leave home and, after several more hearings, was placed in a foster home. L.A.M. (D) was informed that if she left the foster home without permission, she would be found in contempt of court. L.A.M. (D) again ran away and was placed in a Youth Services home. L.A.M. (D) left again. She was declared in criminal contempt, was declared a delinquent, and was confined to a Youth Center. L.A.M. (D) appealed, contending the state improperly infringed upon her liberty rights and institutionalization was improper as a response to L.A.M.'s exercise of those rights. The State (P) argued that its response was justified and institutionalization was appropriate to punish a deliberate violation of a legitimate court order. L.A.M. (D) appealed, alleging her right to liberty could not be restrained and her exercise of this right could not be made a crime requiring institutionalization. The State (P) alleged that its duty to protect the minor and its citizens and the parents' right to custody justified depriving the minor of complete, unfettered liberty. Violations of legitimate court orders were crimes and could be punished by institutionalization.

ISSUE: Does the state's interest in its citizens and the rights of parents to the custody of their children justify depriving minors of liberty to run away or otherwise conduct themselves free of parental interference?

HOLDING AND DECISION: (Erwin, J.) Yes. The state's interest in its citizens and the rights of parents to the custody of their children justifies depriving minors of liberty to run away or otherwise conduct themselves free of parental interference. Minors do not have the right to unfettered freedom. There are competing interests that must be protected, which justify reasonable restrictions on the minor's rights. First, a parent has custodial rights which include normal supervision of the child. These may be enforced by statute by declaring the child to be in need of supervision. It is a judicial method for handling custody disputes between a parent and child. If the child is placed in a foster home, it is for the purpose of eventually affecting a reconciliation of the parties. The state also has a duty to protect minors, who generally are unable to protect themselves. It must also protect its other citizens who may be harmed if the minor turns to crime to obtain money. L.A.M. (D) never has challenged the custodial rights of her mother. So long as these rights exist, the parent may enforce them. Violation of a court order is a crime and is grounds for institutionalization as a delinquent. Courts have the power to enforce their orders by criminal contempt in such situations. Finally, the Youth Center is not for hardened delinquents, but those in need of supervision. The institutionalization is affirmed.

CONCURRENCE: (Boochever, J.) The state has a valid interest in a child's welfare. Institutionalization in this case was appropriate because nothing else worked and this was in the child's best interests.

▌ ANALYSIS

In some states, children in need of supervision must first be placed in minimum security Youth Centers. Only if such restrictions on liberty prove to be ineffective may they be incarcerated in state training schools. *In re Presley*, 47 Ill. 2d 50 (1970). Child-in-need-of-supervision statutes have been upheld as a method of preventing physical violence to minors who are under the control of parents who may use force to restrain or punish the child. *State v. England*, 220 Or. 395 (1960).

■══■

Quicknotes

BEST INTERESTS OF CHILD Standard used by courts when rendering decisions which involve a child or children.

■══■

Matter of Andrew R.

Minor child

N.Y. Fam., 115 Misc. 2d 937, 454 N.Y.S.2d 820 (1982).

NATURE OF CASE: Person in need of supervision proceeding.

FACT SUMMARY: Citing actions his 13-year-old son had taken against being placed at Hawthorne Cedar Knolls and his parents' efforts to return him there when he ran away, Andrew R.'s father brought a petition to have him declared a person in need of supervision.

🏛 RULE OF LAW
A child may not be adjudicated a person in need of supervision (PINS) for refusing to comply with a directive that violates his constitutional rights or is otherwise unlawful, or for the conduct attributable to his reaction to said violation of his rights, rather than a PINS intention on his part.

FACTS: Andrew R. was subjected to a "voluntary" placement at Hawthorne Cedar Knolls with the consent of his parents. Despite his vehement protest against being put in Hawthorne, which mixed voluntarily placed children, persons in need of supervision, and juvenile delinquents, Andrew remained there for seven months without a neutral fact finder reviewing his "voluntary" placement. While at Hawthorne, Andrew was truant and ran away. He went home, where, in the face of his father's insistence that he return to Hawthorne, Andrew threatened his father. In response to a threat to kill him, the father handed Andrew a knife and told him to go ahead, whereupon Andrew thrust the knife into a household item. Andrew's father used these incidents in filing a petition to have his son declared a person in need of supervision (PINS).

ISSUE: May a child be adjudicated a person in need of supervision (PINS) for refusing to comply with a directive that violates his constitutional rights or is otherwise unlawful, or for the conduct attributable to his reaction to said violation of his rights, rather than a PINS intention on his part?

HOLDING AND DECISION: (Leddy, J.) No. A child cannot be adjudicated a person in need of supervision for refusing to comply with a directive that violates his constitutional rights or is otherwise unlawful or for the conduct attributable to his reaction to said violation of his rights, rather than a PINS intention on his part. Andrew's constitutional rights were definitely violated by his placement at Hawthorne for seven months without a neutral fact finder reviewing same. Whatever actions Andrew took in response to his being unconstitutionally placed there for that lengthy period, while not condoned, are attributable to his reaction to such unconstitutional

deprivation of liberty, rather than a PINS intention on his part. Thus, his actions cannot be used to support an adjudication of his status as that of a person in need of supervision. Petition dismissed.

▶ ANALYSIS

The law has come a long way since the late 1600s, when a Massachusetts ordinance provided that a child over 16 who was of sufficient understanding could be put to death for cursing or smiting its natural father and authorized a similar penalty for a "stubborn and rebellious" son over 16 who "will not obey the voice of his father or the voice of his mother."

■ ■ ■

In re M.L.

State agency (P) v. Parents (D)

Pa. Sup. Ct., 562 Pa. 646, 757 A.2d 849 (2000).

NATURE OF CASE: Appeal from judgment that a child is dependent notwithstanding the fact that the child's non-custodial parent is ready, willing, and able to provide adequate care to the child.

FACT SUMMARY: M.L.'s mother (P), the custodial parent, had a mental disorder that led her to repeatedly allege that the non-custodial father was sexually abusing M.L., despite convincing evidence that no such abuse was occurring. Accordingly, the trial court granted a petition for dependency and awarded custody to the father.

> ## RULE OF LAW
> A child, whose non-custodial parent is ready, willing, and able to provide adequate care to the child, cannot be found dependent.

FACTS: M.L.'s natural parents never married, but shared custody from the time of her birth. About two years after the child's birth, a custody dispute ended with M.L.'s mother (P) being the primary custodial parent, and R.G., M.L.'s father, having custody every other weekend. Before the custody dispute, however, M.L.'s mother (P) had alleged that R.G. was sexually abusing the child, and that he did not properly take care of M.L. During the five months that preceded the custody dispute, M.L.'s mother (P) subjected M.L. to six separate physical examinations for possible sexual abuse, none of which revealed any such abuse. Despite the lack of evidence, the mother (P) kept alleging that R.G. was sexually abusing M.L. This led to the filing of a dependency petition by the county's Children and Youth Service (CYS). The trial court found that because the mother suffered from a mental disorder, M.L. was dependent, and the court awarded custody to R.G. The mother (P) appealed, the Superior Court affirmed, and the mother (P) appealed to the Pennsylvania Supreme Court, which granted review.

ISSUE: Can a child, whose non-custodial parent is ready, willing, and able to provide adequate care to the child, be found dependent?

HOLDING AND DECISION: (Castille, J.) No. A child, whose non-custodial parent is ready, willing, and able to provide adequate care to the child, cannot be found dependent. A dependent child is defined by statute as a child who is without proper parental care or control, has been abandoned, or "is without a parent, guardian, or legal custodian." A court may find that a child is dependent if the child meets the statutory definition. However, as here, a child whose non-custodial parent is ready, willing,

and able to provide appropriate care to the child, does not meet this definition. Where a non-custodial parent is available to take care of the child, the power of the trial court to declare dependency and thereby place the child is an unwarranted intrusion into the family. Reversed.

DISSENT: (Cappy, J.) The majority today violates the intent and language of the Juvenile Act due to a fundamental misapprehension of dependency proceedings.

▌ANALYSIS

The dissent, although agreeing with the ultimate result of the majority's opinion, found that the majority's approach did not comport with the goal of a dependency hearing, which is to obtain a disposition that is consistent with the child's best interests. The dissent found that the fundamental flaw in the majority's approach was that it authorized an automatic transfer of custody to the non-custodial parent without requiring a finding of dependency and without assessing whether such a transfer would be in the child's best interests.

Quicknotes

BEST INTERESTS OF CHILD Standard used by courts when rendering decisions which involve a child or children.

CHILD ABUSE Conduct harmful to a child's physical or mental health.

CUSTODIAL PARENT A parent who is awarded the care and control of a child by the court in a dissolution or separation proceeding.

DEPENDENT One who depends upon another person for support.

In re Juvenile Appeal (83–CD)

Commissioner of children's services (P) v. Mother (D)

Conn. Sup. Ct., 189 Conn. 276, 455 A.2d 1313 (1983).

NATURE OF CASE: Appeal from an order granting temporary custody to the Department of Children and Youth Services.

FACT SUMMARY: After the death of her nine-month-old child, a mother was visited by a caseworker, and her children were placed in the temporary custody of the Commissioner of the Department of Children and Youth Services, despite no substantial evidence that she had caused the death or that she was not caring for her children.

🏛 RULE OF LAW
A child must be at risk of harm before the state's interest becomes a compelling one justifying temporary removal of the child from the home.

FACTS: A caseworker was sent to investigate the home of a mother of six after her nine-month-old child died. No cause of death could be determined at the time, but the pediatrician noticed some unexplained superficial marks on the child's body. It was later determined they could not have caused the death and that the child had a viral lung infection. Meantime, her five other children were ordered by the court into the temporary custody of the Commissioner of the Department of Children and Youth Services (P), which temporary custody went on for three years, while the mother fought the aforementioned order. At no time during the visits to the mother's home did caseworkers observe abuse or neglect of the children, although evidence was offered as to the presence of dirt and roaches, that the mother had been observed drinking beer and may have been drunk on occasion, that the two older children occasionally came to school without eating breakfast, and that a neighbor had reported the children as being left all alone one night. Mother (D) challenged the constitutionality of the temporary custody and removal statute on the grounds that it impermissibly infringed on her right to family integrity and was void for vagueness. Mother (D) also claimed that the trial court employed the wrong standard of proof when it used "probable cause" as the standard in the temporary custody proceeding.

ISSUE: Must a child be at risk of harm before the state's interest becomes a compelling one justifying temporary removal of the child from the home?

HOLDING AND DECISION: (Speziale, C.J.) Yes. A child must be at risk of harm before the state's interest becomes a compelling one justifying a temporary removal of the child from the home. Mother (D) contends the removal statute is unconstitutional, so the state must demonstrate its compelling interest and narrowly drawn legislative enactments. A child's best interest is typically served by remaining with his or her family. Only when that child's safety and welfare is at risk does the state's intrusion become justified. The language of the statute clearly limits the state's intervention ability to situations where the state's interest in the safety of the child becomes compelling. Temporary custody is only permitted where necessary to "safeguard his welfare." Read in connection with the criteria of the child welfare statutes, the challenged statute is constitutional. The focus then turns to the facts of the case and whether temporary custody was justified because of risk to the children. Here, the facts did not warrant a conclusion that the children were at risk. Their removal, temporary in name only, was not warranted. Reversed.

▶ ANALYSIS

The American Bar Association Juvenile Justice Standards Project has developed Model Standards Relating to Abuse and Neglect, which attempt to set forth the six general circumstances in which a child is sufficiently "at risk" to make state intervention permissible. They include sexual abuse of the child by its parent or a member of the household and a child's committing delinquent acts as a result of parental encouragement, guidance, or approval.

■■■

Quicknotes

PROBABLE CAUSE A reasonable basis for believing that a crime has been committed.

■■■

Johnson v. State

Convicted drug user (D) v. State (P)

Fla. Sup. Ct., 602 So.2d 1288 (1992).

NATURE OF CASE: Review of two convictions for delivering a controlled substance to a minor.

FACT SUMMARY: Johnson (P) contested her conviction of delivery of a controlled substance, cocaine, to her baby through her umbilical cord after birth, arguing the criminal statute did not apply to her.

🏛 RULE OF LAW
A pregnant mother who takes a controlled substance and knows the substance will pass to her newborn baby by way of the umbilical cord cannot be criminally prosecuted for "delivery" of a controlled substance to a minor.

FACTS: In 1987, Johnson (P) gave birth to a son with no signs of fetal distress. Johnson (P) admitted that she used cocaine the night before. In 1988, Johnson (P) was pregnant again and suffered an overdose due to crack cocaine. While she was in labor, she admitted to the doctor that she used crack cocaine the morning before. In both instances, the umbilical cord was still attached for approximately one to one and half minutes after birth. The State (D) charged Johnson with "delivery" of cocaine to her two children through the umbilical cord during those sixty to ninety seconds. Johnson (P) was convicted and appealed.

ISSUE: Can a pregnant mother who takes a controlled substance and knows the substance will pass to her newborn baby be criminally prosecuted for "delivery" of a controlled substance to a minor?

HOLDING AND DECISION: (Harding, J.) No. A pregnant mother who takes a controlled substance and knows the substance will pass to her newborn baby cannot be criminally prosecuted for "delivery" of a controlled substance to a minor. There is no evidence that an actual "delivery" of a controlled substance occurred from Johnson's (P) placenta through the umbilical cord to her newborn in the first sixty to ninety seconds of the baby's life. Furthermore, the legislature did not intend the general drug delivery statutes to be used to prosecute pregnant mothers who take illegal drugs. Prosecuting pregnant mothers who take illegal drugs may discourage women from seeking prenatal care for fear of self-incrimination. This would be contrary to the public interest and the express policy of keeping families together. Reversed.

▶ ANALYSIS

In an attempt to address the growing number of newborns born with fetal alcohol syndrome or born with addictions caused by their mother's use of illegal drugs, some states have broadened child protection statutes to include "fetal abuse" that endangers fetal health and development. These statutes have been challenged as an impermissible infringement on privacy rights and as the first step down a slippery slope that would ultimately regulate a wide variety of maternal habits and lifestyles.

Quicknotes

CONTROLLED SUBSTANCE A drug whose medical distribution is regulated by the federal government; certain classifications are unlawful.

Sanders v. State

Convicted murderer (D) v. State (P)

Ga. Sup. Ct., 251 Ga. 70, 303 S.E.2d 13 (1983).

NATURE OF CASE: Appeal from conviction for murder.

FACT SUMMARY: Sanders (D) contended the trial court erred in allowing the State (P) to present evidence in its case in chief that she suffered from the battering-parent syndrome.

RULE OF LAW
The state may not introduce evidence that the defendant suffers from the battering-parent syndrome, or that she has character or personality traits indicating she has the characteristics of a battering parent, unless she has placed her character in issue or asserted a defense which such evidence would rebut.

FACTS: Sanders (D) was charged with the murder of her infant daughter. In its case in chief, the State (P) presented expert testimony concerning the "battering-parent syndrome." The testimony described the typical profile of a parent who batters her child, including the fact that the parent is the product of a violent environment, that she is under chronic environmental stress, and that she has a history of poor social judgment. She was convicted of murder and appealed, contending this testimony was improper character evidence.

ISSUE: May the prosecution present evidence indicating the defendant suffered from the battering-parent syndrome in its case in chief?

HOLDING AND DECISION: (Bell, J.) No. The State (P) may not introduce evidence that the defendant suffers from the battering-parent syndrome, or that she has character or personality traits indicating she has the characteristics of a battering parent, unless she has placed her character in issue or asserted a defense which such evidence would rebut. Even though the expert never concluded that Sanders's (D) history fit the profile of a battering parent, his testimony clearly implicated her character. The construction of the profile coupled with other testimony that Sanders (D) possessed many of the characteristics described could lead a reasonable juror to infer she fit the profile. As a result, such testimony offered in the case in chief was improper. However, because the remaining evidence of guilt was so overwhelming, the error was not prejudicial. Affirmed.

ANALYSIS

Many jurisdictions allow defendants to offer evidence that they suffer from a particular syndrome in order to mitigate their culpability or to establish a defense. In *Smith v. Smith*, 277 S.E.2d 678 (1981), a defendant was permitted to show she suffered from the battered-woman syndrome to support her claim of self-defense in a murder trial.

People v. Jennings

State (P) v. Convicted child abuser (D)

Colo. Sup. Ct., 641 P.2d 276 (1982) (en banc).

NATURE OF CASE: Appeal from dismissal of child abuse prosecution.

FACT SUMMARY: The trial court held that a Colorado statute, which provided that those who "cruelly punish" were guilty of child abuse, was unconstitutionally vague.

RULE OF LAW
A child abuse law is not unconstitutionally vague merely because it does not specify the exact acts which constitute criminally punishable abuse.

FACTS: Jennings (D) was convicted of child abuse under a Colorado statute which defined felony child abuse as knowingly, intentionally, or negligently, permitting a child to be "cruelly punished." He moved to dismiss, contending the language "cruelly punished" was unclear and susceptible to subjective interpretation because what one juror might define as justifiable parental action might be defined as "cruel" by another. The trial court found the statute unconstitutionally vague and granted the motion to dismiss. The People (P) appealed.

ISSUE: Is a child abuse statute unconstitutionally vague if it fails to specify the particular acts which constitute punishable abuse?

HOLDING AND DECISION: (Dubofsky, J.) No. A child abuse statute is not unconstitutionally vague merely because it does not specify the acts which constitute punishable abuse. Punishment can be adequately distinguished from abuse by evaluating the reasonableness of the act in light of the child's age, condition, acts of misconduct being punished for, and the kind of punishment inflicted. As a result, what is "cruelly punished" can be determined as a matter of fact. Therefore, given these available guidelines, the Colorado (P) statute was not unconstitutionally vague. Reversed and remanded.

ANALYSIS

Every state has enacted a form of reporting statute, which requires certain persons who normally come in contact with children to report evidence of abuse. Generally these include teachers and health care professionals. Generally the reporting is done to child protective services. Requiring people to report potential crimes to law enforcement agencies tends to dissuade reporting.

Quicknotes

CHILD ABUSE Conduct harmful to a child's physical or mental health.

Baltimore City Dept. of Social Services v. Bouknight

City social services (P) v. Accused child abuser (D)

493 U.S. 549 (1990).

NATURE OF CASE: Review of order voiding a contempt citation.

FACT SUMMARY: Bouknight (D) claimed a Fifth Amendment privilege against complying with a juvenile court order to produce an allegedly battered child.

🏛 RULE OF LAW
A custodian of an allegedly battered child may not claim a Fifth Amendment privilege against complying with an order demanding production thereof.

FACTS: Based on substantial evidence that Bouknight (D) was abusing her small child, the Baltimore City Department of Social Services (P) obtained an order giving it jurisdiction over the child. Bouknight (D) was at first allowed to keep custody, but the Dept. (P) later obtained an order that Bouknight (D) surrender the child. Bouknight (D) refused to produce the child and was imprisoned for contempt. The Maryland Court of Appeals vacated the citation, holding that production of the child by court order would constitute a Fifth Amendment violation. The U.S. Supreme Court granted review.

ISSUE: May a custodian of an allegedly battered child claim a Fifth Amendment privilege against complying with an order demanding production thereof?

HOLDING AND DECISION: (O'Connor, J.) No. A custodian of an allegedly battered child may not claim a Fifth Amendment privilege against complying with an order demanding production thereof. The Fifth Amendment only protects against coerced testimonial self-incrimination. While production of an object may be merely testimonial if production is tantamount to authentication, such a situation does not exist here. Further, the Fifth Amendment may not be invoked to resist compliance with a state regulatory framework affecting purposes unrelated to criminal law. Here, the set of laws and regulations at issue deals with the child's welfare, a matter of a civil nature. For these reasons, the Fifth Amendment is inapplicable here. Reversed and remanded.

DISSENT: (Marshall, J.) Production of the child would be testimonial in this instance, as it would constitute an admission of her custody and control over the child. While a regulatory framework is involved here, criminal law elements are also implicated, thus making the Fifth Amendment applicable.

▶ ANALYSIS

The main difference between the approaches taken by the majority and the dissent here appears to be the extent to which criminal law must be applicable for a production of a thing to implicate the Fifth Amendment. The majority would seem to require that criminal law be the main focus of the production. The dissent would seem to require only the possibility of criminal sanctions.

■━■

Quicknotes

CONTEMPT OF COURT Conduct that is intended to obstruct the court's effective administration of justice or to otherwise disrespect its authority.

CUSTODIAN Person having responsibility for a person or his property pursuant to law.

FIFTH AMENDMENT Provides that no person shall be compelled to serve as a witness against himself, or be subject to trial for the same offense twice, or be deprived of life, liberty, or property without due process of law.

■━■

In re Michael C.

Suspected abused child

R.I. Sup. Ct., 557 A.2d 1219 (1989).

NATURE OF CASE: Appeal from a judgment finding sexual abuse and neglect of a child.

FACT SUMMARY: The parents of Michael C. contended the trial court erred in allowing the child to testify on camera concerning alleged sexual molestation and neglect, arguing that such deprived them of their due process rights.

🏛 RULE OF LAW
It is not an abuse of discretion for the trial court to allow minor children to testify on camera concerning acts of the parents to avoid undue pressure on the child.

FACTS: The Department of Children and Their Families brought a proceeding against the parents of Michael C., contending the child had been sexually abused by his father and neglected by both parents. The child, 13 years old at the time of the hearing, expressed to his guardian ad litem extreme reticence in wanting to testify in open court against his parents. Based upon this, the trial court ordered that his testimony would be taken on camera in the presence of a court stenographer. After his testimony was read to the attorneys, written questions were solicited from both sides to be read by the trial judge on camera for purposes of cross-examination. Following this, the trial court found that Michael C. had been sexually abused and neglected. Both parents appealed, contending the on-camera examination violated their due process rights.

ISSUE: Does on-camera examination of a minor child concerning sexual abuse and neglect charges violate the due process rights of the parents?

HOLDING AND DECISION: (Kelleher, J.) No. The taking of testimony on camera from a minor child concerning the sexual abuse and neglect of the parents does not violate the parents' due process rights. The tender age of the child indicates that he would be reluctant to testify truthfully against the parents in open court. Further, testimony from the father on cross-examination indicated a violent temper, and thus led the trial court to exercise its discretion in allowing the on-camera testimony. The determination as to whether or not on-camera examination is appropriate must be left to the trial judge, who is in the unique position to evaluate the various demeanors of the potential witnesses. Affirmed.

▶ *ANALYSIS*

The court pointed out that there is no confrontation right resting on the parties to a civil action. Child neglect pro-

ceedings are not criminal in nature. Therefore, no due process right to confront witnesses against the parents is present. The court is charged with obtaining the truth, and if it believes that such will be facilitated by the taking of on-camera testimony, it is within the court's discretion to do so.

■≡■

Quicknotes

ABUSE OF DISCRETION A determination by an appellate court that a lower court's decision was based on an error of law.

CHILD ABUSE Conduct harmful to a child's physical or mental health.

CHILD NEGLECT Conduct on the part of a parent or guardian that demonstrates unfitness on the part of that individual to provide the proper care and control over the child, resulting in harm or potential harm to the child's physical or mental health.

DUE PROCESS RIGHTS The constitutional mandate requiring the courts to protect and enforce individuals' rights and liberties consistent with prevailing principles of fairness and justice, and prohibiting the federal and state governments from such activities that deprive its citizens of a life, liberty or property interest.

GUARDIAN AD LITEM Person designated by the court to represent an infant or ward in a particular legal proceeding.

■≡■

DeShaney v. Winnebago County DSS

Abuse victim (P) v. County social services agency (D)

489 U.S. 189 (1989).

NATURE OF CASE: Appeal from dismissal of action for denial of due process.

FACT SUMMARY: DeShaney (P) contended that Winnebago (D) denied him due process by failing to take steps to protect him from his abusive father once such abuse was made known to the County (D).

RULE OF LAW
A state or local government is not constitutionally required to protect its citizens from private violence not attributable to its own employees.

FACTS: DeShaney (P) brought suit against Winnebago (D), the county in which he lived. He had been a victim of frequent and severe abuse at the hands of his father, and County (D) employees were aware of such. His suit contended that the County's (D) failure to protect him from abuse by his father constituted a deprivation of life and liberty without due process. He argued that the County (D) owed him a duty of protection due to a special relationship of trust created by the County's (D) knowledge of the abuse. The County (D) successfully moved for summary judgment, and the court of appeals affirmed. The U.S. Supreme Court granted review.

ISSUE: Is a state or local government constitutionally required to protect its citizens from private violence not attributable to its own employees?

HOLDING AND DECISION: (Rehnquist, C.J.) No. A state or local government is not constitutionally required to protect its citizens from private violence not attributable to its own employees. The Due Process Clause of the Fourteenth Amendment simply does not require such protection. While liberty is protected against governmental encroachment, no duty to affirmatively provide protection exists. Private violence does not give rise to a constitutional remedy unless performed under color of state law. There being no governmental act in this case, no relief is available. Affirmed.

DISSENT: (Brennan, J.) The Constitution requires a more active governmental role than that taken by officials in this case. The majority holds that the Due Process Clause does not require affirmative protection, but that was not the case appealed, briefed, argued, or presented to this court. The focus should have been on what action was taken to protect DeShaney (P) and whether that action was constitutionally sufficient. Wisconsin has a clear view to protecting children and established the defendant agency. The facts support that the agency's (D) inaction failed DeShaney (P). DeShaney (P) should have the opportunity to demonstrate that the department's (D) inaction was deliberately irresponsible.

DISSENT: (Blackmun, J.) The facts of this case reveal active state intervention in the life of DeShaney (P), which triggered a duty to aid the boy once the State learned of the danger he was in. The question presented by this case is an open one, and the Fourteenth Amendment can be read broadly or narrowly, as it was designed in part to undo formalistic legal reasoning, in order to resolve the issue. Moreover, it should be read to comport with justice and compassion.

ANALYSIS

The proper remedy, according to the Court, would have been a civil action under state tort law. No special relationship existed, and no general duty to act existed. The flood of litigation that would follow a different result would put unbearable strain on state and local governments.

Quicknotes

DUE PROCESS CLAUSE Clauses found in the Fifth and Fourteenth Amendments to the United States Constitution providing that no person shall be deprived of "life, liberty, or property, without due process of law."

Hermanson v. State

Convicted child abusers (D) v. State (P)

Fla. Sup. Ct., 604 So. 2d 775 (1992).

NATURE OF CASE: Appeal from conviction for child abuse resulting in third-degree murder.

FACT SUMMARY: The Hermansons (D) were convicted of child abuse resulting in third-degree murder upon the death from juvenile diabetes of their daughter, to whom they denied medical therapy in accordance with the teachings of their religion.

🏛 RULE OF LAW
The legislature must clearly indicate the point at which parents' reliance on their religious beliefs in the treatment of their children becomes criminal conduct.

FACTS: The Hermansons' (D) daughter died as a result of juvenile diabetes, which they were treating according the dictates of Christian Science Church. Christian Scientists believe in healing by spiritual means rather than through the use of traditional medical practice. In accord with their beliefs, the Hermansons (D) sought the assistance of a Christian Science practitioner and a Christian Science nurse. They did not provide their daughter medical treatment. Their daughter died, and the Hermansons (D) were tried for and convicted of child abuse resulting in third-degree murder under Florida Statute § 827.04(1). They received four-year suspended prison sentences and were ordered to serve fifteen years' probation. The district court affirmed. The Hermansons (D) appealed, raising four issues, but the Florida Supreme Court only addressed the issue of due process, which it considered dispositive.

ISSUE: Must the legislature clearly indicate the point at which parents' reliance on their religious beliefs in the treatment of their children becomes criminal conduct?

HOLDING AND DECISION: (Overton, J.) Yes. The legislature must clearly indicate the point at which parents' reliance on their religious beliefs in the treatment of their children becomes criminal conduct. If the legislature decides to provide for religious accommodation while protecting the children of the state, it must clearly indicate when parents' conduct becomes criminal. One of the purposes of due process is "to insure that no individual is convicted unless 'a fair warning [has first been] given to the world in language that the common world will understand, of what the law intends to do if a certain line is passed.'" *Mourning v. Family Publications Serv., Inc.,* 411 U.S. 356 (1973). In the statutes in question, the point at which parents' actions become criminal is not clear. Therefore, no standard existed against which to determine when (and

if) the Hermansons' (D) conduct became criminal. Reversed and remanded.

▶ ANALYSIS

In *State v. McKown,* 461 N.W.2d 720 (Minn. Ct. App. 1990), *aff'd,* 475 N.W.2d 63 (Minn. 1991), *cert. denied,* 112 S. Ct. 882, a child's parents utilized a Christian Science practitioner and a Christian Science nurse and did not seek conventional medical treatment. The parents were indicted for second-degree manslaughter when their child died of untreated diabetes. The issue in that case was whether the child abuse statute, which contained an exception for spiritual treatment similar to the Florida statute in the instant case, was to be construed in conjunction with a manslaughter statue that was based on culpable negligence resulting in death. In finding a violation of due process, the Minnesota Court concluded that there was a "lack of clarity in the relationship between the two statutes." Here, the statues in question did not establish a line of demarcation at which a person of common intelligence would know their conduct became criminal, thus denying the parents due process.

∎≡∎

Quicknotes

CHILD ABUSE Conduct harmful to a child's physical or mental health.

DUE PROCESS The constitutional mandate requiring the courts to protect and enforce individuals' rights and liberties consistent with prevailing principles of fairness and justice and prohibiting the federal and state governments from such activities that deprive its citizens of life, liberty, or property interest.

MURDER Unlawful killing of another person, either with deliberation and premeditation or by conduct demonstrating a reckless disregard for human life.

∎≡∎

Newmark v. Williams

Christian Scientist parents (D) v. Director of protective services (P)

Del. Sup. Ct., 588 A.2d 1108 (1991).

NATURE OF CASE: Appeal from Family Court order granting temporary custody of a minor child to the Division of Child Protective Services.

FACT SUMMARY: The Delaware Division of Child Protective Services (DCPS) (P) sought temporary custody of the Newmarks' (D) son in order to provide the child with the cancer treatment that the Newmarks (D) were unwilling to provide due to their religious beliefs.

🏛 RULE OF LAW

Refusal by parents of a minor child to provide radical medical treatment that has only a limited chance of success does not constitute child neglect.

FACTS: Three-year-old Colin Newmark was diagnosed with an extremely aggressive form of a pediatric cancer. Although Morris and Kara Newmark (D) were Christian Scientists, they consented to a great deal of medical treatment for Colin, including surgery, to determine the causes of their son's lingering illness. Colin's doctors prescribed radical and extensive chemotherapy treatment which offered only a 40 percent chance of survival. The treatment was so intensive that it, in itself, could cause the child's death. Despite the fact that, without treatment, Colin was expected to live for only six to eight months, the Newmarks (D) chose instead to provide Colin with spiritual aid and prayer according to their religious belief. The DCPS (P) petitioned the court for custody of Colin in order to provide him with the prescribed medical treatment. The lower court granted DCPS (P) custody of Colin. The Newmarks (D) appealed.

ISSUE: Does refusal by parents of a minor child to provide radical medical treatment that has only a limited chance of success constitute child neglect?

HOLDING AND DECISION: (Moore, J.) No. Refusal by parents of a minor child to provide medical treatment that has only a limited chance of success does not constitute child neglect. The rights of parental autonomy must be weighed against the best interests of the child. In analyzing the best interests of the child, one must weigh the seriousness of the illness versus the invasiveness of the treatment and its potential for success. Although Colin's illness was life threatening, the treatment denied by the Newmarks (D) was in itself lethal and provided less than a 40 percent chance of survival. Because the treatment was not clearly in the best interests of the child, DCPS's (P) interest in protecting a minor does not outweigh the Newmarks' (D) parental rights. Reversed.

▶ ANALYSIS

More problematic are the cases where parents choose more unconventional medical treatment rather than the traditional treatment. *In the Matter of Hofbauer*, 393 N.E.2d 1009 (1979), the court found that parents who are aware of the alternatives available and the consequences of the recommended treatment should be allowed to follow the advice of their chosen physician. In that case the parents of the child involved elected to follow one physician's advice to provide nutritional therapy and laetrile as treatment for Hodgkin's disease rather than traditional radiation therapy advised by the attending physician.

Quicknotes

BEST INTERESTS OF CHILD Standard used by courts when rendering decisions which involve a child or children.

CHILD NEGLECT Conduct on the part of a parent or guardian that demonstrates unfitness on the part of that individual to provide the proper care and control over the child, resulting in harm or potential harm to the child's physical or mental health.

3/20/15

Parham v. J.R.

Administrator (D) v. Institutionalized child (P)

442 U.S. 584 (1979).

NATURE OF CASE: Class action to enjoin and declare unconditional voluntary commitment procedures for minors.

FACT SUMMARY: The lower court had held, inter alia, that the voluntary commitment procedures for children under 18, like J.R. (P), were unconstitutional for failing to provide for an adversary proceeding.

🏛 RULE OF LAW
An adversary proceeding prior to or after commitment is not required to render constitutional the process by which parents or guardians of minor children can seek to voluntarily admit them for institutional mental health care.

FACTS: J.R. (P) and other minors who had been committed to mental institutions by their parents or guardians, including the State of Georgia, brought a class action alleging that the process involved in such commitment did not meet due process requirements and asked for an injunction against future enforcement of the statutes involved. The district held Georgia's statutory scheme unconstitutional. It ordered Georgia to expend whatever amount was "reasonably necessary" to provide nonhospital facilities for the treatment of those members of the class who could be treated in a less drastic, nonhospital environment. It also held that a post-commitment adversarial proceeding was required. On appeal, Parham (D) and the others involved in administering the scheme argued that parents or guardians could only apply for admission to the hospitals, and that the superintendent of the hospital was obliged to find evidence of mental illness and suitability for treatment in the hospital before the child would be admitted "for such period and under such conditions as may be authorized by law." Furthermore, they noted, by statute each superintendent has an affirmative duty to release any "child who has recovered from his mental illness or who has sufficiently improved that the superintendent determines that hospitalization of the patient is no longer desirable." On top of this, review of the case by a medical team is conducted once a week in many cases and at least once every two months in all cases.

ISSUE: Must there be an adversarial proceeding prior to or after commitment in order for the process by which parents or guardians can voluntarily commit their children to mental hospitals to be deemed constitutional?

HOLDING AND DECISION: (Burger, C.J.) No. No adversary proceeding prior to or after commitment is required in order to render constitutional the process by

which parents or guardians of minors can seek to voluntarily admit them for institutional mental health care. A child has a liberty interest in not being confined unnecessarily for medical treatment, but the parents have an equally recognized interest in taking care of their child. This includes a "high duty" to recognize symptoms of illness and to seek and follow medical advice. The courts will simply not deny the historical supposition that natural bonds of affection generally lead parents to act in the best interests of their children and that they should be presumed to be so acting until it is otherwise shown in a particular case. Often, parents must act contrary to the wishes or desires of their children to do what they deem to be in the child's eventual best interests. Of course, this would not mean that parents have an absolute right to institutionalize their children, but in this case there is the interposing of a physician's independent examination and medical judgment. Turning to the state's interest, it includes seeing to it that no procedural obstacles be imposed which would discourage the mentally ill or their families from seeking needed help. The family discord and embarrassment at having their motives questioned in an adversary proceeding would have just such an undesirable effect. Furthermore, it would take up much more of the valuable time of the hospital personnel, whose main business should be providing treatment and not testifying in an adversary proceeding for each of the thousands of cases which would arise. Of course, the risk of error inherent in the parental decision to have a child institutionalized is sufficiently great to require that some kind of inquiry be made by a "neutral fact finder" to determine whether the statutory requirements for admission are satisfied. He must have the authority to refuse to admit any child who does not satisfy the medical standards for admission. Finally, it is necessary that the child's continuing need for commitment be reviewed periodically by a similarly independent procedure. This fact finder need not be law-trained, but could be a staff physician. Nor need he conduct a formal or quasi-formal hearing to satisfy due process. The record, in this case, supports the conclusion that the admissions staffs of the hospitals have acted in a neutral and detached fashion in making medical judgments in the best interests of the children. This court is satisfied by the record that Georgia's general administrative and statutory scheme for the voluntary commitment of children is not per se unconstitutional under the aforementioned standards. However, the record is insufficient to show whether every child in the class received an adequate, independent diagnosis of his emotional condition and need for commitment under those standards. On remand, the district court is free

Continued on next page.

to and should consider any individual claims in that regard. It also is free to decide whether or not the periodic reviews are sufficient to justify continuing a voluntary commitment. Furthermore, while the initial admission procedures need not vary, children admitted by the state as their guardian may be more susceptible to simply being lost in the administrative shuffle thereafter. Thus, the district court might well consider if wards of the state should be treated, with respect to continuing therapy, differently from children with natural parents. Reversed and remanded.

CONCURRENCE AND DISSENT: (Brennan, J.) The concerns justifying postponement of hearings until after commitment in the case of children admitted by their natural parents do not exist when children are admitted as wards of the state. In those cases, precommitment hearings should be required in the absence of exigent circumstances. Furthermore, parentally admitted children are entitled to postcommitment hearings, and the postadmission procedures Georgia uses do not quality as such.

▌ ANALYSIS

Much of the argument advanced in this case revolved around the allegation that parents were simply "warehousing" unwanted children or children whose actions they found unacceptable. In response, the tone of the decision reflects continued judicial adherence to the traditional rebuttable presumption that parents act in the best interests of their children. It remains one of the most strongly guarded notions in the family law area, even though the courts have recognized that the state can exercise some control over parents when a child's physical or mental health is jeopardized.

Quicknotes

BEST INTERESTS OF CHILD   Standard used by courts when rendering decisions which involve a child or children.

CLASS ACTION   A suit commenced by a representative on behalf of an ascertainable group that is too large to appear in court, who shares a commonality of interests and who will benefit from a successful result.

DUE PROCESS   The constitutional mandate requiring the courts to protect and enforce individuals' rights and liberties consistent with prevailing principles of fairness and justice and prohibiting the federal and state governments from such activities that deprive its citizens of life, liberty, or property interest.

VOLUNTARY COMMITMENT   A voluntary proceeding to commit a person either to a prison or mental health facilities.

3/20/15 (handwritten)

Stump v. Sparkman

Judge (D) v. Mother (P)

435 U.S. 349 (1978).

NATURE OF CASE: Appeal from dismissal of action for violations of constitutional rights.

FACT SUMMARY: Sparkman (P) sued Stump (D), contending his judicial approval of a petition filed by Sparkman's (P) mother to have an involuntary tubal ligation performed on Sparkman (P) constituted state action upon which a suit for deprivation of constitutional rights could be based.

🏛 RULE OF LAW
A judicial officer is immune from suit for authorizing involuntary sterilization procedures so long as the officer's court had subject matter jurisdiction.

FACTS: McFarlin, Sparkman's (P) mother, petitioned an Indiana state court for approval of her intention to have Sparkman (P) sterilized due to her mental retardation. Stump (D), the circuit court judge, approved the plan. Sparkman (P), then 15, was told she was having an appendectomy and entered the hospital where she underwent tubal ligation. Subsequently she married, and her inability to become pregnant led to her discovery of the involuntary sterilization. She sued her mother and others, including Judge Stump (D), for violation of her constitutional rights. The trial court held that a cause of action existed only if state action caused the sterilization and that only Stump's (D) actions could be held to be state action. It dismissed the complaint, holding Stump (D) immune from suit. Sparkman (P) appealed, contending Stump (D) had no immunity due to his court's lack of subject matter jurisdiction over the petition. The court of appeals held Stump's (D) court had no jurisdiction, under its general jurisdiction and under Indiana statutes, allowing sterilization of institutionalized patients under some circumstances. Stump (D) appealed.

ISSUE: Can a judicial officer be held liable for allowing involuntary sterilizations of handicapped people?

HOLDING AND DECISION: (White, J.) No. A judicial officer cannot be sued for allowing involuntary sterilizations so long as his court had subject matter jurisdiction. In this case, Stump's (D) court had general jurisdiction over all cases in law and equity. The absence of specific authority for him to act in an area does not infer a lack of jurisdiction. He may have erred as a matter of law in recognizing a nonexistent parental right, but he had jurisdiction to entertain the petition. As a result, he was immune from prosecution. Reversed and remanded.

▶ ANALYSIS

This case recognizes judicial immunity from suits to redress wrongs imposed on minors. Sparkman's (P) cause of action against the private defendants stated they conspired with Stump (D) to deny her her constitutional rights. Lacking state action, this was dismissed. However, she also filed pendant state claims against these defendants for assault and battery and loss of potential parenthood. These claims would seem meritorious, yet the case was resolved on the basis of the constitutional claims.

■—■

Quicknotes

GENERAL JURISDICTION Refers to the authority of a court to hear and determine all cases of a particular type.

OFFICIAL IMMUNITY Immunity of an official from civil liability for injuries sustained by an individual as a result of actions performed in the discharge of his official duties.

■—■

3/20/15

In re Green

[Parties not identified.]

Pa. Sup. Ct., 448 Pa. 338, 292 A.2d 387 (1972).

NATURE OF CASE: Appeal from reversal of petition's dismissal in guardianship action.

FACT SUMMARY: If nothing were done in regard to Ricky Green's spinal condition, he could become bedridden. Green, his mother, consented to surgery on the condition that he not have a blood transfusion since transfusions conflicted with her religious beliefs.

RULE OF LAW
The state does not have an interest of sufficient magnitude to outweigh a parent's religious beliefs to interfere with a parent's control over his or her child in order to enhance the child's physical well-being when the child's life is in no immediate danger.

FACTS: Ricky Green, a 15-year-old suffering from paralytic scoliosis, had a severe curvature of the spine. He was unable to stand but could sit. If nothing were done, he was in danger of becoming bedridden. A spinal fusion was recommended, to which his mother consented on the condition that he not be given a blood transfusion. A transfusion was necessary for the surgery but was forbidden by the Greens' religious beliefs. There was no evidence that Ricky Green's life was in danger or that the operation had to be performed immediately. A neglect petition was filed to have a guardian appointed for Ricky. The guardian could then consent to the surgery on Ricky's behalf. The court dismissed the petition and that decision was appealed. The Superior Court reversed the dismissal and that decision was appealed.

ISSUE: Can the state interfere with a parent's control over his or her child in order to enhance the child's physical well-being when the child's life is in no immediate danger and when the state's intrusion conflicts with the parents' religious beliefs?

HOLDING AND DECISION: (Jones, C.J.) No. As between a parent and the state, the state does not have an interest of sufficient magnitude to outweigh a parent's religious beliefs when the child's life is not immediately imperiled by his or her physical condition. However, here there was no evidence as to the child's wishes. The wishes of the 15-year-old boy should be ascertained. Hence, this court reserves any decision regarding a possible parent-child conflict and remands the matter for an evidentiary hearing to determine Ricky Green's wishes. Reversed and remanded.

DISSENT: (Eagan, J.) If there is a substantial threat to health, then the courts can, and should, intervene to protect the child. The court's remand to determine Ricky

Green's wishes is an inadequate solution. He has been crippled most of his life and consequently has been under the direct control of his parents. To now presume he could make an independent decision is unreasonable. Moreover, the court's solution will force him to choose between his parents' wishes and his chance for a normal life.

▶ ANALYSIS

Compare *In re Sampson*, 317 N.Y.S.2d 641, wherein a 15-year-old suffered from a severe facial deformity, which prevented him from attending school. A lengthy and dangerous operation might improve his appearance but would not cure him of his disease. His mother would not consent to transfusions. The court held that it could not shift the responsibility onto the child nor permit his mother's religious beliefs to stand in the way of his obtaining, through corrective surgery, whatever chance he might have for a normal, happy existence.

Quicknotes

CHILD NEGLECT Conduct on the part of a parent or guardian that demonstrates unfitness on the part of that individual to provide the proper care and control over the child, resulting in harm or potential harm to the child's physical or mental health.

GUARDIANSHIP A legal relationship whereby one party is responsible for the care and control over another and his property due to some legal incapacity on the part of the ward.

3/20/15

Hart v. Brown

Parents (P) v. Physician (D)

Conn. Super. Ct., Fairfield Cty, 29 Conn. Sup. 368, 289 A.2d 386 (1972).

NATURE OF CASE: Action for declaratory judgment.

FACT SUMMARY: Brown (D), a physician, refused to perform a kidney transplant on K. Hart as donee and M. Hart as donor unless the court declared that the Hart parents (P) had the right to give their consent to the operation on the children who were seven-year-old identical twins.

🏛 RULE OF LAW
The power of a court of equity to act for an incompetent is recognized as the doctrine of substituted judgment and is broad enough to cover all matters concerning the well-being of legally incapacitated persons, including infants.

FACTS: A kidney transplant was necessary to save the life of K. Hart. A transplant from one of her parents (P) might be cruel and inhuman because of the possible side effects of immunosuppressive drugs. These drugs would not be necessary if the transplant were from K. Hart's identical twin, M. Hart. The twins were seven years old. The risks to either of them from a transplant from M. Hart were negligible, and the prognosis for good health and long lives for both twins was excellent. M. Hart strongly identified with her sister and would suffer a great loss if she were to die. She desired to donate her kidney to her. Brown (D), a physician, refused to perform the operation on K. Hart as donee and M. Hart as donor unless the court declared that the Hart parents (P) had the right to give their consent to the operation. The Harts' (P) decision to consent to the operation was approved by physicians, by guardians ad litem of both twins, and by clergymen.

ISSUE: Is the power of a court of equity to act for an incompetent, recognized as the doctrine of substituted judgment, broad enough to cover all matters concerning the well-being of legally incapacitated persons, including infants?

HOLDING AND DECISION: (Testo, J.) Yes. The power of a court of equity to act for an incompetent is recognized as the doctrine of substituted judgment and is broad enough to cover all matters concerning the well-being of legally incapacitated persons, including infants. There is authority that non-therapeutic operations can be legally permitted on a minor so long as the parents or other guardians consent to the procedure. Here the operation is necessary to K. Hart's life, and the risks involved to her and M. Hart are negligible. The prognosis for good health and long life for both children is excellent. To subject K. Hart to

a transplant from her parents (P) may be cruel and inhuman due to the side effects. There is no opposition, and it will be most beneficial to K. Hart and of some benefit to M. Hart. Under these circumstances the natural parents of a minor should have the right to give their consent to a kidney transplant. Judgment for the parents.

▶ ANALYSIS

Some courts have developed a "mature minor rule," which allows hospitals or physicians to make a subjective appraisal of a minor's capacity to consent in at least some cases. Such a rule commonly has been applied in situations involving less than major risk treatment for the personal benefit of a minor near majority or clearly of sufficient capacity to understand the nature of and importance of the procedure.

∎═∎

Quicknotes

COURT OF EQUITY A court that determines matters before it consistent with principles of fairness and not in strict compliance with rules of law.

∎═∎

In re Doe

Terminally ill child

Ga. Sup. Ct., 262 Ga. 389, 418 S.E.2d 3 (1992).

NATURE OF CASE: Appeal from a declaratory judgment.

FACT SUMMARY: Because Jane Doe's parents disagreed about the appropriate course of medical treatment for her degenerative neurological disease, the hospital sought a legal judgment regarding its duty of care.

🏛 RULE OF LAW
Those legally responsible for an incompetent patient may consent to treatment without seeking prior judicial approval, but where two parents have legal custody of a child, each parent must share equal decision-making responsibility for that child.

FACTS: Jane Doe suffered from a degenerative neurological disease and was placed on feeding and respiratory support systems. Jane's mother agreed to a Do Not Resuscitate (DNR) order, but her father did not. Neither parent favored a de-escalation of life support. The hospital brought a declaratory judgment action to determine its legal obligation to Jane Doe. The State contended that the hospital had no standing and that Jane's parents could not legally decide to deescalate her treatment. The trial judge enjoined the hospital from de-escalating treatment or from enforcing a DNR order unless both parents agreed. The State appealed.

ISSUE: May those legally responsible for an incompetent patient refuse treatment or consent to treatment without seeking prior judicial approval?

HOLDING AND DECISION: (Clarke, J.) Yes. Those legally responsible for an incompetent patient may refuse or consent to treatment without seeking prior judicial approval, but where two parents have legal custody of a child, each parent must share equal decision-making responsibility for that child. Since medical technology and societal views about death and dying are constantly evolving, there cannot be a single, static formula for deciding when de-escalation is appropriate. Instead, that decision is best left to the patient's family and the patient's doctors. In this case, the life support system was prolonging Jane's death, not her life. Therefore, her parents could have decided to de-escalate treatment. Since they chose not to, the trial court correctly enjoined the hospital from doing so. As to the DNR order, both parents must agree on its appropriateness, if they are present and actively participating in the decision process. Therefore, since Jane's father revoked his consent, the court also determined, correctly, that the hospital could not enter a DNR order. Affirmed.

CONCURRENCE: (Hunt, J.) This opinion should not be read to confer standing to a hospital under circumstances other than those presented here.

▶ ANALYSIS

The Supreme Court has stated that "natural bonds of affection lead parents to act in the best interests of their children." *Parham v. J.R.*, 442 U.S. 584 (1979). Therefore, the law presumes that the parents are the appropriate parties to make their children's medical decisions. However, this right to make medical decisions is not absolute and may be overridden by a conflicting state interest.

■—■

Quicknotes

CUSTODY The granting of care and control of a child or children to a parent pursuant to an action for dissolution or separation.

DUTY OF CARE A principle of negligence requiring an individual to act in such a manner as to avoid injury to a person to whom he or she owes a duty.

■—■

Montalvo v. Borkovec

Parent (P) v. Physician (D)

Wis. Ct. App., 256 Wis. 2d 472, 647 N.W.2d 413, *appeal denied*, 257 Wis. 2d 118, 653

N.W.2d 890, *cert. denied*, 124 S. Ct. 1485 (2003).

NATURE OF CASE: Appeal from complaint dismissal in medical malpractice action.

FACT SUMMARY: Montalvo (P) gave birth by cesarean section to a premature son. She sued the physicians and hospital involved alleging that the defendants violated the informed consent statute. Montalvo (P) sought recovery because the risks of a cesarean section and "extraordinary care measures" were not fully explained to her.

🏛 **RULE OF LAW**
Informed consent disclosure is not triggered in an emergency situation where life-sustaining treatments are necessary for a child.

FACTS: Nancy Montalvo (P) began labor prematurely at St. Mary's Hospital. Physicians attempted to delay labor because the baby was just 23-weeks old and weighed 679 grams. Montalvo (P) executed an informed consent agreement and Dr. Terre Borkovec [*sic*] (D) performed a cesarean section. Borkovec (D) immediately handed the baby, Emanuel, to Dr. Arnold (D), a neonatologist, who successfully resuscitated Emanuel. Montalvo (P) filed suit against the physicians and the hospital arguing that they violated the informed consent statute when performing the c-section and performing life-saving resuscitation on Emanuel. Montalvo (P) claimed she was not fully informed of the risks of both procedures. Montalvo (P) voluntarily dismissed Borkovec (D) from the petition. The remaining defendants moved to dismiss the petition for failure to state a claim. The trial court determined that Montalvo (P) was not arguing Emanuel was disabled because of the actions taken, but was claiming that the "extraordinary care measures" should have been her decision. The trial court held that Montalvo (P) could not sustain a claim against Arnold (D) for violating the informed consent statute regarding the c-section because he was not involved with that surgery. The trial court also found that the life-saving resuscitation is not a decision left solely to the parents because the state has an interest in saving lives and the physicians have a duty to preserve life. The trial court dismissed the petition and Montalvo (P) appealed.

ISSUE: Is informed consent disclosure triggered in an emergency situation where life-sustaining treatments are necessary for a child?

HOLDING AND DECISION: (Wedemeyer, J.) No. Informed consent disclosure is not triggered in an emergency situation where life-sustaining treatments are necessary for a child. The trial court properly dismissed

the claim involving the cesarean section because the informed consent statute does not require compliance by non-treating physicians. Arnold (D) was a bystander during the surgery and cannot be held liable here. The remaining claim involves informed consent for life-saving measures. The informed consent statute intends to provide persons with legitimate alternatives so that the person may make a reasoned, informed, intelligent decision. Six exceptions exist to the disclosure statute and one exception is "in emergencies where failure to provide treatment would be more harmful to the patient than treatment." The disclosure requirement is a case-by-case basis and the physician must properly provide viable alternatives. Montalvo (P) is essentially arguing here that one viable alternative was to omit life-saving measures for Emanuel because of the risk of him developing a disability due to his prematurity. The court cannot make judgments on the quality of a life as weighed against life at all. Withholding life-sustaining treatment was simply not a viable option triggering informed consent disclosure. Disclosure was also not triggered because of the United States Child Abuse Protection and Treatment Act (CAPTA) applicable in Wisconsin. CAPTA prohibits withholding life-sustaining treatment when such treatment is appropriate. Montalvo (P) does not make the ridiculous argument that life-sustaining treatment should have paused while a physician explained all possible alternatives, viable or not, during the emergency situation. Informed consent was simply not required here. The trial court's decision was primarily based on public policy, which supports the physicians in this case. The physicians could face liability for allowing an infant to die and Montalvo (P) also seeks for them to be liable for acting to allow an infant to live. Physicians do not have to practice in "damned if you do, damned if you don't" circumstances. Affirmed.

▶ **ANALYSIS**

Courts often speak for children who cannot speak for themselves. Here, Emanuel's parents were essentially arguing that Emanuel should have died rather than be saved by the physicians. States remove such a decision from the parents' sole responsibility because the state has an interest in infant survival. States also must respect parents' and children's religious beliefs, however. Some states have amended their child abuse statutes to permit a parent or an older child to elect to forgo necessary treatment due to religious or spiritual beliefs. As the child ages, the state's

Continued on next page.

involvement is less necessary and states respect the informed choices of its citizens.

■■■■

Quicknotes

INFORMED CONSENT An individual's consent to a particular occurrence following full disclosure of the consequences of that consent.

PUBLIC POLICY Policy administered by the state with
respect to the health, safety and morals of its people
in accordance with common notions of fairness and
decency.

■■■■

Newman v. Cole

Personal representative (P) v. Decedent's parents (D)

Ala. Sup. Ct., 872 So. 2d 138 (2003).

NATURE OF CASE: Appeal from dismissal of complaint in wrongful-death action.

FACT SUMMARY: The Coles (D) beat their sixteen-year-old son as punishment over household duties and the son died. Newman (P), the personal representative, sued in a wrongful-death action. The Coles (D) claimed the protection of the parental immunity doctrine.

🏛 RULE OF LAW
A parent's willful and intentional conduct, shown by clear and convincing evidence, which causes the death of his child, is an exception to the parental immunity doctrine.

FACTS: Clinton Patterson Cole, 16, got into an altercation over chores with his father, John Cole (D). John (D) allegedly punched Clinton several times in the chest and then held him on the ground in a chokehold. Clinton's stepmother, Tara Cole (D), sprayed Clinton in the face with a garden hose while John (D) held Clinton down. A police officer arrived and Clinton was taken to the hospital where he died the next day. Anna Belle Newman (P) is Clinton's estate's personal representative. She sued the Coles (D) claiming wrongful death due to their negligent, willful, and intentional behavior. The Coles (D) moved to dismiss based on parental immunity and the trial court dismissed the petition. Newman (P) appeals, contending the doctrine of parental immunity should be amended or abolished.

ISSUE: Is a parent's willful and intentional conduct, shown by clear and convincing evidence, which causes the death of his child an exception to the parental immunity doctrine?

HOLDING AND DECISION: (Per curiam) Yes. A parent's willful and intentional conduct, shown by clear and convincing evidence, which causes the death of his child, is an exception to the parental immunity doctrine. Alabama is the last state to modify or abolish the parental immunity doctrine, but the Coles (D) argue that the legislature is the appropriate body to change the law. The court today can decline to interfere, abolish the doctrine, or craft an exception. In *Hurst v. Capitell*, 539 So. 2d 264 (1989), this court crafted an exception in sexual abuse cases on the grounds that the doctrine was judicially created and may be judicially modified. The Legislature made no further modifications since *Hurst*. Courts, however, are historically reluctant to interfere with the parent-child relationship and the doctrine remains useful. Juries may show their distaste for a particular child-rearing technique without

the doctrine's applicability. The court today, therefore, leaves the doctrine unchanged regarding a parent's unintentional conduct. A parent's responsibilities to his child and the child's dependence on the parent are terminated on that child's death. The child's wrongful death needs redress. The standard of proof to demonstrate a parent's intentional conduct is clear-and-convincing evidence. Affirmed in part; reversed in part; and remanded.

▶ ANALYSIS

The parental immunity doctrine is actually not English common law, but was judicially created in the late 1800s by the Mississippi Supreme Court. The primary purpose was to preserve parental authority and keep the family unit intact without facing judgment from outsiders or rebellion from the children. Some states never adopted the parental immunity doctrine at all, most states have abrogated it entirely, and the rest have modified it to address intentional conduct, such as sexual abuse, physical injury, or death.

■=■

Quicknotes

CLEAR AND CONVINCING EVIDENCE An evidentiary standard requiring a demonstration that the fact sought to be proven is reasonably certain.

PARENTAL IMMUNITY The immunity of a parent from liability in actions brought by his or her child claiming negligence.

WILLFUL AND WANTON MISCONDUCT Unlawful intentional or reckless conduct without regard to the consequences.

WRONGFUL DEATH An action brought by the beneficiaries of a deceased person, claiming that the deceased's death was the result of wrongful conduct by the defendant.

■=■

Vying for Custody

Quick Reference Rules of Law

Johnson v. Johnson

Father (P) v. Mother (D)

143-146

Alaska Sup. Ct., 564 P.2d 71, *cert. denied*, 34 U.S. 1048, 54 L.Ed.2d 800 (1977).

NATURE OF CASE: Appeal from a child custody decree.

FACT SUMMARY: Rudy Johnson (Rudy) (P) challenged a trial court award of custody to his wife, Linda (D), which was based on the tender years presumption that the mother should be given a preference in custody litigation involving very young children.

⬛ RULE OF LAW

Child custody is determined by the best interests of the child and requires an evaluation of several factors including, but not limited to, the age of the child.

FACTS: Rudy (P) filed for divorce from his wife, Linda (D), and sought custody of their two young children. The trial court awarded custody to Linda (D) based solely on the "tender years presumption," which provided that the mother of young children be given a preference in custody litigation. Rudy (P) appealed, contending reliance on this presumption was error, as the standard to be applied in child custody was the best interests of the child.

ISSUE: Is child custody determined by the best interest of the child based on an evaluation of several factors?

HOLDING AND DECISION: (Burke, J.) Yes. Child custody is determined based on an evaluation of several factors indicating the best interest of the child. These factors include, but are not limited to, the age of the child. Other factors which must be considered are: the moral fitness of the parties; the home environment offered by each; the emotional ties to each; and the sex and health of the child. In this case, the trial court erred in basing its award solely on the basis of the children's age. Therefore, the case must be remanded for an evaluation of the other factors.

▶ ANALYSIS

This case shows the Alaska court's abandonment of the tender years doctrine in favor of the best interest test. New York also abandoned the tender years doctrine on the basis it created an invalid sex-based presumption and did not adequately protect the best interests of the child. See *State ex rel. Watts v. Watts*, 350 N.Y.S.2d 285 (1973).

Quicknotes

BEST INTERESTS OF CHILD Standard used by courts when rendering decisions which involve a child or children.

TENDER YEARS DOCTRINE Presumption traced back to 1830 that it would violate the laws of nature to remove an infant from the care of its mother; thus, children under the age of four should reside with their mother.

In re Marriage of Carney

Quadriplegic father (P) v. Noncustodial mother (D)

Cal. Sup. Ct., 157 Cal. Rptr. 383, 24 Cal. 3d 725, 598 P.2d 36 (1979).

NATURE OF CASE: Appeal from interlocutory decree of dissolution transferring custody.

FACT SUMMARY: After his children had lived with William Carney (P) for virtually all their lives, their mother Ellen (D) sought custody of them because William (P) had become a quadriplegic.

🏛 RULE OF LAW
If a person has a physical handicap, the court may not simply rely on that condition as prima facie evidence of the person's unfitness as a parent.

FACTS: William (P) and Ellen (D) Carney, residents of New York, separated after a four-year marriage. Ellen (D) relinquished custody of their two sons to William (P), who later moved with the children to California. Four years later, William (P) was injured in a jeep accident, leaving him a quadriplegic. He subsequently filed for dissolution of his marriage. Ellen (D) moved for an order awarding her immediate custody of both boys because of William's (P) physical condition, although she had never visited them or contributed to their support. The court so ordered, and William (P) appealed.

ISSUE: If a person has a physical handicap, may the court simply rely on that condition as prima facie evidence of the person's unfitness as a parent?

HOLDING AND DECISION: (Mosk, J.) No. If a person has a physical handicap, the court may not simply rely on that condition as prima facie evidence of the person's unfitness as a parent. Rather, the court must view the handicapped person as an individual and the family as a whole. To achieve this, the court should inquire into the person's actual and potential physical capabilities, learn how he and the other members of the family have adapted, and consider the special contributions the person may make to the family despite or even because of the handicap. The court should then carefully determine whether the person's condition will in fact have a substantial and lasting adverse effect on the best interests of the child. The judge in this case made no such determinations. To the contrary, he assumed that because William (P) could not play sports or engage in other activities with his sons, he was unable to be a good parent. But the essence of the parent-child relationship lies in the ethical, emotional, and intellectual guidance the parent gives to the child. Since no evidence was presented to show that William (P) could not provide such guidance, the order to transfer custody is reversed.

▶ ANALYSIS

In order to justify ordering a change of custody, there must generally be a persuasive showing of changed circum-stances affecting the child. Moreover, such change must be substantial: a child will not be removed from the prior custody of one parent and given to the other unless the facts and circumstances are of a kind to render it essential or expedient for the welfare of the child that there be a change. The reasons for the rule are clear: courts are reluctant to order a change of custody and will not do so except for imperative reasons; it is desirable that there ultimately be an end of litigation, and undesirable to change the child's established mode of living.

■=■

Quicknotes

CHILD CUSTODY DECREE A court order awarding responsibility for the care and control over a child or children in a dissolution or separation proceeding.

DISSOLUTION DECREE A decree terminating a marriage.

INTERLOCUTORY ORDER An order entered by the court determining an issue that does not resolve the disposition of the case, but is essential to a proper adjudication of the action.

■=■

Palmore v. Sidoti

Mother (D) v. Father (P)

466 U.S. 429 (1984).

NATURE OF CASE: Appeal from a child custody decree.

FACT SUMMARY: The trial court terminated Palmore's (D) custody of her daughter because after being awarded custody, Palmore (D) had remarried a man of a different race.

🏛 RULE OF LAW
A natural mother cannot be divested of the custody of her child merely because of her remarriage to a person of a different race.

FACTS: Sidoti (P) petitioned for a modification of a prior judgment awarding custody of his daughter to his former wife, Palmore (D), due to Palmore's (D) remarriage to a man outside her race. The trial court found that Palmore (D) and her husband adequately cared for the child; however, the social pressure that would be imposed on the child due to the mixed marriage would be so great that it would be in her best interest to award Sidoti (P) custody. Palmore (D) appealed.

ISSUE: Can a natural mother be divested of custody of her child merely because of her remarriage to a person of a different race?

HOLDING AND DECISION: (Burger, C.J.) No. A natural mother cannot be divested of custody of her child merely because of her remarriage to a person of different race. Private biases and their prejudicial impact cannot be made to determine judicial decisions. Racial discrimination is wholly contrary to public policy, and custody decisions cannot turn on racial considerations. The trial court held that but for the mixed marriage, Palmore (D) was fit for custody. To deny custody would be to deny basic constitutional rights. Reversed.

▌ ANALYSIS

The recurring theme permeating child custody determinations is the best interest of the child. What is in the best interest must be decided after evaluating all relevant factors. As such, cases in which a court has based its determination on essentially a single factor are uniformly reversed. In *Moye v. Moye*, 627 P.2d 799 (1981), the Idaho Supreme Court reversed a lower court judgment denying custody to a mother because she was epileptic. Similarly, in *In re Marriage of G.B.S.*, 641 S.W.2d 776 (1982), a Missouri court held that adultery alone could not preclude custody. The reason these are rejected is that these factors alone do not render a parent unfit for custody.

Quicknotes

CHILD CUSTODY DECREE A court order awarding responsibility for the care and control over a child or children in a dissolution or separation proceeding.

NATURAL MOTHER The biological mother of a child, as opposed to a mother whose rights have either been assigned or are recognized by law.

In re Marriage of Weidner

Wife (P) v. Father (D)

Iowa Sup. Ct., 338 N.W.2d 351 (1983).

NATURE OF CASE: Appeal from denial of joint custody.

FACT SUMMARY: Marvin Weidner (Marvin) (D) contended the trial court erred in granting sole custody of his children to his wife, Betsy (P).

🏛 RULE OF LAW
Joint custody will be awarded only where the parents demonstrate they are able to communicate and reach shared decisions that are in the best interests of the children.

FACTS: Marvin (D) and Betsy (P) Weidner separated briefly due to disagreements between them. They subsequently filed for divorce, and their children lived with Betsy (P) pending trial. During this time, the two parties had several arguments concerning who was going to have the children at what time, and on one occasion the police were called to keep the peace. By the time of trial, neither party trusted the other nor enjoyed sharing each other's company. At trial, Marvin (D) petitioned for joint custody, yet the trial court awarded sole custody to Betsy (P), finding the parties could not cooperate sufficiently to meet the best interests of the children. Marvin (D) appealed.

ISSUE: Will joint custody be awarded only where the parents demonstrate they are able to communicate and reach shared decisions that are in the best interest of the children?

HOLDING AND DECISION: (Wolle, J.) Yes. Joint custody will be awarded only where the parents demonstrate they are able to communicate and reach shared decisions that are in the best interests of the children. Constant conflict and mistrust, as shown in this case, has a traumatic effect on children. It is clear from the record that the conflicts over custody and the mistrust and dislike between Marvin (D) and Betsy (P) would preclude them from making joint decisions, after due deliberation, concerning and in the best interests of the children. Therefore, joint custody was properly denied. Affirmed.

▶ ANALYSIS

Under the Iowa custodial statute, a court will entertain granting joint custody upon the application of either parent. In making its determination, the court is directed to evaluate several factors besides the ability to reach joint decisions. These factors include: (1) whether the child will suffer psychologically from a separation from either parent;

and (2) whether joint custody is in accord with the child's wishes.

■━■

Quicknotes

BEST INTERESTS OF CHILD Standard used by courts when rendering decisions which involve a child or children.

SPLIT CUSTODY Arrangement whereby the care and control of the child or children is divided between both parents, each having absolute control over the child during his or her visitation period.

■━■

Schutz v. Schutz

Father (P) v. Mother (D)

Fla. Sup. Ct., 581 So. 2d 1290 (1991).

NATURE OF CASE: Appeal of child custody decree.

FACT SUMMARY: A trial court ordered Mrs. Schutz (D) to refrain from making negative comments to her children regarding Mr. Schutz (P).

🏛 RULE OF LAW
A court may order one parent to refrain from making negative comments to her children regarding the other parent.

FACTS: The Schutzes divorced. Mrs. Schutz (D) was given custody of their children; Mrs. Schutz (D) and the children later moved away, and Mr. Schutz (P) was unable to locate them for several years. When he did locate them, the children were extremely hostile. Apparently, Mrs. Schutz (D) had falsely told the children that Mr. Schutz (P) had abandoned them. Mr. Schutz (P) filed a petition for an order compelling Mrs. Schutz (D) to allow visitation and to refrain from making untrue comments about him. The petition was granted. Mrs. Schutz (D) appealed, contending that the order violated her free speech rights.

ISSUE: May a court order one parent to refrain from making negative comments to her children regarding the other parent?

HOLDING AND DECISION: (Kogan, J.) Yes. A court may order one parent to refrain from making negative comments to her children regarding the other parent. A custodial parent has an affirmative duty to encourage and nurture the relationship between the child and the noncustodial parent. This duty is owed to both the noncustodial parent and the child. Pursuant to this, the custodial parent must take measures to promote positive interaction between the noncustodial parent and the children. One aspect of this is to not make negative misstatements. While this does to some extent burden free speech, such burden is incidental and does not rise to a constitutional violation. This is precisely the situation here. Affirmed.

▌ ANALYSIS

The order here essentially prohibited Mrs. Schutz from committing slander. Slander, of course, is not a constitutional right, but ordinarily speech is not restrained; once spoken, any resultant injury can give rise to an action for damages. It would be quite different if the order had compelled her to say positive things. This almost surely would be unconstitutional.

Quicknotes

AFFIRMATIVE DUTY An obligation to undertake an affirmative action for the benefit of another.

CHILD CUSTODY DECREE A court order awarding responsibility for the care and control over a child or children in a dissolution or separation proceeding.

CUSTODIAL PARENT A parent who is awarded the care and control of a child by the court in a dissolution or separation proceeding.

SLANDER Defamatory statement communicated orally.

Harrington v. Harrington

Ex-husband with new girlfriend (P) v. Ex-wife

Miss. Sup. Ct., 648 So. 2d 543 (1994).

NATURE OF CASE: Appeal from a chancellor's decision to modify visitation.

FACT SUMMARY: Mark Harrington's (P) overnight visitation with his two daughters was modified upon a motion of his ex-wife Donnett Harrington when he began to live with an unmarried woman. The court found his living arrangement detrimental to his children.

🏛 RULE OF LAW
It is in the children's best interest to have overnight visitation with their father while he cohabitates with an unmarried woman.

FACTS: Upon his divorce, Mark Harrington (Mark) (P) was granted overnight visitation with his two daughters on the first and third weekends of every month. The children's mother, Donnett Harrington (Donnett) (D) filed a Motion to Modify Judgment of Divorce alleging a material chance in circumstances affecting the children, namely that Mark (P) was living with a woman without the benefit of marriage. After a hearing, Donnett (D) agreed that Mark (P) was in compliance with all other terms of the child custody, child support, and the property settlement. However, she indicated that Mark's living arrangement was detrimental to the children and that there had been arguments between the children and Mark's (P) girlfriend. The presiding chancellor found there to be a conflict in Mark's (P) life (living with a woman to which he was not married while advocating Christian principles) that was detrimental to and not in the best interests of the children, and cited the fact that the oldest child was upset. The chancellor granted the modification denying Mark (P) overnight visitation, restricting his physical custody schedule, prohibiting the children from seeing Mark's (P) girlfriend and prohibiting Mark (P) from speaking to the children about his relationship with his girlfriend. Mark (P) then appealed.

ISSUE: Is it in the children's best interest to have overnight visitation with their father while he cohabitates with an unmarried woman?

HOLDING AND DECISION: (Sullivan, J.) Yes. It is in the children's best interest to have overnight visitation with their father while he cohabitates with an unmarried woman. The chancellor has broad discretion when determining visitation and the limitations thereon. When the chancellor determines visitation, he must keep the best interests of the child as his paramount concern while always being attentive to the rights of the non-custodial parent, recognizing the need to maintain a healthy, loving relationship between the non-custodial parent and his child. This Court will not reverse a chancellor's findings of fact so long as they are supported by substantial evidence in the record. However, this court will reverse when a chancellor is manifestly in error in his finding of fact or he has abused his discretion.

This court has stated that there must be evidence presented that a particular restriction on visitation is necessary to avoid harm to the child before a chancellor may properly impose the restriction. The chancellor should approach the fixing of visitation rights with the thought in mind that, absent extraordinary circumstances militating to the contrary, the non-custodial parent will have broad authority and discretion with respect to the place and manner of the exercise during periods of visitation. Overnight visitation with a non-custodial parent is the rule, not the exception. Indeed the non-custodial parent is presumptively entitled during reasonable times to overnight visitation with the children.

As noted in recent decisions, the court will set aside its own notions of morality and ethics and set aside its own understanding of Christian principles and must make the decision before it, based on whether or not it is in the best interests of the minor children to continue the visitation schedule as it currently existed. Here, the chancellor accorded great weight to the fact that Mark (P) was professing one lifestyle while living another. One could conclude from the chancellor's analysis that if Mark (P) were agnostic or atheist, there would be no problem with overnight visitations because the hypocrisy would be removed. The chancellor maintained that Mark's (P) living arrangement is detrimental to the children because (1) it is in conflict with his religion; and (2) this conflict leads to his children being confused. Mark (P) is Catholic. The divorce itself is in conflict with his religion.

There is simply not substantial evidence in the record supporting the chancellor's findings that the children are confused. Although there was testimony that one child had an argument with Mark's (P) girlfriend, there is no indication from the record that the child was suffering from harm because of confusion resulting from her father's alleged hypocrisy. It was admitted by Donnett (D) that the other daughter thought it was fine that her father lives with his girlfriend. Even if there was confusion by one child, this is not the type of harm that rises to the level necessary to overcome the presumption that a non-custodial parent is entitled to overnight visitation.

Continued on next page.

The chancellor also gave weight to the fact that the children were aware of Mark's (P) living arrangement and were concerned to the point of asking him if he would marry his girlfriend. These facts do not constitute substantial evidence of harm or detriment to the children. In further support of his ruling, the chancellor relied on Donnett's (D) testimony that Mark's girlfriend has spoken harshly to one child. While not condoning this behavior, harsh language in order to discipline a child is not substantial enough evidence of harm to restrict visitation.

In response to a question from the chancellor, Mark (P) said that if his visitation were to be continued as it was, that perhaps he would not allow his girlfriend to be present. This goes further than the law requires. There are numerous cases that would allow Mark (P) to have visitation with his children without any restriction on his relationship with his girlfriend. The better course of action would be that his girlfriend not stay overnight in the home with the children during visitation. The chancellor was absolutely without authority to prohibit Mark (P) from discussing his girlfriend with his children. The chancellor was manifestly wrong on the record in this case to restrict visitation and amend the prior visitation order. Reversed.

CONCURRENCE IN PART AND DISSENT IN PART:

(Lee, J.) The majority is correct that the chancellor abused his discretion when he ordered Mark (P) not to discuss his girlfriend while in the presence of his two daughters. However, the chancellor did not abuse his discretion when he restricted Mark (P) overnight visitation rights. Visitation and restrictions placed upon it are within the sound discretion of the chancellor. Visitation should be established with the best interests of the children as the paramount consideration, keeping in mind the rights of the non-custodial parent and the objective that parent and child should have as normal a relationship as possible despite the fact that they do not live together.

In this case, the chancellor, after hearing all of the testimony, found that Mark should not have overnight visitation as long as he cohabitated with his girlfriend. The chancellor's decision was not an abuse of discretion nor was it manifest error to restrict the children's overnight visits. The issue is quite simple. Shall the court condone Mark's (P) violation of state law by reversing the chancellor's ruling, or shall the court uphold the chancellor's decision and require Mark (P) to follow the law of the state. The law of the state deems it immoral for two persons of the opposite sex who are not married to cohabit. It is quite clear that the legislature proscribed this behavior as immoral for all citizens, be they religious or not. Therefore, it is quite clear that the chancellor found Mark's (P) living arrangement violated state law and was detrimental to his children.

▶ ANALYSIS

The *Harrington* court affirmed the standard that a restriction on visitation will not occur absent substantial evidence that a child is harmed. The harsh rebuke of the chancellor in this case shows that the presumption of overnight visits and reasonable visitation conditions are not to be limited by narrow views or the imposition of the court's view of its morality or ethical standards. Noting that it was likely unwise for the father to have his girlfriend stay overnight when the children were present, the court was not going to affect the non-custodial parent's rights if it was not in the children's best interest.

━━■

Quicknotes

NON-CUSTODIAL PARENT A parent who is not awarded the primary care and control of a child by the court in a dissolution or separation proceeding.

VISITATION Rights awarded by the court in a divorce or custody proceeding to a parent who does not have custody over the child or children, permitting that parent to visit with the child or children.

━━■

Troxel v. Granville

Grandparents (P) v. Mother (D)

530 U.S. 57 (2000).

NATURE OF CASE: Petition seeking visitation rights.

FACT SUMMARY: The Troxels (P) petitioned a Washington Superior Court for the right to visit their grandchildren over the protest of the children's mother (D).

🏛 RULE OF LAW
A parent has a fundamental right in the care, custody and control of his or her child.

FACTS: Tommie Granville (D) and Brad Troxel had two daughters together but never married. The couple separated and Brad later committed suicide. Granville (D) notified the Troxels (P) that she wished to limit their visitation to one short visit per month and they brought suit seeking to obtain visitation rights. Their petition was based on Wash. Rev. Code § 26.10.160(3), which provides that "any person may petition the court for visitation rights at any time, including, but not limited to, custody proceedings." The superior court entered a visitation decree ordering visitation for one weekend per month, one week during the summer and four hours on each of the grandparents' (P) birthdays. Granville (D) appealed and the case was remanded, during which time she married. Her husband later adopted the children. The court of appeals reversed the lower court's decision and dismissed the petition, holding that nonparents lack standing to seek visitation unless a custody action is pending. The Washington Supreme Court found that the Troxels (P) had standing to seek visitation under the statute, but concluded that they could not obtain visitation because § 26.10.160(3) unconstitutionally infringes on the fundamental rights of parents to rear their children. This Court granted certiorari.

ISSUE: Does a parent have a fundamental right in the care, custody and control of his or her child?

HOLDING AND DECISION: (O'Connor, J.) Yes. A parent has a fundamental right in the care, custody and control of his or her child. The Fourteenth Amendment prohibits states from "depriving any person of life, liberty or property, without due process of law." The clause also provides heightened protection against government interference with certain fundamental rights and liberty interests. The liberty interest at issue here is that of parents in the care, custody and control of their children. Section 26.10.160(3) here unconstitutionally infringes on Granville's (D) fundamental parental right. The statute is extremely broad, permitting any third party to subject any decision by a parent concerning visitation of the parent's children to state-court review placing the best-interests determination exclusively in

the hands of the judge. Several factors here compel the conclusion that the section as applied violates due process. First, the Troxels (P) did not allege, nor did the court find, that Granville (D) was an unfit parent. There is a presumption that fit parents act in the best interests of their children. Where this is the case, there is usually no reason for the state to interject itself into the private realm of the family. The superior court's decision directly contravened this presumption and failed to provide any protection for Granville's fundamental constitutional right to make decisions regarding the rearing of her own daughters. Affirmed.

DISSENT: (Stevens, J.) The Court should identify the two flaws in the Washington Supreme Court's ruling and remand for further deposition. That court's holding that "the Federal Constitution requires a showing of actual or potential 'harm' to the child before a court may order visitation continued over a parent's objections" has no support in case law. This Court has never held that a parent's liberty interest is so inflexible as to establish a shield protecting every parental decision from challenge absent a shoeing of harm. The Due Process Clause should allow the states to consider the impact on a child of potentially arbitrary decisions that neither serve nor are motivated by the child's best interests.

▎ *ANALYSIS*

In *V.C. v. M.J.B.*, 319 N.J. Super. 103, 725 A.2d 13 (1999), a New Jersey court held that a lesbian partner was entitled to visitation with the other partner's child. The court established a four-part test for determining whether a third party is entitled to visitation rights: (1) the biological parent's consent to the establishment of a parent-like relationship with the child; (2) the party seeking visitation and the child lived together in the same home; (3) the party seeking visitation assumed parental obligations; and (4) the party seeking visitation had been in a parental role for sufficient amount of time to establish a parental relationship.

▰▰▰

Quicknotes

BIOLOGICAL PARENTS A man and woman who conceive and give birth to a child.

DUE PROCESS CLAUSE Clauses found in the Fifth and Fourteenth Amendments to the United States Constitution providing that no person shall be deprived of "life, liberty, or property, without due process of law."

Continued on next page.

FOURTEENTH AMENDMENT Declares that no state shall make or enforce any law that shall abridge the privileges and immunities of citizens of the United States. No state shall deny to any person within its jurisdiction the equal protection of the laws.

LIBERTY INTEREST A right conferred by the Due Process Clauses of the state and federal constitutions.

VISITATION Rights awarded by the court in a divorce or custody proceeding to a parent who does not have custody over the child or children, permitting that parent to visit with the child or children.

Painter v. Bannister

Father (P) v. Grandparents (D)

Iowa Sup. Ct., 258 Iowa 1390, 140 N.W.2d 152, *cert. denied*, 385 U.S. 949 (1966).

NATURE OF CASE: Action for a writ of habeas corpus.

FACT SUMMARY: When Painter's (P) wife died, he gave their child to the maternal grandparents temporarily, but when he sought return of the child, the court refused because Painter's (P) life was too unstable, insecure, artsy, and "Bohemian."

🏛 RULE OF LAW
Where return of custody to the parent is likely to have a seriously disruptive and disturbing effect upon the child after the child has become adjusted to his foster parents, it would not be in the child's best interest to reunite him with his parent.

FACTS: Painter (P) left his son, Mark, with the boy's maternal grandparents, the Bannisters (D), after his wife was killed in a car accident. Painter (P) led a "Bohemian" lifestyle and had left to his wife the task of dealing with family finances and other responsibilities. He was never steadily employed but sought work in the photography and art worlds. At the time Mark was left with the Bannisters (D), the child was insecure and hostile to classmates and cruel to animals. Under the Bannisters' (D) care, Mark had become secure, well adjusted, and happy in the stable, conventional, middle-class, and mid-western Bannister (D) home. Subsequently, Painter (P) remarried, and his new wife appeared to be a leveling influence, who would be a loving mother to Mark. The Bannisters (D) refused to return the boy when Painter (P) decided that he could thereafter care for him. Painter (P) consequently sought a writ of habeas corpus to compel the Bannisters (D) to turn Mark (who was now seven years old) over to him.

ISSUE: Is it in the child's best interests to reunite him with his parent, where return of custody to the parent is likely to have a seriously disruptive and disturbing effect upon the child after the child has become adjusted to his foster parents?

HOLDING AND DECISION: (Stuart, J.) No. Where return of custody to the parent is likely to have a seriously disruptive and disturbing effect upon the child after the child has become adjusted to his foster parents, it would not be in the child's best interest to reunite him with his parent. A child of seven years needs stability and security, which he had found in his stay with his grandparents. It is not in his best interests to trade these qualities, which he had lacked, for the love and affection of his father. Painter's (P) lifestyle would be likely to have a disrupting and disturbing effect on the child if he were returned. The court cannot determine custody on its own choice of two lifestyles within normal and proper limits. However, philosophies are important as they relate to the needs and best interests of this particular child. The child's life would be more exciting and more artistically and intellectually rewarding if he were returned to his father, but the child needs stability and security, and that the father cannot provide. Writ denied. Reversed and remanded.

▶ ANALYSIS

Where the parent leaves the child with a friend or relative who later refuses to return him on request, the crucial issue is whether the child will be harmed by a shift in custody back to the parent. This is determined on the basis of the length of the stay with the foster parents, the nature of his relationship with them, the degree of contact maintained with the parent, and the circumstances in which the child would live with his parent. However, this case illustrates the danger that courts may decide custody on their own subjective, parochial view of what is best for the child.

■■■

Quicknotes

BEST INTERESTS OF CHILD Standard used by courts when rendering decisions which involve a child or children.

FOSTER PARENTS Parents appointed by law to serve as guardians of a child by virtue of their voluntary assumption of parental rights and responsibilities, and otherwise acting as the child's advocate in place of the child's natural parents.

WRIT OF HABEAS CORPUS A proceeding in which a defendant brings a writ to compel a judicial determination of whether he is lawfully being held in custody.

■■■

Bennett v. Jeffreys

Biological mother (P) v. Caregiver (D)

N.Y. Ct. App., 40 N.Y.2d 543, 356 N.E.2d 277 (1976).

NATURE OF CASE: Appeal from custody award.

FACT SUMMARY: Bennett (P), the natural mother of the child in question, sued for custody from Jeffreys (D) who had been the custodian of the child for most of its life.

RULE OF LAW
Where there has been a prolonged separation between mother and child, the natural mother should only be granted custody where it is established that it is in the child's best interests.

FACTS: Bennett (P) was the natural mother of an eight-year-old child. The child had been in the custody of Jeffreys (D), a friend of the maternal grandmother, since birth. Bennett (P) filed a custody action which was denied. Custody was awarded on appeal on the sole basis that Bennett (P) had not surrendered, abandoned, or persistently neglected the child. Bennett (P) had borne the child when she was 15 and unwed. Her mother had pressured her to give the child to a friend (D) of her grandmother. There had been some contact over the years between Bennett (P) and child, but its kind and quality were challenged. Jeffreys (D) appealed on the basis that such a prolonged absence required a consideration of the child's best interests.

ISSUE: Where there has been a prolonged separation between mother and child, should the natural mother be granted custody only when it is in the child's best interests?

HOLDING AND DECISION: (Breitel, C.J.) Yes. Where there has been a prolonged separation between mother and child, the natural mother should be granted custody only when it is in the child's best interests. A parent's right to rear its child is not absolute. Extraordinary situations may require a different result. The rights of the child must be considered. Its welfare is deemed paramount where the mother's fitness is in question. The presumption that its best interest lies with the natural mother no longer applies where a prolonged absence is present. Such extraordinary circumstances trigger the "best interests of the child" test. Removal from the custodian after a long period of time may cause psychological difficulties. The trial court considered the long delay, and the appellate court considered the statutory presumption favoring the natural mother. Neither court carefully investigated what would be in the best interest of the child. The case must be remanded for such a determination. Reversed and remanded.

CONCURRENCE: (Fuchsberg, J.) Where the natural mother has consented to the custodial relationship and it has endured for a number of years, weight should be given to the natural mother's status. Further, the "best interests of the child" test should be applied in all situations regardless of abandonment, etc.

ANALYSIS

The majority holds that the best interests of the child are conclusively presumed to lie with the natural mother absent abandonment, neglect, etc. Indeed, the fitness of the mother to raise the child is subsumed to the primacy of parental rights. *People ex rel. Anonymous v. Anonymous*, 10 N.Y.2d 332. The state as parens patriae is not deemed to have a sufficient interest to supplant such rights except in cases of grievous cause or necessity. *Stanley v. Illinois*, 405 U.S. 645 (1972).

Quicknotes

BEST INTERESTS OF CHILD Standard used by courts when rendering decisions which involve a child or children.

NATURAL MOTHER The biological mother of a child, as opposed to a mother whose rights have either been assigned or are recognized by law.

PARENS PATRIAE Maxim that the government as sovereign is conferred with the duty to act as guardian on behalf of those citizens under legal disability.

Bennett v. Marrow

Biological mother (P) v. Foster mother (D)

N.Y. App. Div., 59 A.D.2d, 492, 399 N.Y.S.2d 697 (1977).

NATURE OF CASE: Appeal from a custody decree.

FACT SUMMARY: The family court awarded custody of Gina Marie to Marrow, her foster mother, denying the petition for custody of Bennett (P), her natural mother.

🏛 RULE OF LAW
A court may, in the best interests of the child, award custody to a foster parent over a petition for custody by a natural parent.

FACTS: Bennett (P) petitioned the court for custody of her daughter, Gina Marie, who had been living with Marrow (D), her foster mother. At the original hearing, the child was living with Marrow (D), yet she went to live with Bennett (P) for 15 months. At the second hearing, expert testimony was presented, showing the child went from being happy and well adjusted while living with Marrow (D), with whom she had developed a parent-child relationship, to being unhappy and uncomfortable with Bennett (P). The court awarded custody to Marrow (D), finding that although Bennett (P) provided the child with all her material needs, she failed to fulfill her emotional needs, and therefore it was in her best interest to award Marrow (D) custody. Bennett (P) appealed. [Note that, although not stated in the casebook excerpt, it appears that "Marrow" was the new name of Jeffreys, the party in the earlier case of *Bennett v. Jeffreys*, 40 N.Y.2d 453 (N.Y. Ct. App. 1976), apparently by marriage.]

ISSUE: May a court award custody to a non-blood relation over a petition for custody by a natural parent?

HOLDING AND DECISION: (O'Connor, J.) Yes. A court may, in the best interests of the child, award custody to a foster parent over a natural parent. The overriding consideration in child custody disputes is not the relationship between the litigants and the child but what is in the best interest of the child. In this case, the trial court did not abuse its discretion in awarding custody to the foster parent, as this clearly preserved the more beneficial relationship from the child's point of view. Therefore, no error was committed. Affirmed.

▌ *ANALYSIS*

Since the holding in this case was published in 1977, the New York courts have followed it yet have declined to extend its scope. In cases such as *Dickson v. Lasearis*, 423 N.E.2d 361 (1981), the court limited its application where there were allegations of abandonment.

Quicknotes

BEST INTERESTS OF CHILD Standard used by courts when rendering decisions which involve a child or children.

BIOLOGICAL PARENTS A man and woman who conceive and give birth to a child.

CHILD CUSTODY DECREE A court order awarding responsibility for the care and control over a child or children in a dissolution or separation proceeding.

FOSTER PARENTS Parents appointed by law to serve as guardians of a child by virtue of their voluntary assumption of parental rights and responsibilities, and otherwise acting as the child's advocate in place of the child's natural parents.

Guardianship of Phillip B.

Psychological parents (P) v. Biological parents (D)

Cal. Ct. App., 139 Cal. App. 3d 407, 188 Cal. Rptr. 781 (1983).

NATURE OF CASE: Appeal from an order of guardianship.

FACT SUMMARY: Phillip B.'s natural parents (D) challenged an award of custody to Herbert and Patsy H. (P), who contended they had protectable rights as Phillip's "psychological parents."

🏛 RULE OF LAW
A person who assumes the role of parent by raising and nurturing a child may acquire a protectable interest in the companionship, care, custody, and management of the child as a psychological parent.

FACTS: Phillip B. was born with Down's syndrome and was placed in a board and care facility by his parents, Warren and Patricia B. (D). After some time, the B.s (D) failed to visit him regularly, and Patsy H. (P), a volunteer at the facility, developed a relationship with him, which led to his spending time at her home and with her family. His attitude and mental ability flourished as a result of this relationship. Subsequently, he was accepted as a member of the H. (P) family, was given his own bedroom, and was included in family activities. Phillip's parents (D) subsequently refused to consent to heart treatment for him, and terminated any further contact with the H.s (P). This led to a severe shift in Phillip's behavior and a constant demand to be allowed to return to the H.s' (P) home. The H.s (P) petitioned for an order appointing them Phillip's legal guardians. The trial court granted the order, finding an award of custody to the B.s (D) would be harmful in light of the psychological parental relationship with the H.s (P). The B.s (D) appealed.

ISSUE: May a person who assumes the role of a parent by raising and nurturing a child acquire a protectable interest in the companionship, care, custody, and management of the child as a psychological parent?

HOLDING AND DECISION: (Racanelli, J.) Yes. A person who assumes the role of a parent by raising and nurturing a child may acquire a protectable interest in the companionship, care, custody, and management of the child as a psychological parent. In this case the relationship existing between Phillip and the H.s (P) was clearly as close and beneficial to him as any natural relationship could have been. The termination was correctly viewed by the trial court as severely detrimental to his well-being. As a result, it was in Phillip's best interests to recognize the H.s (P) as his psychological parents with rights to custody. Affirmed.

▶ ANALYSIS

This case illustrates judicial recognition that biological parental relationships do not guarantee a child will receive the essential intangible support vital to his development. The recognition of psychological or de facto parenthood dates back at least to the case of the *Guardianship of Shannon*, 218 Cal. 490 (1933). The relationship is developed through day-to-day interaction and shared experiences.

■■■

Quicknotes

BIOLOGICAL PARENTS A man and woman who conceive and give birth to a child.

GUARDIANSHIP A legal relationship whereby one party is responsible for the care and control over another and his property due to some legal incapacity on the part of the ward.

NATURAL PARENTS The biological parents of a child as opposed to those parents whose rights have either been assigned or are otherwise recognized by law.

■■■

Smith v. Organization of Foster Families for Equality & Reform

Foster care agency (D) v. Foster family organization (P)

431 U.S. 816 (1977).

NATURE OF CASE: Appeal from a judgment declaring a state foster-care statute unconstitutional.

FACT SUMMARY: The district court held that a New York statute allowing agency removal of children from foster homes without a hearing was a denial of the constitutional right to due process.

🏛 RULE OF LAW
A state foster-care statute which allows an agency to remove children from foster homes after notifying the foster parents in advance and allowing them an opportunity to contest the decision does not violate due process requirements.

FACTS: The Organization of Foster Families for Equality and Reform (Organization) (P) challenged a New York statute which allowed the state Department of Social Services (D) to remove children from foster homes, contending it constituted a denial of due process. The statute provided that the Department (D) could, in its discretion, remove a child from a foster home. It required that the agency give the foster parents ten-day written notice, and gave the foster parents the right to request a conference where they could be represented by counsel and informed of the reasons for the removal, and to contest the removal. The foster parents could then seek a full hearing and then judicial review. The district court held that due process required a child be afforded a hearing at which all relevant parties could testify prior to removal. The Department (D) appealed.

ISSUE: Does a state foster-care statute which allows an agency to remove children from a foster home after notifying the foster parents and affording them an opportunity to contest the removal violate due process?

HOLDING AND DECISION: (Brennan, J.) No. A state foster-care statute which allows an agency to remove children from a foster home after notifying the foster parents and affording them an opportunity to contest the removal does not violate due process. Foster-parent rights are created by the state. As a result, any relationship between foster parents and children includes the state as a partner. Therefore, the state may prescribe removal procedures. In this case, the procedures involved adequately protected the public and private interests and did not present an unsatisfactory potential for error. Reversed.

state removed one of two siblings from a foster parent who was a half-sister. The sister did not waive any familial interest protected by due process when she consented to be a foster parent.

◼▬◼

Quicknotes

DUE PROCESS RIGHTS The constitutional mandate requiring the courts to protect and enforce individuals' rights and liberties consistent with prevailing principles of fairness and justice, and prohibiting the federal and state governments from such activities that deprive its citizens of a life, liberty or property interest.

FOSTER PARENTS Parents appointed by law to serve as guardians of a child by virtue of their voluntary assumption of parental rights and responsibilities, and otherwise acting as the child's advocate in place of the child's natural parents.

LIBERTY INTEREST A right conferred by the Due Process Clauses of the state and federal constitutions.

◼▬◼

▶ ANALYSIS

In *Rivera v. Marcus*, 696 F.2d 1016 (2d Cir. 1982), the federal court held that due process was denied when a

In re Amberley D.

Guardians (P) v. Mother (D)

Me. Sup. Jud. Ct., 775 A.2d 1158 (2001)

NATURE OF CASE: Appeal by out-of-state parent from judgment appointing co-guardians of her minor (teenage) child.

FACT SUMMARY: Amberley D. (Amberley) ran away from her neglectful mother Joann R. (Joann) (P), who lived in New Hampshire, to be with her stepfather's parents in Maine. The step-grandparents (D) were appointed as co-guardians of Amberley, and Joann (P) challenged the appointment on several grounds.

🏛 RULE OF LAW

(1) The Uniform Child Custody Jurisdiction and Enforcement Act (UCCJEA) is not preempted by the Parental Kidnapping Prevention Act (PKPA), and, therefore, an out-of-state parent is not entitled to notice of an emergency guardianship hearing.

(2) Where a child has no home state, jurisdiction and venue in a guardianship proceeding are properly vested in the state where the child is present and with which the child has significant contacts.

(3) Where a court must find in a guardianship proceeding by clear and convincing evidence that a child's living conditions are at least temporarily intolerable and that the proposed guardian(s) will provide a living situation that is in the child's best interests, the court's findings are not clearly erroneous where it finds a history of abuse, neglect, and mistreatment of the child by the parent and finds that the proposed guardian offers the child a stable, loving home and meets the child's other needs.

(4) A guardianship statute that provides an opportunity for a parent to petition for the removal of a guardian is not unconstitutional.

FACTS: Amberley's mother, Joann (P), and her stepfather, Charles R., were itinerant, constantly moving all over New England. The year that Amberley was in eighth grade, Joann (P) and Charles divorced, and Joann (P) stayed in New Hampshire. By that point, Amberley, who was 14, had been enrolled in approximately 27 different schools and had stopped going to school altogether. Joann (P) was being abusive to and neglectful of Amberley, whose living situation became intolerable, and Amberley ran away to Charles's parents, Diana and Richard B. (D), who lived in Maine, and with whom Amberley had stayed for periods of time during several years. Joann (P) reported Amberley missing, and left for a California vacation. Upon her return, she was informed by

Maine county officials of Amberley's whereabouts. In the meantime, Diana and Richard (D) had filed a petition requesting appointment as temporary (six-month) co-guardians of a minor, which petition was granted. Joann (P) was served notice of the appointment, and she filed a motion to dismiss it. Her motion was denied. At a hearing on full guardianship, which was held by the probate court, of which Joann (P) had notice and participated in, Diana and Richard (D) were appointed full co-guardians, and Joann (P) appealed on several grounds, namely: (1) the court erred by appointing temporary guardians without notice to her; (2) the court lacked jurisdiction and venue over the guardianship petition; (3) no clear and convincing evidence supported the petition; and (4) the guardianship statute was unconstitutional as applied. There were no prior or pending orders from any other court in any state addressing custody or parental rights for Amberley during this time.

ISSUE:

(1) Is the Uniform Child Custody Jurisdiction and Enforcement Act (UCCJEA), preempted by the Parental Kidnapping Prevention Act (PKPA), thereby entitling an out-of-state parent to notice of an emergency guardianship hearing?

(2) Where a child has no home state, are jurisdiction and venue in a guardianship proceeding properly vested in the state where the child is present and with which the child has significant contacts?

(3) Where a court must find in a guardianship proceeding by clear and convincing evidence that a child's living conditions are at least temporarily intolerable and that the proposed guardian(s) will provide a living situation that is in the child's best interests, are the court's findings clearly erroneous where it finds a history of abuse, neglect, and mistreatment of the child by the parent and finds that the proposed guardian offers the child a stable, loving home and meets the child's other needs?

(4) Is a guardianship statute that provides an opportunity for a parent to petition for the removal of a guardian unconstitutional?

HOLDING AND DECISION: (Alexander, J.) No as to issue #1. Yes as to issue #2. No as to issue #3. No as to issue #4.

(1) As to the first issue regarding notice, the probate court waived notice of hearing to Joann (P) pursuant to a Maine statute (18-A M.R.S.A. § 5-207) that permits such waiver upon a showing of good cause and where a minor at least 14 years old is involved. Joann (P) contends that the Uniform Child Custody Jurisdic-

Continued on next page.

tion and Enforcement Act (UCCJEA), which defers to state notice provisions for child custody determinations, is preempted by the Parental Kidnapping Prevention Act (PKPA), and that she was entitled to notice of the emergency guardianship hearing under the PKPA. The UCCJEA provides that notice to persons outside the state "may be given in a manner prescribed by the law of this State for service of process or by the law of the state in which the service is made." In the event of a conflict, the PKPA preempts the UCCJEA, but only when existing orders regarding custody or visitation have been entered by courts of other states. Here, the PKPA is inapplicable because there was no such order. Joann (P) also claimed that the waiver violated due process by depriving her of fundamental parental rights. Here, Joann (P) does have a fundamental parental right, but it is balanced by the state's significant interest in protecting children. Because the temporary guardianship is time-limited and the parent, upon notice of the appointment, has an opportunity to petition for the removal of the guardian, which here Joann (P) did, the guardianship statute, providing for waiver of notice in limited circumstances, but with subsequent opportunity to be heard, did not violate Joann's (P) due process rights.

(2) As to the second issue regarding jurisdiction and venue, Joann (P) contends that New Hampshire has jurisdiction over the guardianship petition pursuant to the PKPA and the UCCJEA. Both statutes provide that a state has jurisdiction over a child custody proceeding if the state is the "home state" of the child on the date the proceeding is commenced, or was the home state within six months before the date the proceeding is commenced. They define the home state as the state in which the child lived with a parent, or a person acting as a parent, for at least six consecutive months immediately before the commencement of a child custody proceeding, and include periods of temporary absence as part of the period. Here, Joann (P) contends that New Hampshire is Amberley's home state. However, Amberley did not live there for the requisite six-month period, and, therefore, New Hampshire cannot be considered her home state. When the child has no home state, the statutes require the court to examine if there is a sufficiently significant connection to exercise jurisdiction, and, under the PKPA, a state can exercise jurisdiction when it is in the child's best interest and there is substantial evidence of a connection between the child and at least one applicant and the state. The UCCJEA basically tracks this provision but omits the "best interest" language. Here, there was a significant connection with Maine—Amberley lived and attended school there for periods of time during six years—and the substantial evidence requirements were satisfied under the UCCJEA and PKPA. Accordingly, the probate court had jurisdiction over the guardianship petition. Regarding Joann's (P) claim that venue did not exist, venue for guardianship proceedings for minors is "in the place where the minor resides or is present." Amberley's presence within Maine was, therefore, determinative in establishing venue.

(3) As to the third issue, regarding the sufficiency of the evidence, absent consent from the parent, the probate court must find by clear and convincing evidence that the child's living conditions are at least temporarily intolerable and that the proposed guardian(s) will provide a living situation that is in the child's best interest. Here, the probate court found that the evidence established a history of abuse, neglect, and mistreatment of Amberley by her mother. The court also found that Diana and Richard (D), with whom Amberley had spent considerable time during her life, offered her a stable, loving home and met her physical, educational, emotional, and social needs. This evidence was sufficient to support the court's finding of an intolerable living situation and its "best interests" finding, and, therefore, the probate court's finding was not clearly erroneous. The fact that Amberley was 15 at the time the petition was filed and granted also bolsters the probate court's best interest finding because older minors are permitted to exercise a greater degree of choice.

(4) As to the fourth issue regarding the constitutionality of the guardianship statute, Joann (P) claimed that her parental rights were effectively terminated. However, guardianship determinations are not final, and there is opportunity for Joann (P) or Amberley to petition for removal of the guardians. Because the parent retains the right to regain custody, the same degree of procedural safeguards as in termination proceedings is not constitutionally required. Affirmed.

▶ ANALYSIS

It should be kept in mind that the goal of the Uniform Child Custody Jurisdiction and Enforcement Act (UCCJEA), and the Parental Kidnapping Prevention Act (PKPA), is to limit the ability of sister states to modify custody decrees. This decision, in all its aspects, supports that goal.

■═■

Quicknotes

BEST INTERESTS OF CHILD Standard used by courts when rendering decisions which involve a child or children.

CHILD CUSTODY DECREE A court order awarding responsibility for the care and control over a child or children in a dissolution or separation proceeding.

CLEAR AND CONVINCING EVIDENCE An evidentiary standard requiring a demonstration that the fact sought to be proven is reasonably certain.

DUE PROCESS RIGHTS The constitutional mandate requiring the courts to protect and enforce individuals' rights

Continued on next page.

and liberties consistent with prevailing principles of fairness and justice, and prohibiting the federal and state governments from such activities that deprive its citizens of a life, liberty or property interest.

GUARDIANSHIP A legal relationship whereby one party is responsible for the care and control over another and his property due to some legal incapacity on the part of the ward.

TERMINATION OF PARENTAL RIGHTS The purposeful cessation of lawfully recognized rights between a child and its parents and of the parent to the child, including physical possession of the child, companionship and support, the right to discipline the child, and control over the child's property.

In re Heinrich and Curotto

Father (P) v. Mother (D)

N.H. Sup. Ct., 7 A.3d 1158 (2010).

NATURE OF CASE: Appeal of the trial court's decision to deny relocation of a custodial parent.

FACT SUMMARY: Upon the dissolution of Mary Ellen Curotto's (D) marriage to Eric W. Henrich (P), Mary sought to move from New Hampshire to Florida.

🏛 RULE OF LAW

The proper test for the relocation of children is what is in their "best interests."

FACTS: During their 12-year marriage, Mary Ellen Curotto (Mary) (D) and her then husband Eric W. Henrich (Eric) (P) moved from Florida to New Hampshire, following employment opportunities for the husband, who works as a professional chef. Mary (D) worked part-time in the hospitality industry as a waitress and bartender. When the parties relocated to New Hampshire, Mary (D) alleges the move was meant to be temporary, no longer than five years, after which they intended to return to Florida. Eric (P) disputes this. Upon Eric's (P) filing for divorce, alleging that irreconcilable differences between the parties caused an irremediable breakdown of the marriage, Mary (D) filed an answer and cross-motion to petition for divorce and asked the court to award her primary residential responsibility for the children so that she could relocate the children to Florida where her extended family lives and where she would have employment opportunities. Eric (P) opposed this move, primarily because he did not believe it was in the children's best interests because the children would not be able to see him weekly and would have to move from the only home they have known. After a hearing, a temporary parenting plan gave primary residential (custodial) responsibility to Mary (D) but awarded Eric (P) regular parenting time. The court barred any relocation outside of New Hampshire and appointed a guardian ad litem (GAL) to study, among other issues, whether relocation would be in the children's best interests. The GAL submitted a detailed preliminary report in which she reported that "the children are strongly bonded to both parents," that both "are good parents," and that the children would "suffer a loss" if they were separated from either parent. Based upon this report, the trial court partially modified the existing temporary parenting plan giving Eric (P) greater parenting time and denied Mary's (D) wife's request to relocate temporarily to Florida with the children. At the final hearing, the trial court agreed with the prior decision to bar relocation to Florida. Mary (D) then appealed the final divorce decree.

ISSUE: Is the proper test for the relocation of children what is in their "best interests"?

HOLDING AND DECISION: (Hicks, J.) Yes. The proper test for the relocation of children is what is in their "best interests." The wife (D) first argues that the trial court erred when it applied certain state code provisions in denying her petition to relocate with the children to Florida. She (D) contends that the state code provisions apply only to a post-divorce relocation request to modify an existing permanent parenting decree. Here, she (D) asserts, there was no permanent parenting decree in place, and, therefore, the court should have applied the best interests of the child standard.

The wife's (D) argument requires us to construe the pertinent statutes. The state code provisions she cites govern parenting plans and the determination of parental rights and responsibilities. It directs that "[i]n developing a parenting plan under this section, the court shall consider only the best interests of the child and the safety of the parties." The state code provisions lay out a two-part test, known as the burden-shifting test, for a court to apply if a parent seeks to relocate the residence of a child. Under this test, the parent petitioning for relocation must demonstrate that the relocation is for a legitimate purpose and is reasonable in light of that purpose. If the petitioning parent meets this burden, the opposing party then has the burden of proving that the relocation is not in the best interests of the child. Nothing in the state code provisions purport to limit its applicability to relocations proposed after a final divorce decree has been entered.

Mary (D) next argues that the trial court unsustainably exercised its discretion in denying her request to relocate to Florida with the children. Specifically, she (D) contends that the trial court failed to give proper weight to evidence and testimony proffered by her relative to the opportunities available to the children in Florida. These opportunities include the ability of the children to attend private school, participate in their family's hotel legacy, and attend monthly scheduled parenting time with their father (P). Mary (D) further asserts that she would be able to provide a better lifestyle for the children in Florida than in New Hampshire and that the parties had agreed to move from New Hampshire to Florida after five years. By ignoring these factors, the trial court placed too much emphasis on how the relocation would negatively affect the husband's (P) relationship and parenting time with the children. She (D) asserts there would be no negative effect; the husband (P) would have the same quality of parenting time whether the children live in New Hampshire or Florida.

Continued on next page.

Under the state code provisions, the parent seeking to relocate has the initial burden of demonstrating by a preponderance of the evidence that the relocation is for a legitimate purpose and is reasonable in light of that purpose. Once the parent has met this prima facie burden, the burden shifts to the other parent to prove by a preponderance of the evidence that relocating is not in the child's best interests.

Whether Mary (D) met her prima facie burden is not at issue here. This appeal concerns only whether the trial court properly concluded that Eric (P), the father, met his burden of showing the relocation was not in the children's best interests. Here, the trial court, after reviewing the GAL's final report, hearing testimony from witnesses, and listening to the parties and reading their written submissions, found that the father (P) had established that a relocation to Florida was not in the children's best interests. In reaching this conclusion, the trial court carefully analyzed each of the factors listed in *Tomasko v. DuBuc*, 145 N.H. 169, 761 A.2d 407 (2000). These factors include: (1) each parent's reasons for seeking or opposing the move; (2) the quality of the relationships between the child and the custodial and noncustodial parents; (3) the impact of the move on the quantity and quality of the child's future contact with the noncustodial parent; (4) the degree to which the custodial parent's and child's life may be enhanced economically, emotionally, and educationally by the move; (5) the feasibility of preserving the relationship between the noncustodial parent and child through suitable visitation arrangements; (6) any negative impact from continued or exacerbated hostility between the custodial and noncustodial parents; and (7) the effect that the move may have on any extended family relations.

The trial court focused upon how the relocation would affect the quality of the relationship of the husband, "an involved father," with his children. The court found that this relationship would suffer because the husband's day-to-day contact with the parties' minor children will be eliminated. Mary (D) asserted that these factors are far outweighed by the economic, emotional, and educational benefits of the move. Trial court found that the "quality of life argument raised by Mary (D) do not overcome the negative impact to the quality of Eric's (P) relationship with the parties' minor children if Mary (D) were to relocate to Florida."

The record supports the trial court's findings. There is evidence that the husband (P) was an involved, caring father. His family gathers together regularly at his parents' house on Sundays to relax, play games, and swim. He (P) is involved in extra-curricular activities as an assistant coach, helps the children with their homework, and attends school activities. The GAL noted that there are times when the husband (P) could not exercise his parenting time because of his work schedule and relies upon a third party for day care. Nevertheless, the GAL opined that she believed it was important for the children "to have access to their dad" regularly. The GAL noted in her report that while the

Florida parenting plan would allow the husband (P) and children "to maintain a relationship, it will not be the same type of relationship, which exists now. The reality is that the ability to have day to day contact with the boys will be eliminated." She concluded that the boys "will suffer a loss."

The trial court, therefore, was able to consider these differences in philosophy and to weigh the GAL's report accordingly. This court defers to the judgment of the trial court in these matters because a trial court is in the best position to assign weight to evidence and to assess the credibility of witnesses. Based upon the review of the record, it cannot be said that the trial court unsustainably exercised its discretion in finding that it would not be in the children's best interests to relocate to Florida. Affirmed.

Next, Mary (D) contends that the trial court erred in ruling that the husband (P) was entitled to reimbursement of money spread over 12 months. The parties do not dispute that the husband (P) overpaid child support. The court incorrectly calculated the overpayments. Vacated and remanded for recalculation of the overpayments. Finally, Mary (D) asserted that the trial court unsustainably exercised its discretion in requiring the children to be in the care of a third-party caretaker for greater than 48 hours before the other parent is offered the right to care for the children. Based upon the review of the record, it cannot be said that the trial court unsustainably exercised its discretion in imposing a 48 hour period. Affirmed in part; vacated in part; and remanded.

▶ ANALYSIS

In addressing the contentious issue of relocation, the court upheld the "best interests of the child" standard and reaffirmed the state code provisions that place the burden on the party seeking relocation. Rather than simply look at the financial situation of the custodial parent, the effect of relocation on the children was put in primary focus. Despite the obvious benefits to the wife, the lack of parenting time with the father was significant and fatal to her request.

Quicknotes

BEST INTERESTS OF CHILD Standard used by courts when rendering decisions which involve a child or children.

Delvoye v. Lee

Father (P) v. Mother (D)

329 F.3d 330 (3d Cir. 2003).

NATURE OF CASE: Appeal from denial of petition to remove minor child from country.

FACT SUMMARY: Delvoye (P) was a Belgian citizen with a New York apartment. Lee (D) was a United States citizen residing in New York. The couple began a relationship and Lee (D) got pregnant. She had Baby S in Belgium but returned to the United States with Delvoye's (P) reluctant consent. When the relationship deteriorated, Delvoye (P) claimed Lee (D) had wrongfully taken Baby S out of Belgium.

RULE OF LAW
Habitual residence requires a degree of settled purpose.

FACTS: Delvoye (P), a Belgian citizen, kept an apartment in New York. He met Lee (D), a United States citizen, in New York in early 2000, and a romantic relationship developed. Lee (D) moved into Delvoye's (P) New York apartment and he visited about a quarter of his time. Lee (D) became pregnant and Delvoye (P) insisted she come to Belgium to have the child because healthcare was free. Lee (D) agreed, obtained a 3-month visa, and went to Belgium in November 2000. Lee (D) left most of her belongings in the New York apartment, lived out of suitcases in Belgium, and did not renew her visa when it expired. The relationship deteriorated by the time the child, Baby S, was born in May 2001. Delvoye (P) reluctantly signed the consents to permit the child to obtain an American passport and agreed that Lee (D) could return with Baby S to the United States in July 2001. Delvoye (P) visited often over the next two months and the couple tried to reconcile, but failed. Delvoye (P) then filed a petition claiming Baby S had been wrongfully removed from Belgium under the Hague Convention on the Civil Aspects of International Child Abduction. The trial court denied the petition on the basis that Delvoye (P) did not meet his burden of proof that Baby S's habitual residence was Belgium. Delvoye (P) appealed.

ISSUE: Does habitual residence require a degree of settled purpose?

HOLDING AND DECISION: (Schwarzer, J.) Yes. Habitual residence requires a degree of settled purpose. The Hague Convention on the Civil Aspects of International Child Abduction (the "Convention") provides that a child is wrongfully taken if a breach of custody rights occurs under the law of the state wherein the child was "habitually resident" prior to the taking. The issue is whether Baby S was a habitual resident of Belgium and

determination of habitual residence is a mixed question of fact and law. Habitual residency depends upon the circumstances of the child's presence in a particular place, the child's acclimatization to that place, and the parents' intentions of the child's presence. The trial court determined that Baby S, at just four months old and still nursing, could not have acclimatized to Belgium. Whether an infant can acclimatize is an issue of first impression. It may occur that an infant does not have a separate residence from its custodial parent. The mother's residence is not the automatic residence of the infant, however. Here, the mother traveled temporarily to Belgium at the father's insistence, did not evidence an intention to stay, and showed no "degree of settled purpose" to demonstrate habitual residence. Baby S did not become a habitual resident there because the parents did not share an intention that he remain. The infant has no habitual residence until the mother leaves the country of temporary residence and finds her "degree of settled purpose." Affirmed.

ANALYSIS

Habitual residence will require a more fact-intensive analysis due to the increasing globalization of our communities. People travel more often and for longer periods of time because of the ease of transportation and communication networks. Military personnel may be stationed all over the world and may choose to become residents of a new country even if only temporarily. Medical advancements make it safer for late-term pregnant women to travel internationally and give birth out of the country. Additionally, the traditional family is disappearing and parents may not be married or even in a committed relationship after a child is born. The child could then be a "resident" of two different countries with two individuals seeking custody, as the case here. Courts will need to look carefully at the circumstances of each case.

■══■

Quicknotes

HABITUAL RESIDENCE Location where a person lives with the intent to remain for an unspecified time.

■══■

Friedrich v. Friedrich

Father (P) v. Mother (D)

78 F.3d 1060 (6th Cir. 1996).

NATURE OF CASE: Appeal from district court's decision on remand to allow a petition to return a child.

FACT SUMMARY: Jeana (D), an American citizen, removed her son with Emanuel (P), a German citizen, from Germany, where her son was born and had lived his entire life, without Emanuel's (P) consent, and Emanuel (P) petitioned to have him returned.

RULE OF LAW

If a person has valid custody rights to a child under the law of the country of the child's habitual residence, that person cannot fail to "exercise" those custody rights under the Hague Convention short of acts that constitute clear and unequivocal abandonment of the child. A grave risk of harm, for purposes of the convention, can exist only when return of the child puts the child in imminent danger prior to the resolution of the custody dispute and/or where there is serious abuse or neglect or extraordinary emotional dependence and the court in the country of habitual residence is incapable of giving or unwilling to give the child adequate protection.

FACTS: Emanuel Friedrich (P), a German citizen, and Jeana Friedrich (D), an American citizen working in Germany, were married in Germany and had a son, Thomas, who was born in Germany. When Thomas was two years old, the couple separated after an argument in which Emanuel (P) placed Thomas's and Jeana's (D) belongings in the hallway outside of their apartment. Jeana (D) shortly thereafter took Thomas to Ohio without telling Emanuel (P). Emanuel (P) subsequently obtained an order from a German family court awarding him custody and then filed the present action in the United States District Court for the Southern District of Ohio seeking the return of his son. The appeals court reversed the district court's denial of Emanuel's (P) claim for the return of his son to Germany and remanded for a determination of whether, as a matter of German law, Emanuel (P) was exercising custody rights to Thomas at the time of removal and if Jeana (D) could prove any of the four affirmative defenses provided by the Hague Convention on the Civil Aspects of International Child Abduction and the International Child Abduction Remedies Act. On remand the district court determined that Emanuel (P) was exercising custody rights, that affirmative defenses had not been established, and that Thomas was to be returned to Germany. Jeana (D) appealed.

ISSUE: What does it mean to "exercise" custody rights, and when can a court refuse to return a child who has been wrongfully removed from a country because return of the abducted child would result in a "grave" risk of harm?

HOLDING AND DECISION: (Boggs, J.) If a person has valid custody rights to a child under the law of the country of the child's habitual residence, that person cannot fail to "exercise" those custody rights under the Hague Convention short of acts that constitute clear and unequivocal abandonment of the child. Once it determines that the parent exercised custody rights in any manner, the court's job is done. The question of whether the parent exercised the custody rights well or badly is to be left to the court in the foreign country, because it goes to the merits of the custody dispute and are beyond the subject matter jurisdiction of the federal courts. A court in the abducted-to nation has jurisdiction to decide the merits of an abduction claim, but not the merits of the underlying custody dispute. The removal of a child from the country of its habitual residence is "wrongful" under the Hague Convention if a person in that country is, or would otherwise be, exercising custody rights to the child under that country's law at the moment of removal. Emanuel (P) was exercising custody rights over Thomas at the time of Thomas's removal. The fact that Emanuel (P) placed Thomas's belongings in the hallway outside of his apartment after he argued with Jeana (D) is insufficient to terminate parental rights as a matter of German law. Under German law, both parents retain joint rights of custody until a decree has been entered limiting one parent's rights. The exercising of custody rights is to be liberally found whenever a parent with de jure custody rights keeps, or seeks to keep, any sort of regular contact with his or her child. This definition is appropriate because American courts are not well suited to determine the consequences of parental behavior under the law of a foreign country, an American decision about the adequacy of one parent's exercise of custody rights is dangerously close to the merits of the custody dispute, and it is difficult to assess adequately the acts and motivations of a parent when informal separations are involved. In this case, Jeana (D) was in Germany for four days after she left Emanuel's (P) apartment. The day after she left the apartment, Emanuel (P) met and visited with Thomas and also scheduled to visit with Thomas a few days later. The night before the scheduled visit, Jeana (D) left with Thomas to America. Emanuel (P) thus had custody rights and did not clearly abandon those rights prior to Thomas being removed and, therefore, the removal of Thomas was wrongful under the Convention. Furthermore, a grave risk of harm for purposes of the convention can

Continued on next page.

exist only when return of the child puts the child in imminent danger prior to the resolution of the custody dispute and/or where there is serious abuse or neglect or extraordinary emotional dependence and the court in the country of habitual residence is incapable of giving or unwilling to give the child adequate protection. Jeana (D) did not prove her affirmative defense by clear and convincing evidence that there was grave risk that the return of the child would expose it to physical or psychological harm. This defense requires more than evidence of adjustment problems that would attend to the relocation of most children without any allegation of abuse. Emanuel's (P) home that he prepared appeared to be adequate, he did not work long hours, and Emanuel's (P) mother was ready to care for the child when Emanuel (P) could not. There was no evidence that Thomas would experience permanent harm or unhappiness. Moreover, the issue of where the child would be happiest is to be reserved for the country of habitual residence. Jeana (D) also failed to prove her defense that Emanuel (P) consented to and acquiesced in the removal of Thomas to America. The deliberately secretive nature of her actions in removing Thomas is evidence that Emanuel (P) would not have consented to the removal of Thomas, and an isolated statement to a third party does not qualify as subsequent acquiescence. Acquiescence requires either an act or a statement with the requisite formality, and since Emanuel (P) immediately sought custody of his son once he was removed he did not acquiesce. Affirmed and stay order vacated.

► ANALYSIS

This court is placing a lot of confidence in a foreign court to determine what is best for the child in regard to custody.

Quicknotes

AFFIRMATIVE DEFENSES An assertion raised by the defendant in the answer, permitting the introduction of additional evidence to address or refute a plaintiff's allegations; affirmative defenses shift the burden of proof to the defendant to establish all the elements of the defense.

CHILD CUSTODY DECREE A court order awarding responsibility for the care and control over a child or children in a dissolution or separation proceeding.

CLEAR AND CONVINCING EVIDENCE An evidentiary standard requiring a demonstration that the fact sought to be proven is reasonably certain.

HABITUAL RESIDENCE Location where a person lives with the intent to remain for an unspecified time.

CHAPTER 9

Parental Rights Termination and Adoption

Quick Reference Rules of Law

Santosky v. Kramer

Parents (D) v. Commissioner of child services agency (P)

455 U.S. 745 (1982).

NATURE OF CASE: Appeal from judgment upholding constitutionality of a state child-neglect law.

FACT SUMMARY: The Santoskys (D) challenged the constitutionality of a New York statute which allowed the state to terminate the parental relationship by establishing the merits of its charges by a preponderance of the evidence.

🏛 RULE OF LAW
The Fourteenth Amendment guarantee of due process requires that before a state may completely sever parental rights, it must support its allegations by at least clear and convincing evidence.

FACTS: Kramer (P), Commissioner of the Ulster County Department of Social Services, initiated proceedings to terminate the Santoskys' (D) parental rights because of their alleged neglect. Under a New York statute, the trial court found Kramer (P) had proven the charges by a fair preponderance of the evidence and ordered the rights terminated. The Santoskys (D) appealed, contending the use of this standard of proof violated due process. The appellate court held the standard properly recognized and sought to balance rights possessed by the child with those of the parents. The Santoskys (D) appealed.

ISSUE: Does due process require that assertions be proved by clear and convincing evidence before parental rights may be terminated?

HOLDING AND DECISION: (Blackmun, J.) Yes. The Fourteenth Amendment guarantee of due process requires that before a state may completely sever parental rights, it must support its allegations by clear and convincing evidence. A parent's right to the companionship, care, custody, and management of his child is a far greater interest than an ordinary property right and requires more procedural protections. The risk of error in terminating such rights is unacceptably increased through the use of the preponderance standard. Further, because the state's ability to prepare its case is vastly superior to that of the parents, the risk of error rises even more. Therefore, the standard of proof allowed by the statute allowed the state to terminate parental rights without due process and was invalid. Vacated and remanded.

DISSENT: (Rehnquist, J.) The statutory procedures render the process fundamentally fair. The Court was shortsighted in invalidating it merely because of the standard of proof. The removals occurred after shockingly abusive treatment. The Santoskys (D) received extensive counseling and rehabilitative services, but minimally responded or participated. The agency attempted to reunite the family for an extraordinary four years with the Santoskys (D) failing to respond at every level. The majority almost completely disregards these facts. The standard of proof, in any event, clearly evidences a constitutionally permissible balance of interests. The focus should be on the interests to be protected rather than solely on the standard applied. One interest is in the protection of the family unit and parental interests in custody. The other interest is that of the child's in a stable, loving home environment. The State also has an interest in the welfare of the child. The risk of error should not be allocated to one interest over another. The preponderance of the evidence standard permissibly balances the risk of error among all interests.

▶ ANALYSIS

In *In re T.R.*, 502 Pa. 165 (1983), the Pennsylvania Supreme Court expanded the rule articulated in this case by holding that the clear and convincing evidence standard did not apply only to state action to terminate parental rights. Even where the party asserting the charges is a parent or an interested third party, the preponderance standard violates due process.

■━■

Quicknotes

CHILD NEGLECT Conduct on the part of a parent or guardian that demonstrates unfitness on the part of that individual to provide the proper care and control over the child, resulting in harm or potential harm to the child's physical or mental health.

CLEAR AND CONVINCING EVIDENCE An evidentiary standard requiring a demonstration that the fact sought to be proven is reasonably certain.

DUE PROCESS RIGHTS The constitutional mandate requiring the courts to protect and enforce individuals' rights and liberties consistent with prevailing principles of fairness and justice, and prohibiting the federal and state governments from such activities that deprive its citizens of a life, liberty or property interest.

PREPONDERANCE OF THE EVIDENCE A standard of proof requiring the trier of fact to determine whether the fact sought to be established is more probable than not.

TERMINATION OF PARENTAL RIGHTS The purposeful cessation of lawfully recognized rights between a child and its parents and of the parent to the child, including physical

Continued on next page.

possession of the child, companionship and support, the right to discipline the child, and control over the child's property.

■■═■

In re K.A.W.

Division of family services (P) v. Mother (D)

Mo. Sup. Ct., 133 S.W.3d 1 (2004) (en banc).

NATURE OF CASE: Appeal from termination of parental rights.

FACT SUMMARY: T.W. (D) had her parental rights terminated based on her decision to place her twins with multiple adoptive parents and her alleged emotional instability.

🏛 RULE OF LAW
The trial court must make findings on all statutory factors when terminating parental rights and the evidence must be clear, cogent, and convincing.

FACTS: T.W. (D), a single working mother of three and Missouri resident learned she was pregnant with twin girls. T.W. (D) decided to give them up for adoption. The twins were born three months premature and were in the hospital for two months. T.W. (D) expressed breast milk for them, visited with them daily, took a class for parents of premature infants, and then gave them their required medications hourly when they were released to go home. T.W. (D) investigated potential adoptive families during this time. T.W. (D) consulted with adoption professionals and attorneys during her search. She and the twins spent ten days with a couple in California and then traveled from California to Arkansas with a British couple. Media reports suggested that T.W. (D) sold the twins on the Internet, but an investigation failed to substantiate the allegations. T.W. (D) selected the British couple as the adoptive parents for the twins. She wanted an open adoption but was informed that Missouri did not permit such adoptions. She was encouraged to claim Arkansas residency but decided not to do so and simply listed a relative's Arkansas address on the adoption paperwork. An Arkansas judge signed the adoption order and the British couple took the twins to England. British authorities later found the couple to be unfit. The Arkansas court set aside the adoption judgment on the basis that no one was an Arkansas resident and thus the court lacked jurisdiction. The twins returned to Missouri and were placed in the custody of the Missouri Division of Family Services (DFS) (P). T.W. (D) decided to raise the twins and entered into a parenting plan with DFS to regain custody. T.W. (D) complied fully with the parenting plan and met each of her goals. Despite her compliance, DFS (P) filed a petition to terminate T.W.'s (D) parental rights. The petition claimed that T.W. (D) committed emotional abuse toward the twins by placing them in multiple homes within the first few months of their life, that T.W. (D) was emotionally unable to care for the twins, that the twins suffered from "Reactive Detachment (*sic*) Disorder" because of T.W.'s (D) ongoing

emotional abuse, and that the twins' adoption would be in their best interests. The trial court terminated T.W.'s (D) parental rights and T.W. (D) appeals.

ISSUE: Must the trial court make findings on all statutory factors when terminating parental rights and must the evidence be clear, cogent, and convincing?

HOLDING AND DECISION: (Teitelman, J.) Yes. The trial court must make findings on all statutory factors when terminating parental rights and the evidence must be clear, cogent, and convincing. In terminating parental rights based on abuse or neglect, a court must consider whether a child will be harmed by a continued relationship with his parent. The court cannot rest on past behavior or circumstances because a parent must be given the opportunity to correct past wrongs and learn new behaviors. Another consideration is whether the cited conduct justifying the termination actually has had or will have a detrimental impact on the child, and whether that impact is severe enough to constitute abuse. Severity may be measured by statutory guidance or can be a case-by-case basis if a pattern is demonstrated. Here, the trial court cited T.W.'s (D) multiple placements of the twins in unstable and temporary homes as a basis for termination. To the contrary, the evidence does not show that the first home in California was unstable. Second, the trial court's reference to placements "in Arkansas and Great Britain" is referring to a single placement with one couple. T.W. (D) admittedly placed the twins for adoption twice, but that does not constitute abuse. It certainly does not constitute severe abuse, even if it is a character flaw. The trial court also found that T.W. (D) could not emotionally care for the twins because of her stress level. It is hardly unimaginable that a single working mother of five would be stressed. The expert hired by DFS (P) found that T.W.'s (D) stress level was average with other single parents. T.W.'s (D) emotional fortitude is not so lacking to justify termination. The trial court found that the twins suffered from "Reactive Detachment (sic) Disorder." The actual diagnosis, Reactive Attachment Disorder, was made by one physician and vehemently disagreed with by two clinical psychologists. The physician did not observe the twins with T.W. (D) and the two psychologists did. Finally, the trial court erred in not considering all requisite factors when terminating T.W.'s (D) parental rights pursuant to the abuse/neglect statute. The trial court does not have discretion in determining which factor to consider. The termination occurred because T.W. (D) tried to find an appropriate adoptive family for her twins. The evidence does not support the

Continued on next page.

supposition that T.W. (D) did so for personal gain. Termination of parental rights without consent requires clear, cogent, and convincing evidence of at least one statutory basis. The evidence fails here. Reversed and remanded.

DISSENT: (Price, J.) The trial court is in the best position to determine the credibility of witnesses and the trial court can believe all, part, or none of a witness's testimony. Here, the trial court found that T.W. (D) committed a pattern of emotional abuse when she placed her children for adoption in multiple homes with multiple couples. The evidence fully supports this finding. The trial court also found that T.W.'s (D) pattern was ongoing and of such duration that she would be unable to adequately care for the twins in the future. The evidence also supports this finding. T.W. (D) was on medication to prevent premature labor, but she was "tired of being pregnant" and stopped taking the medication on her own volition. T.W. (D) missed a vital first medical appointment for the twins. She testified that the twins' father told her no man would want five children. T.W. (D) first placed the twins with the California couple because they were wealthy. She did so despite knowing of the criminal record of one of them. She testified that she called them on a daily basis after placing the twins with them and then felt put out when they made her feel like a pest. She later learned they were having financial trouble, so she removed the twins from their home on false pretenses six weeks later. She almost immediately transferred custody of the twins to the British couple. A DFS (P) investigator testified that T.W. (D) gave them custody because she thought they would fly her to Great Britain annually for the twins' birthday. T.W. (D) only objected to the twins' placement with the British couple when media reports surfaced that she had sold her twins on the internet. T.W. (D) violated Missouri statutory law when she placed the twins with the sets of parents because parents cannot give away their children to "new owners." The twins have only been with their mother a total of 52 days since their birth. After her repeated placements with other parents, the twins have resided with foster parents where they have an adopted sibling. They are living in a stable environment responsive to their needs and the evidence does not show that their mother can provide that for them. The majority improperly searches the trial record for evidence contrary to the trial court's finding. The standard of review is such that the trial court's decision should be upheld so long as credible evidence supports it. Substantial, clear, cogent evidence supports the termination of T.W.'s (D) parental rights.

► ANALYSIS

Media reports on T.W.'s actions were sensational and worldwide. CNN, Oprah, American news, Canadian news, and British news outlets sparked outrage internationally. The media generally reported that Tranda Wecker placed her twin girls with an Internet-based adoption agency.

Richard and Vickie Allen, the California couple, applied through the agency to adopt the girls and paid $6,000.00 for them. Wecker placed the girls with the Allens for two months and then took them away suddenly because she got a higher offer from Alan and Judith Kilshaw, the British couple. The Kilshaws paid $17,000 for the twins. The world waited while the case went before the Arkansas court and the judge vacated the adoption. At the time, Gloria Allred represented Wecker. The truth likely lies somewhere between the media reports and the majority's opinion. Later the same year, Wecker pled guilty to federal welfare fraud charges. She and the twins' father, Aaron Wecker, began their fight for custody of the girls. The foster parents that had adopted the girls retained custody, but the Missouri Supreme Court overturned the adoption when it reversed the termination of Wecker's parental rights. In 2006, Wecker, now remarried, was allowed visitation rights with her girls, then five years old, and the foster parents were named their legal guardians.

Quicknotes

CHILD ABUSE Conduct harmful to a child's physical or mental health.

TERMINATION OF PARENTAL RIGHTS The purposeful cessation of lawfully recognized rights between a child and its parents and of the parent to the child, including physical possession of the child, companionship and support, the right to discipline the child, and control over the child's property.

New Jersey Division of Youth and Family Services v. B.G.S.

State social services department (P) v. Biological mother (D)

N.J. Super. Ct., 291 N.J. Super. 582, 677 A.2d 1170 (1996).

NATURE OF CASE: Appeal from order terminating parental rights.

FACT SUMMARY: B.G.S. (D) challenged an order terminating her parental rights of natural mother to her son, contending that the statutory criteria for termination were not satisfied by clear and convincing evidence.

🏛 RULE OF LAW
Parental rights may be terminated when a child's physical or mental health is jeopardized.

FACTS: M.A.S. had been in foster care for most of his five and one-half years. His mother, B.G.S. (D), had a bipolar disorder—manic depression—and a drug problem that rendered her incapable for caring for M.A.S. on a sustained basis. She also was involved in a highly dysfunctional relationship with a man who had abused both her and M.A.S. on occasion. For these reasons, the Division of Youth and Family Services (DYFS) (P) sought to terminate her parental rights. Although B.G.S. (D) conceded that she was unable to care for M.A.S. and did not seek to interfere with the custody arrangement with his foster family, she did assert that the termination of her parental rights was improper since it was not based on clear and convincing evidence.

ISSUE: May parental rights be terminated when a child's physical or mental health is jeopardized?

HOLDING AND DECISION: (Petrella, J.) Yes. Parental rights may be terminated when a child's physical or mental health is jeopardized. An action shall be initiated to terminate parental rights in the child's best interest if (1) the child's health and development would be endangered by the parental relationship; (2) the parent is unwilling or unable to eliminate the harm facing the child; (3) the court has considered alternatives to termination; and (4) termination of parental rights will not do more harm than good. In this case, DYFS (P) satisfied the four-prong test. M.A.S. is subject to continued psychological damage because of his need for a permanent home and identity. B.G.S. (D) is unable or unwilling to resolve the problems with respect to her mental health and substance abuse. DYFS (P) diligently tried to assist B.G.S. (D), but to no avail. Termination here would not do more harm than good since DYFS (P) has a permanent plan to satisfy M.A.S.'s needs in the form of adoption. Therefore, the order of termination of B.G.S's (D) parental rights is affirmed.

▶ ANALYSIS

As this case demonstrates, parental rights are not inviolate. New Jersey law effectuates a legislative policy that chil-

dren be placed in stable and permanent homes instead of indefinite long-term foster case. Once there is no longer any prospect that the natural parent can be rehabilitated and there is no available family member to provide care for the child, the child's need for stability and attachment to an adoptive family become paramount.

■■■

Quicknotes

CLEAR AND CONVINCING EVIDENCE An evidentiary standard requiring a demonstration that the fact sought to be proven is reasonably certain.

NATURAL MOTHER The biological mother of a child, as opposed to a mother whose rights have either been assigned or are recognized by law.

TERMINATION OF PARENTAL RIGHTS The purposeful cessation of lawfully recognized rights between a child and its parents and of the parent to the child, including physical possession of the child, companionship and support, the right to discipline the child, and control over the child's property.

■■■

Matter of Gregory B.

Child care agency (P) v. Incarcerated father (D)

N.Y. Ct. App., 74 N.Y.2d 77, 542 N.E.2d 1052 (1989).

NATURE OF CASE: Appeal from a termination of parental rights.

FACT SUMMARY: In two separate cases, the matter of Gregory B. and the matter of Willie John B., both biological fathers contended the trial courts erred in finding permanent neglect because of their incarceration. Their only alternative plan for the care of their children was to keep them in foster care until their release.

RULE OF LAW

Parental rights of incarcerated parents may be terminated where a good-faith effort at familial reconciliation has occurred and no biological familial custodial option is available.

FACTS: In two separate cases, *In re Gregory B.* and *In re Willie John B.*, the biological fathers, the only parents available of minor children, were incarcerated throughout the period of their children's minority. In both cases, the fathers attempted to have the children placed with relatives. However, due to certain medical and psychological needs, the available relatives were not able to provide adequate care. The foster parents, through the state agency, petitioned for the termination of parental rights in anticipation of adopting the children. The parental rights were terminated, and the biological parents appealed, contending that due to statutory reforms, their incarceration could not be used as the basis for the termination of parental rights. It is only based upon such incarceration that they were adjudged permanently neglectful of their children. The appellate court affirmed, and the court of appeals granted a hearing.

ISSUE: May parental rights of incarcerated parents be terminated where a good-faith effort at familial reconciliation has occurred and no biological familial custodial option is available?

HOLDING AND DECISION: (Alexander, J.) Yes. Parental rights of incarcerated parents may be terminated where a good-faith effort at familial reconciliation has occurred and no biological familial custodial option is available. Incarceration alone cannot be the basis for a finding of permanent neglect and then termination of parental rights. The option of foster care until a release from prison or the child reaches majority is simply not viable. The Legislature has acknowledged the special circumstances of the incarcerated parent and has made allowances for meeting his or her obligations during incarceration. Indefinite foster care, however, was not the intended consequence. A child has a right to permanency and a loving, stable home environment. Affirmed.

ANALYSIS

While in the final analysis, the incarceration of the biological parents was at the source of the termination of the parental rights in this case, if there had been a viable option other than foster care, the parental rights would not have been terminated. If there had been a relative able to care for the minor children, then the nurturing of the familial relationship would have been completed due to the use of other family resources. However, because these were not available in these cases, the parental rights were terminated.

Quicknotes

BIOLOGICAL PARENTS A man and woman who conceive and give birth to a child.

CHILD NEGLECT Conduct on the part of a parent or guardian that demonstrates unfitness on the part of that individual to provide the proper care and control over the child, resulting in harm or potential harm to the child's physical or mental health.

TERMINATION OF PARENTAL RIGHTS The purposeful cessation of lawfully recognized rights between a child and its parents and of the parent to the child, including physical possession of the child, companionship and support, the right to discipline the child, and control over the child's property.

In re Jeffrey E.

State (P) v. Biological parents (D)

Me. Sup. Ct., 557 A.2d 954 (1989).

NATURE OF CASE: Appeal from a termination of parental rights.

FACT SUMMARY: The parents of Jeffrey E., Linda and James E., appealed from a termination of their parental rights on the basis that the trial court entered a termination order that was not supported by clear and convincing evidence of neglect.

> ## 🏛 RULE OF LAW
> The termination of parental rights must be supported by clear and convincing evidence of neglect.

FACTS: Jeffrey E., the fourth son of Linda and James E., was diagnosed with pneumonia and hospitalized. The physicians released him to his parents' custody with complicated instructions as to his care. The parents were unable to follow these instructions, even with the aid of a nurse. Jeffrey was therefore removed from the familial residence and placed in foster care, where he improved both physically and mentally. He had been developmentally underachieved at this point. However, he improved substantially in foster care. A proceeding was brought to terminate the parental rights of the parents based upon neglect. Evidence was presented of three reunification plans following Jeffrey's placement in foster care. All of these plans failed due to a lack of effort and interest on the part of the parents. Further evidence was presented that the father was completely uninvolved in the nurturing of the children. Based upon such evidence, the trial court found by clear and convincing evidence that neglect had taken place and that the parents were unable or unwilling to protect Jeffrey from further medical, physical, and psychological jeopardy. The parental rights were therefore terminated. The parents appealed, contending the trial court's order was not based upon clear and convincing evidence.

ISSUE: Must the termination of parental rights be based upon clear and convincing evidence of neglect?

HOLDING AND DECISION: (Clifford, J.) Yes. The termination of parental rights must be supported by clear and convincing evidence of neglect. In this case, the evidence was clear that there were three reunification plans which were rejected by the parents. Further, Jeffrey's substantial increase in mental and physical health following his placement in foster care is clearly evidence of the parents' neglect. The trial court's finding that the parents were unable or unwilling to protect Jeffrey from further physical and psychological jeopardy was clearly supported by clear

and convincing evidence on the record. As a result, the order must be affirmed.

▶ ANALYSIS

This case should be contrasted with *Rivera v. Minnich*, 483 U.S. 574 (1987). In that case, an argument was made by a putative father that the establishment of a parental relationship must be based upon the same standard of proof that the termination of a parental relationship uses. In this case, the clear and convincing evidence standard was applied to terminate the parental relationship. In *Rivera*, a preponderance of the evidence standard was applied and was upheld as consistent with due process principles in the creation of a parental relationship. The court in *Rivera* indicated that the creation and termination of parental relationships do not involve the same public interests, and therefore the standards do not necessarily have to be the same.

Quicknotes

CHILD NEGLECT Conduct on the part of a parent or guardian that demonstrates unfitness on the part of that individual to provide the proper care and control over the child, resulting in harm or potential harm to the child's physical or mental health.

CLEAR AND CONVINCING EVIDENCE An evidentiary standard requiring a demonstration that the fact sought to be proven is reasonably certain.

TERMINATION OF PARENTAL RIGHTS The purposeful cessation of lawfully recognized rights between a child and its parents and of the parent to the child, including physical possession of the child, companionship and support, the right to discipline the child, and control over the child's property.

Wyatt v McDermott

Biological father (P) v. Adoption attorney (D)

Va. Sup. Ct., 283 Va. 685, 725 S.E.2d 555 (2012).

NATURE OF CASE: Certification of a question to the state's highest court.

FACT SUMMARY: A child identified as E.Z. was born to Colleen Fahland (Colleen) and Wyatt Fahland (Wyatt) (P), who were unmarried. Wyatt (P) brought suit against Colleen's attorney McDermott (D) and others for inducing Colleen to give the child away to an out-of-state couple for adoption.

🏛 **RULE OF LAW**

The Commonwealth of Virginia recognizes tortious interference with parental rights as a cause of action.

FACTS: Colleen Fahland (Colleen) gave birth to a child identified as "E.Z.," whose biological father is Wyatt Fahland (Wyatt) (P). Colleen and Wyatt (D) were unmarried. [It is not explained in the opinion why Colleen and Wyatt (P) have the same last name.] During the course of the pregnancy, Colleen continuously informed Wyatt (P) that they would raise the baby as a family. She did, however, consult with an adoption attorney, Mark McDermott (D) and others who encouraged here to make false statements to Wyatt (P) while contemplating and effectuating an adoption with an out-of-state couple. Colleen (D) concealed the fact that she was in labor and did not tell Wyatt (P) that she did give birth to E.Z. Colleen (D) later signed an affidavit of relinquishment and transferred custody to the out-of-state couple, who had travelled to Virginia to pick up the child. Wyatt (P) brought suit alleging that all the defendants, including McDermott (D), had induced Colleen to waive her parental rights although they knew she did not want to relinquish rights to the baby and that Wyatt (P) believed he would have parental rights. Although Wyatt (P) was ultimately awarded custody by the juvenile and domestic relations courts; the out-of-state courts have awarded custody of E.Z. to the adopting family. Wyatt (P) filed an action in the district court against McDermott (D) and others, seeking compensatory and punitive damages for the unauthorized adoption as well as a declaratory judgment asserting numerous claims, including one for tortious interference with parental rights. Upon consideration of a motion to dismiss filed by McDermott (D) and the other defendants, the district court denied the motion as to the claim for tortious interference with parental rights pending its request to the appellate court as to whether Virginia recognized such a cause of action.

ISSUE: Does the Commonwealth of Virginia recognize tortious interference with parental rights as a cause of action?

HOLDING AND DECISION: (Millette, J.) Yes. The Commonwealth of Virginia recognizes tortious interference with parental rights as a cause of action. As the statutory basis for tortious interference with parental rights is clearly absent from the Virginia Code, the court must therefore focus our analysis on whether this tort exists at common law. The conclusion is that, although no Virginia court has had occasion to consider the cause of action, the tort in question has indeed existed at common law and continues to exist today. Furthermore, rejecting tortious interference with parental rights as a legitimate cause of action would leave a substantial gap in the legal protection afforded to the parent-child relationship.

There is an essential value of protecting a parent's right to form a relationship with his or her child. The court has previously acknowledged that "the relationship between a parent and child is constitutionally protected by the Due Process Clause of the Fourteenth Amendment." Indeed, the Supreme Court of the United States has characterized a parent's right to raise his or her child as "perhaps the oldest of the fundamental liberty interests recognized by this Court." It follows, then, that a parent has a cause of action against third parties who seek to interfere with this right. In the analogous case of *Chaves v. Johnson*, 230 Va. 112, 335 S.E.2d 97 (1985), the court explicitly recognized the common-law tort of tortious interference with contract rights for the first time, noting its historical basis in the Commonwealth. In *Chaves*, the court did not create a new tort but rather recognized that the common law provided a cause of action for tortious interference with contract rights. The historical happenstance that the tort in question had not previously been invoked in Virginia did not prevent the court from recognizing that the common-law right of contract necessarily brought with it, as a corollary, a right to seek recompense against those who interfered with a valid contract. Noting the recognition of tortious interference with contract by many of our sister states, by many English courts, and in the Restatement of Torts, the court concluded that a claim for tortious interference with contract could be brought in Virginia. It would be remarkable indeed if the common-law right to be free from interference in contract were to be deemed to be more valuable than the common-law right of a parent to be free from interference in a relationship with his or her child.

In this case, following the blueprint set forth in *Chaves*, we would not be creating a new tort, but rather recognizing that the common-law right to establish and maintain a relationship with one's child necessarily implies a cause of

Continued on next page.

action for interference with that right. To hold otherwise in this case would be to recognize "a right without a remedy—a thing unknown to the law."

It is acknowledged that the most direct and proper remedy, the return of the child and restoration of the parent-child relationship, may never be achieved through a tort action. When a parent has been unduly separated from a child by a third party for a substantial period of time without due process of law, however, other legitimate harms may be suffered that are properly recoverable in tort, including loss of companionship, mental anguish, loss of services, and expenses incurred to recover the child.

An examination of our law shows that the redress of these wrongs is in some circumstances otherwise unavailable in the Commonwealth. Wrongful custodial interference is codified as a criminal offense, but this statute provides no civil recovery. Virginia also has well-developed custody laws to manage intra-familial disputes, but custody disputes do not implicate rights or duties of third parties, such as are at issue here. The Commonwealth provides for causes of action for fraud and constructive fraud, but a third party can wrongfully interfere with parental rights without engaging in fraudulent behavior. There remain many cognizable scenarios in which intentional tortious interference with parental rights could be invoked not as a legal redundancy, but as a unique remedy. The recognition of tortious interference with parental rights finds precedent in our common law. Prior to 1607, a comparable cause of action did lie in England, providing a father with recourse for the abduction of his heir or sons rendering services.

Clearly, there are ways in which this ancient writ is markedly different from the modern cause of action urged by Wyatt (P), which would permit recourse for either parent, regardless of gender, and which encompasses a recovery not merely for loss of services but also for loss of companionship. This difference reflects society's changing values as reflected in this Court's rulings over the centuries, including principles of gender equality, an inherent value in the relationship between parents and their children beyond the value of services rendered, and the modern trend in tort law to make plaintiffs whole by compensating not only pure pecuniary loss but also emotional harm. The overwhelming majority of the high courts of our sister states that have considered the issue have also recognized such a tort, many of them tracing its evolution in the common law.

The Court is now left to determine what elements are essential to the tort as it exists today, consistent with the original writ, but in line with equal protection and modern law. *Kessel v. Leavitt*, 204 W.Va. 95, 511 S.E.2d 720 (1998) succinctly lays out the elements of this cause of action, consistent with Virginia law: (1) the complaining parent has a right to establish or maintain a parental or custodial relationship with his/her minor child; (2) a party outside of the relationship between the complaining parent and his/her child intentionally interfered with the complaining parent's parental or custodial relationship with his/her

child by removing or detaining the child from returning to the complaining parent, without that parent's consent, or by otherwise preventing the complaining parent from exercising his/her parental or custodial rights; (3) the outside party's intentional interference caused harm to the complaining parent's parental or custodial relationship with his/her child; and (4) damages resulted from such interference.

Given the nature of the original English common-law writ, the court must consider whether the harm and recoverable damages must be limited solely to tangible loss of service. As has been previously stated, if a tortfeasor's tort was intentional rather than negligent, i.e., deliberately committed with intent to harm the victim, and if the evidence is sufficient to support an award of compensatory damages, the victim's right to punitive damages and the quantum thereof are jury questions. The court adheres to the ordinary burden in civil actions of preponderance of the evidence. Although, as with many torts, juries may award some compensation for mental anguish in intentional interference cases, the harm lies in the physical interruption of the parent-child relationship, a concrete factor. Thus, the court concludes that the ordinary burden of preponderance of the evidence is appropriate for a claim of intentional interference with parental rights.

The minority of states that have resisted recognition of tortious interference with parental or custodial rights have done so based on policy grounds, citing concern for the best interest of the child. This court shares these courts' concern for the well-being of children caught in intra-familial disputes, a concern that was not as prominent an issue in 1607, when only a male parent could bring this cause of action. The fear that this cause of action would be used as a means of escalating intra-familial warfare can be largely disposed of by barring the use of this tort between parents, as other state courts have done. Additionally, in the interest of the child, this court has noted with approval the affirmative defense of justification as set forth in *Kessel*, wherein the court held that a party should not be held liable if he or she "possessed a reasonable, good faith belief that interference with the parent's parental or custodial relationship was necessary to protect the child from physical, mental, or emotional harm[; or] possessed a reasonable, good faith belief that the interference was proper (i.e., no notice or knowledge of an original or superseding judicial decree awarding parental or custodial rights to complaining parent); or reasonably and in good faith believed that the complaining parent did not have a right to establish or maintain a parental or custodial relationship with the minor child (i.e., mistake as to identity of child's biological parents where paternity has not yet been formally established)."

Often, in considering a certified question of law, the facts of a particular case serve only to define the scope of

Continued on next page.

the inquiry to yield a determinative answer for the presiding court. In this instance, however, the facts as pled are illustrative of the basis and continuing need for this action in tort. It is both astonishing and profoundly disturbing that in this case, a biological mother and her parents, with the aid of two licensed attorneys and an adoption agency, could intentionally act to prevent a biological father—who is in no way alleged to be an unfit parent—from legally establishing his parental rights and gaining custody of a child whom the mother did not want to keep, and that this father would have no recourse in the law. The facts as pled indicate that McDermott (D) and the other defendants went to great lengths to disguise their agenda from the biological father, including preventing notice of his daughter's birth and hiding their intent to have an immediate out-of-state adoption, in order to prevent the legal establishment of his own parental rights. This court has long recognized that the rights of an unwed father are deserving of protection. The tort of tortious interference with parental rights may provide one means of such protection. Finally, there is the hope that the threat of a civil action would help deter third parties such as attorneys and adoption agencies from engaging in the sort of actions alleged to have taken place. For the aforementioned reasons, the certified question is answered in the affirmative

DISSENT: (McClanahan, J.) While the facts as pled by Wyatt (P) are unquestionably disturbing, I cannot join the majority's effort to deter such conduct by legislating public policy in Virginia through judicial pronouncement. Because the tort of interference with parental rights currently exists in Virginia, the decision of whether to create such a cause of action should be left to the legislature in light of the competing and far-reaching public policy considerations that are involved. To recognize a new theory of liability involves a multitude of competing interests.

In creating an action for tortious interference with parental rights arising from an unauthorized adoption, there are many significant and varying interests that will be affected. The interests of the biological parents, the adoptive parents, and the child are impacted as well as the legitimate interest in facilitating adoptions for those who seek to place their child for adoption and for those who wish to be adoptive parents. The recognition of this new cause of action also affects the operations and actions of adoption agencies, adoption attorneys, and other professionals or governmental agencies involved in the adoption process, which may be subject to liability. Furthermore, the General Assembly has already enacted specific provisions governing the rights of the biological and adoptive parents.

▌ ANALYSIS

Analogy to other tort actions assisted the court in affirming Wyatt's (P) belief that there was a right to relief. The key motivation of the court can be found in the portion of the opinion which stated, "To hold otherwise would be to

recognize a right without a remedy—a thing unknown to the law." Having decided that the cause of action existed at common law, the court broke new ground by offering the elements and potential defenses. The dissent's worry is that judge-made causes of action are to be discouraged in light of the conflict with the role of the legislature.

Quicknotes

INTENTIONAL TORT A legal wrong resulting in a breach of duty, which is intentionally or purposefully committed by the wrongdoer.

M.H. and J.L.H. v. Caritas Family Services

Adoptive parents (P) v. Adoption agency (D)

Minn. Sup. Ct., 488 N.W.2d 282 (1992).

NATURE OF CASE: Certified question arising in the context of an intentional and negligent misrepresentation claim.

FACT SUMMARY: Caritas Family Services (D) gave the H.'s (P) some vague warnings about incest in the background of the baby whom the H.'s (P) were arranging to adopt but did not tell them that the baby had been parented by a boy and his sister.

🏛 RULE OF LAW
Public policy does not bar a negligent misrepresentation action against an adoption agency when the agency, having undertaken to disclose information about the child's background, negligently withholds information in such a way that the adoptive parents are misled as to the truth.

FACTS: The H.'s (P) contacted Caritas Family Services (D), a Catholic social service agency, to obtain assistance in adopting a child. When a Caritas (D) social worker told the H.'s (P) that a child was available but that there was a possibility of incest in the family, Mr. H. (P) responded that it did not matter. After being assured that the baby's genetic father was in good health, the H's (P) adopted the baby. They soon discovered that the child had serious behavioral and emotional problems. Caritas (D) subsequently disclosed that the baby's genetic parents were a seventeen-year-old boy and his thirteen-year-old sister, information that Caritas (D) had known all along. Caritas (D) also disclosed that the father was borderline hyperactive. The H.'s (P) filed suit against Caritas (D), alleging negligent and intentional misrepresentation. The district court denied Caritas's (D) motion for summary judgment on negligent misrepresentation on policy grounds, and the court of appeals affirmed. The state supreme court accepted the following certified question.

ISSUE: Does public policy bar a negligent misrepresentation action against an adoption agency?

HOLDING AND DECISION: (Wahl, J.) No. Public policy does not bar a negligent misrepresentation action against an adoption agency when the agency, having undertaken to disclose information about the child's background, negligently withholds information in such a way that the adoptive parents are misled as to the truth. Tort liability depends on whether the party accused of the tort owes a duty to the accusing party. Caritas (D) argues that imposing such a duty on adoption agencies would unreasonably burden them, discourage adoptions of difficult-to-place children, and conflict with confidentiality policies. To the contrary, recognizing such a duty would give potential parents more confidence in the accuracy of the information they receive and in the adoption process itself. In this case, Caritas (D) had a legal duty not to mislead the H.'s (P) by only partially disclosing the truth. However, there is no evidence that Caritas (D) intended to mislead the H.'s (P) by deliberately withholding the full facts regarding incest. Reversed, denial of punitive damages by trial court affirmed, and remanded.

▶ ANALYSIS

A few courts have recognized a cause of action for "wrongful adoption" based on facts similar to the above case. See, e.g., *Burr v. Board of County Commissioners of Stark City*, 491 N.E.2d 1101 (1986), in which the Burrs were promised a nice, healthy baby boy born to an eighteen-year-old mother who turned out to be in actuality a thirty-one-year-old woman institutionalized with mental problems. The court held that the agency would be liable if the Burrs could prove fraud by demonstrating the following: that the agency made a material representation or concealed a material fact, falsely, with the intent of misleading the Burrs and that the Burrs justifiably relied on the misrepresentation, resulting in injury.

Quicknotes

INTENTIONAL MISREPRESENTATION A statement or conduct by one party to another that constitutes a false representation of fact.

NEGLIGENT MISREPRESENTATION A misrepresentation that is made pursuant to a business relationship, in violation of an obligation owed, upon which the plaintiff relies to his detriment.

PUBLIC POLICY Policy administered by the state with respect to the health, safety and morals of its people in accordance with common notions of fairness and decency.

Ann Marie N. v. City and County of San Francisco

Adoptive mother (P) v. Governmental agencies (D)

Cal. Ct. App., 2001 WL 1261958 (2001).

NATURE OF CASE: Appeal from nonsuit on claim of intentional concealment.

FACT SUMMARY: Ann Marie N.'s (P) adopted son, Mathew, was HIV-positive. Ann Marie N. (P) did not learn about his status until after the adoption was finalized. She would not have adopted Mathew had she known of his status.

🏛 RULE OF LAW
An adoption agency is not liable for mere negligence in providing health information of a prospective adoptee but it might be liable for intentional concealment of known information.

FACTS: Ann Marie N. (P) adopted Mathew N. in 1988. Mathew's biological mother abused drugs and alcohol during pregnancy and was involved in prostitution. Ann Marie N. (P) indicated on a form prior to Mathew's adoption that she did not want to adopt a child with a "blood disorder." She later learned Mathew's biological mother died from AIDS and she took her son to be tested. Mathew was positive for HIV. Ann Marie N. (P) would not have adopted Mathew if she had known he was HIV-positive. She filed a petition against the City and County of San Francisco ("the City") (D) alleging intentional misrepresentation of Mathew's health and intentional concealment of Mathew's HIV status. The City (D) had policies in place that employees should inform prospective adoptive parents of children at "high risk" for HIV infection. The trial court granted summary judgment to the City (D) on the intentional misrepresentation claim but found a triable issue of material fact on whether City (D) personnel failed to disclose Mathew's birth mother was involved in prostitution. At trial, Ann Marie N. (P) testified she did not recall much of her conversation with City's (D) social worker, Bill Holman. She did not recall him telling her anything about Mathew's birth mother's involvement with prostitution. City (D) called Holman out of order to testify he did not know Mathew was at risk for HIV infection. Ann Marie N. (P) called the City's then-director of Children's Services as an adverse witness to testify regarding risk factors for HIV infection. The parties stipulated another witness would testify to the number of infants with AIDS in San Francisco in 1987. After Ann Marie N.'s (P) evidence, City (D) moved for nonsuit. The trial court granted the motion, noting Holman denied knowing Mathew was at risk for HIV and no evidence refuted his testimony. Ann Marie N. (P) appealed.

ISSUE: Is an adoption agency liable for mere negligence in providing health information of a prospective adoptee?

HOLDING AND DECISION: (Kay, J.) No. An adoption agency is not liable for mere negligence in providing health information of a prospective adoptee but it might be liable for intentional concealment of known information. Ann Marie N. (P) argues the court should overturn prior case law as other states now recognize negligent misrepresentation. Ann Marie N. (P), however, fails to cite evidence the City (D) failed to comply with the statutory requirement of delivery of a medical report. The summary judgment on the negligence claim was appropriate. On the claim of intentional concealment, Mr. Holman's testimony was out of order, so it should have been disregarded for purposes of the nonsuit. The only relevant testimony was that of Ann Marie N. (P), the adverse witness's testimony favorable to Ann Marie N.'s (P) case, and the stipulated testimony. Ann Marie N. (P) testified Mr. Holman did not give her information about Mathew's health. She was not given his medical records until after the adoption was final, she was not told about the risk of HIV to an infant born addicted to drugs, nor was she told Mathew's biological mother was involved with prostitution. The adverse witness's testimony favorable to Ann Marie N. (P) referenced risk factors for HIV-infection, including drug abuse and a mother who had sexual contact with an infected person. There is no direct evidence Mr. Holman concealed Mathew's HIV risk, but a jury could have inferred concealment from his silence on Mathew's health and his birth mother's history. Reversed as to the nonsuit on intentional concealment; affirmed in all other respects.

▶ ANALYSIS

Some states permit an adoption to be annulled or "disrupted" if state actors or agencies concealed information about an adoptee's disability or mental health. The concealment could be intentional or a failure to adequately investigate known risk factors.

■=■

Quicknotes

INTENTIONAL CONCEALMENT A deliberate lack of full disclosure of facts with the intent that another will rely on the misrepresentation to his detriment.

■=■

Michaud v. Wawruck

Biological mother (P) v. Adoptive parent (D)

Conn. Sup. Ct., 209 Conn. 407, 551 A.2d 738 (1988).

NATURE OF CASE: Appeal from order denying enforcement of a visitation agreement.

FACT SUMMARY: The trial court held that a visitation agreement allowing Michaud (P), the natural mother, visitation with the child adopted by Wawruck (D), violated public policy and was unenforceable.

🏛 RULE OF LAW
Visitation agreements between natural and adoptive parents are not per se violative of public policy.

FACTS: Michaud (P) had her parental rights in her natural child severed by court order pursuant to her alleged consent. She sued to reinstate such rights, contending her consent to such, and a resulting adoption, had been fraudulently procured. Wawruck (D), the adoptive parent, intervened in that action. Michaud (P) agreed to drop the suit in exchange for a written visitation agreement allowing her continued visitation rights. Wawruck (D) agreed; however, after the adoption was finalized, he cut off all rights of visitation. Michaud (P) sued to enforce the visitation agreement, yet the trial court granted Wawruck's (D) motion to strike the complaint. The court held that such "side" agreements were contrary to public policy. The case was transferred to the Connecticut Supreme Court.

ISSUE: Are visitation agreements between natural and adoptive parents against public policy per se?

HOLDING AND DECISION: (Peters, C.J.) No. Visitation agreements between natural and adoptive parents are not per se violative of public policy. If the continued visitation of the natural parents is, under the circumstances of a particular case, in the best interest of the child, the agreement is not against public policy. Thus, it cannot be stated as a matter of law that all such agreements are invalid. This case must be remanded for further findings on the impact of the agreement on the best interest of the child.

▶ ANALYSIS

The case presented here illustrates what is sometimes known as "open adoption." This is somewhat of a misnomer because the adoption itself is complete. The natural parent has had all rights severed. The visitation is analyzed just as if the natural parent had merely developed a relationship with the child. The question thus becomes whether this relationship should be severed or continued.

Quicknotes

ADOPTIVE PARENTS A couple who are not a child's natural parents, but with respect to whom the child is vested with the rights and privileges of a natural child.

BEST INTERESTS OF CHILD Standard used by courts when rendering decisions which involve a child or children.

BIOLOGICAL PARENTS A man and woman who conceive and give birth to a child.

PUBLIC POLICY Policy administered by the state with respect to the health, safety and morals of its people in accordance with common notions of fairness and decency.

Mississippi Band of Choctaw Indians v. Holyfield

Native American tribe (P) v. Adoptive parents (D)

490 U.S. 30 (1989).

NATURE OF CASE: Appeal from adoption order.

FACT SUMMARY: The trial court held that because the minor children were not born on, nor had they ever lived on, the reservation, the Tribe (P) had no jurisdiction over their adoption.

RULE OF LAW

Indian tribes have exclusive jurisdiction over child custody and adoption of Indian children domiciled on the reservation.

FACTS: Twin babies were born to members and domiciliaries of the Choctaw Tribe (P) and reservation. The children were born off the reservation and immediately placed for adoption with Holyfield (D), a non-Indian. The state court confirmed the adoption pursuant to a consent decree signed by the parents. The Tribe (P) moved to vacate the adoption order on the basis that it had exclusive jurisdiction over the adoption under the Indian Child Welfare Act of 1978 (ICWA). The court denied the motion on the basis that because the children were not born on, nor had they ever resided on, the reservation, they were not domiciliaries of the reservation, and thus the Tribe (P) did not have exclusive jurisdiction over the adoption. The court of appeals affirmed, and the Supreme Court granted review.

ISSUE: Do Indian tribes have exclusive jurisdiction over child custody and adoption of Indian children domiciled on the reservation?

HOLDING AND DECISION: (Brennan, J.) Yes. Indian tribes have exclusive jurisdiction over child custody and adoption of children domiciled on the reservation. The definition of domicile under the ICWA must be interpreted in light of national Indian policy; thus, a federal definition providing uniformity must be used. While the children were not born on the reservation and never resided there, they are still domiciliaries because their parents were domiciliaries at the time of birth. Thus, as domiciliaries, their adoption came under the exclusive jurisdiction of the Tribe (P). The state court had no jurisdiction in the matter. Reversed and remanded.

DISSENT: (Stevens, J.) The parents' unambiguous wish was to have the children adopted and invoke the jurisdiction of the state court. The parents expended effort to avoid having the children placed for adoption on the reservation and the parents appear on behalf of the Holyfields (D). The ICWA was intended to prevent the unwarranted removal of children of Indian descent. The ICWA provides safeguards and responsibilities. The ICWA

is not meant to defeat a parent's choice of jurisdiction. The tribe retains exclusive jurisdiction when a child is temporarily off the reservation. That is not the case here.

ANALYSIS

The adoption of Indian children presents a unique problem. Statistics have shown a remarkably high incidence of the removal of such children from natural parents. Along with this has been an unusual placement of such children in non-Indian homes. This was thought to threaten the Indian culture and led to passage of the ICWA. The ICWA is not an all-encompassing statute, and courts are required to supplement its provisions by analogizing from state and federal law.

Quicknotes

ADOPTION DECREE A court order terminating the parental rights of a child's natural parents and vesting the child with the rights and privileges of a natural child in respect to his adoptive parents.

JURISDICTION The authority of a court to hear and declare judgment in respect to a particular matter.

Adoption of F.H.

Native American village and state agency (P) v. Adoptive parents (D)

Alaska Sup. Ct., 851 P.2d 1361 (1993).

NATURE OF CASE: Appeal from adoption decree.

FACT SUMMARY: The Native Village of Noatak and the State of Alaska Division of Family and Youth Services (DFYS) opposed the adoption of F.H., an Indian child, by the Hartleys, a non-Indian couple.

🏛 RULE OF LAW
A court may reverse an adoptive placement preference determination only if there has been an abuse of discretion or if controlling factual findings are clearly erroneous.

FACTS: DFYS took custody of F.H. shortly after her birth, based on her mother's homelessness and high blood alcohol level at the time of her birth. The Hartleys were F.H.'s third foster placement. While F.H. was in foster care, the mother, E.P.D., relinquished her parental rights to the Hartleys, conditioned upon the Hartley's adoption of F.H. and E.P.D.'s retention of contact and visitation rights. F.H.'s native village of Noatak and the State of Alaska DFYS filed a motion for reconsideration, contending that F.H. should be adopted by E.P.D.'s cousin, Mary Penn, instead. Noatak and DFYS relied on the Indian Child Welfare Act (ICWA), which provides that in any adoptive placement of an Indian child, a preference shall be given, in the absence of good cause to the contrary, to a placement with a member of the child's extended family, other members of the child's tribe, or other Indian families. The judge, however, found good cause to deviate from ICWA's preferences based on E.P.D.'s preference for the Hartleys, the bond between Nancy Hartley and F.H., the uncertainty of F.H.'s future if the adoption were not allowed, and the openness of the Hartleys' adoption. The judge denied the motion for reconsideration and the superior court granted a decree of adoption. DFYS and Noatak appealed.

ISSUE: May a court reverse an adoptive placement preference determination only if there has been an abuse of discretion or if controlling factual findings are clearly erroneous?

HOLDING AND DECISION: (Compton, J.) Yes. A court may reverse an adoptive placement preference determination only if there has been an abuse of discretion or if controlling factual findings are clearly erroneous. In this case, the factual findings that support deviation from ICWA preferences—i.e., maternal preference, bonding, the need for permanence, and the openness of the Hartleys' adoption—are not clearly erroneous. Furthermore, such findings address factors which are proper to consider in determining whether good cause exists to deviate from the preferences. The record as a whole reveals no abuse of discretion. Affirmed.

▶ ANALYSIS

ICWA was enacted to discourage the separation of Indian children from their families and tribes and to promote the stability and security of Indian tribes and families. Under Alaskan state law, the non-Indian adoptive parents have the burden of proof by preponderance of the evidence that there is good cause for allowing a non-preferred placement. Whether there is good cause to deviate in a particular case depends on many factors including, but not necessarily limited to, the best interests of the child, the wishes of the biological parents, the suitability of persons preferred for placement, and the child's ties to the tribe.

■=■

In the Matter of the Adoption of B.M.W.

Stepparent adopter (P) v. Father (D)

Kan. Sup. Ct., 268 Kan. 871, 2 P.3d 159 (2000).

NATURE OF CASE: Appeal of the court's denial of stepparent adoption.

FACT SUMMARY: Upon the petition of a stepfather (stepfather) (P) for adoption of minor stepchild, the district court found that even though the child's natural father (D) had failed to provide affection and care for the child and had paid only a portion of the court-ordered child support after a threat of contempt, the consent of the father (D) was still required. The stepfather (P) appealed, claiming a father need not fail both the financial and the affection, care, and interest aspects of parenting under the applicable state code provisions for the court to grant an adoption petition without the consent of the parent. The stepfather (P) asserted that child support payments made in response to a contempt order do not constitute a voluntary assumption of parental duties.

> ## 🏛 RULE OF LAW
> A non-consenting parent, who failed to fulfill all of his parental duties during the required statutory two-year term prior to the filing for a stepparent adoption, does not automatically lose his parental rights.

FACTS: The parents of minor child B.M.W. divorced within one year of B.M.W.'s birth. Pursuant to the divorce decree, the parents received joint legal custody of B.M.W. The mother was awarded primary physical custody of the child and the father (D) liberal and reasonable visitation. The father (D) was ordered to pay monthly child support. Since the divorce, the mother has maintained contact with the father (D), advising him of address changes and permitting visitation when he (D) or his family requested. Several years after the divorce, the mother married the petitioner (stepfather) (P). Throughout the required statutory two years preceding the filing of the stepparent's petition for adoption, the natural father (D) was a self-employed carpet layer. The father (D) was summoned to court for failure to pay child support as ordered in the divorce decree. The judge observed there was an arrearage in child support payments and found the father (D) in contempt for willfully and without good cause failing to pay the child support. The district judge sentenced the father (D) to ten days in jail and ordered him to make child support payments. The judge suspended imposition of the confinement portion of the sentence and set a series of dates for the father (D) to appear in court to demonstrate compliance with the order of child support. The father (D) failed to make the first two support payments

ordered by the court. This pattern of sporadic payments continued until the date the stepfather's (P) petition for adoption was filed.

After hearing the evidence, the court determined that during the two years preceding the filing of the stepfather's (P) petition for adoption, the father's (D) few contacts with B.M.W. were incidental, and found that under these circumstances, the father (D) had failed to provide the love and affection required of a parent under the applicable state code provisions. The district court then determined the father (D) had paid 86 percent of the child support obligation accruing in the two years prior to the filing of the petition. The court found that the consent of the child's natural father (D) was required for a stepparent adoption because the father (D) had paid a substantial portion of the support pursuant to the contempt order. The petition for adoption was denied. The stepfather (P) appealed.

ISSUE: Does a non-consenting parent, who failed to fulfill all of his parental duties during the required statutory two-year term prior to the filing for a stepparent adoption, automatically lose his parental rights?

HOLDING AND DECISION: (Lockett, J.) No. A non-consenting parent, who failed to fulfill all of his parental duties during the required statutory two-year term prior to the filing for a stepparent adoption, does not automatically lose his parental rights. The duties of a parent set out in the applicable state code provisions include not only the duty of financial support, but also the natural and moral duty of a parent to show affection, care, and interest toward his or her child. The stepfather (P) argues that the father's (D) parental rights may be severed if he fails to provide either financial support or care and affection for the child. The stepfather (P) asserts that because the district court found that the child's natural father (P) failed to provide care and affection for the child, the district court erred in denying the petition for adoption. The questions require the interpretation of a statute.

The applicable state code provisions provide that in a stepparent adoption, if a mother consents to the adoption of a child who has a presumed or known father, the consent of the father must be given to the adoption unless such father has failed or refused to assume the duties of a parent for two consecutive years next preceding the filing of the petition for adoption or is incapable of giving such consent. In determining whether a father's consent is required, the court may disregard incidental visitations, contacts, communications or contributions. The statute

Continued on next page.

further provides: "In determining whether the father has failed or refused to assume the duties of a parent for two consecutive years next preceding the filing of the petition for adoption, there shall be a rebuttable presumption that if the father, after having knowledge of the child's birth, has knowingly failed to provide a substantial portion of the child support as required by judicial decree, when financially able to do so, for a period of two years next preceding the filing of the petition for adoption, then such father has failed or refused to assume the duties of a parent."

In re Adoption of K.J.B., 265 Kan. 90, 959 P.2d 853 (1998), is the latest case in which this court has discussed the failure or refusal of a parent to assume the duties of a parent in the context of a stepparent adoption case. In *K.J.B.*, the father of three minor children appealed the district court's finding that he had failed to assume the duties of a parent during the two years preceding the filing of the petition, after the court granted the stepfather's petition for adoption. The Court of Appeals affirmed the district court. The father's petition for review was granted. The father claimed that social security payments the minor children received through his disability benefits qualified as credits against his liability for child support, and if the payments qualified as support, the district court erred in determining he had "failed or refused to assume the duties of a parent." After reviewing prior cases, the *K.J.B* court observed that adoption statutes are to be strictly construed in favor of maintaining the right of a natural parent and concluded that the applicable state code provisions require a father to fail both the financial and the affection, care, and interest aspects of parenting before a court may grant a stepparent adoption petition without the father's consent. The *K.J.B.* court then pointed out that unlike the termination of parental rights the applicable state code provisions, neither the fitness of the natural father nor the best interests of the child are controlling factors in stepparent adoptions. The code provides that the father may rebut the presumption that he failed to assume the financial aspect of parental duties by showing that he provided a substantial portion of the court-ordered child support.

The stepfather (P) argues that *K.J.B.*'s analysis regarding the parental duties "ledger" is incorrect because the effect of that holding is that payment of a substantial portion of court-ordered child support creates an irrebuttable presumption that consent of the father for the stepparent to adopt is required. The stepfather (P) asserts that the legislature did not create such a presumption but, in fact, established a rebuttable presumption that the knowing voluntary failure to pay a substantial portion of support when financially able to pay support is failure to assume the duties of a parent. The stepfather (P) asserts that "love and affection" and financial support were not intended by the legislature to be "two sides of a ledger," and that each side of the ledger must fail before the court can sever parental rights and permit a stepparent adoption. The stepfather (P) argues that the legislature intended that lack of love and affection and the failure to substantially

support are separate criterion for determining whether a father has failed to assumed parental duties. The stepfather (P) further argues that if either the love and affection or the financial support of the natural parent is lacking, the court may, upon consideration of all the circumstances, sever parental rights and permit the stepparent adoption.

The stepfather's interpretation of the applicable state code provisions is contrary to our holding in *K.J.B.* *K.J.B.*'s determination that a parent must fail to provide both "love and affection" and financial support was compelled by the fact that "'basic parental rights are fundamental rights protected by the Fourteenth Amendment to the Constitution of the United States. The right to be the legal parent of a child is one of these rights, which cannot be abrogated except for compelling reasons." The duties of a parent addressed by the statute include not only the common-law duty of financial support, but also the natural and moral duty of a parent to show affection, care, and interest toward his or her child. In making a determination of whether consent of a parent to an adoption is unnecessary due to failure to assume parental duties, neither the best interests of the child nor the fitness of the non-consenting parent are controlling factors, as they would be in a proceeding to sever parental rights.

Generally speaking, adoption statutes are strictly construed in favor of maintaining the rights of natural parents in those cases where it is claimed that, by reason of a parent's failure to fulfill parental obligations as prescribed by statute, consent to the adoption is not required. In making a determination in an adoption proceeding of whether a non-consenting parent has failed to assume his or her parental duties for two consecutive years, all the surrounding circumstances are to be considered. Although a child can be adopted without the consent of one of the natural parents, the facts warranting an exception as prescribed by statute must be clearly proven.

The "ledger" model applied by the *K.J.B.* court is not entirely based on the applicable state code provisions in that the statute does not expressly delineate "love and affection" as a parental duty. The statute refers to "visitations, contacts, communications or contributions" and states that if those are incidental only, the court may disregard them in determining whether a father's consent is required. Therefore, if parental duties as outlined the applicable state code provisions can be charted on a "ledger," "visitations, contacts, communications, or contributions" occupy one side, and "child support as required by judicial decree" occupies the other.

Here, as in *K.J.B.*, although the father (D) failed to visit, contact, or communicate with the child, he paid the child's support for two years preceding the filing of the petition for adoption to escape being held in contempt. Here, the father (D) did provide a substantial portion of the child support required by judicial decree; therefore, the rebuttable presumption of failure to assume parental duties does

Continued on next page.

not arise. The father (D) provided only incidental visitations, contacts, communications, or contributions during the two years prior to the filing of the petition for adoption. He paid a substantial portion of his child support obligation. The child support payments were not voluntary but in response to a contempt order, for the sole purpose of staying out of jail. The applicable state code provisions do not distinguish between voluntary and involuntary support or define the amount of child support that constitutes a substantial portion of court-ordered support. Under the circumstances, the father (D) did not fail to assume the duties of a parent as required. The district court's denial of the petition for adoption is affirmed.

▶ *ANALYSIS*

The presumption is that a non-custodial natural parent is allowed to maintain his or her parental rights, even if he or she does not meet all of his or her financial obligations set forth by the court. Here, the natural parent (D) clearly failed at fulfilling all of his child support obligations and had minimal contact with his child for a two-year statutorily relevant time period. This, however, was not enough to automatically permit the stepfather's (P) petition for adoption. The court was wary of setting forth a strict "ledger" to calculate the point at which the natural parent would lose his parent rights. Consent for a stepparent adoption was maintained as the preferred method.

Lankford v. Wright

Adoptee (P) v. [Party not identified.] (D)

N.C. Sup. Ct., 347 N.C. 115, 489 S.E.2d 604 (1997).

NATURE OF CASE: Appeal from denial of equitable adoption.

FACT SUMMARY: The Newtons died intestate and without legally adopting their foster daughter, Barbara, despite a stated intention of doing so and a lifetime of holding her out as their only child. Barbara sought a declaration of her rights as an heir to the estate, but North Carolina did not recognize the doctrine of equitable adoption.

🏛 RULE OF LAW
North Carolina does recognize the doctrine of equitable adoption.

FACTS: Barbara Ann Newton Lankford (P) lived with Clarence and Lula Newton pursuant to the Newtons' agreement with her birth mother. The Newtons held Barbara (P) out to be her child, she took their last name, and she obtained a social security number as Barbara Ann Newton. Clarence Newton passed away, but Lulu and Barbara (P) maintained a typical mother-daughter relationship throughout Barbara's adult years. At Lulu's death, her will, which named Barbara (P) as co-administrator and provided specific bequests to her, could not be probated because an unknown person defaced a portion of it. The result was that Lulu died intestate. Barbara (P) filed a declaratory action to determine her rights as heir to the estate, but administrators and named heirs moved for summary judgment. The trial court granted the motion as Barbara (P) was never legally adopted. The court of appeals affirmed on the basis that North Carolina does not recognize equitable adoption. Barbara (P) petitioned the state supreme court for discretionary review.

ISSUE: Does North Carolina recognize the doctrine of equitable adoption?

HOLDING AND DECISION: (Frye, J.) Yes. North Carolina does recognize the doctrine of equitable adoption. Equitable adoption exists to give legal force to the adoptive parent's intent when appropriate legal steps were never taken. Equitable adoption is not the equivalent to legal adoption, because it merely confers inheritance rights upon the adoptee. A foster child acting as a biological child is placed into the position she would be in had she been legally adopted. Necessary elements include: (1) express or implied agreement to adopt the child; (2) reliance on that agreement; (3) biological parents' relinquishing custody; (4) the child lives with and acts toward the foster parents as a natural child; (5) foster parents taking the child into their home and treating her as a natural child;

and (6) intestacy of the foster parents. This case presents clear and convincing evidence of each element. Equitable adoption does not interfere with legal adoption and has been accepted by the majority of states. Reversed and remanded.

DISSENT: (Mitchell, C.J.) An equitable remedy should not be fashioned where statutory and legal rights exist to control inheritance. The legislative scheme to control intestate succession regarding adopted children is comprehensive and unambiguous. The foster parents here may have held the child out as their own, but they never legally adopted her. Equity cannot overrule statutory schemes.

▶ ANALYSIS

The states that recognize equitable adoption do so solely for inheritance purposes and not to avoid the legal requirements of termination of biological parents' rights and legal adoption by adoptive parents. Equitably adopted children typically have no additional rights other than a determination as to rights to the intestate estate of a foster parent. No one can establish custody through equitable adoption.

Quicknotes

EQUITABLE ADOPTION An oral contract to adopt a child, not executed in accordance with statutory requirements, giving rise to rights of inheritance in the child upon the death of the promisor.

INTESTATE To die without leaving a valid testamentary instrument.

MOTION FOR SUMMARY JUDGMENT Judgment rendered by a court in response to a motion by one of the parties, claiming that the lack of a question of material fact in respect to an issue warrants disposition of the issue without consideration by the jury.

Adoption of Swanson

Adult adoptee

Del. Sup. Ct., 623 A.2d 1095 (1993).

NATURE OF CASE: Appeal from denial of adoption petition.

FACT SUMMARY: Sorrels, a sixty-six-year-old man, sought to adopt his companion, Swanson, fifty-one, in order to facilitate their estate planning.

🏛 RULE OF LAW
A preexisting parent-child relationship is not required in order for one adult to adopt another.

FACTS: Under the Delaware adult adoption statutes, a person seeking an adoption was required only to sign and file a petition containing certain basic personal data and obtain the adoptee's consent. Sorrels, a sixty-six-year-old man, attempted to adopt his companion of seventeen years, fifty-one-year-old Swanson, in order to formalize their close emotional relationship and to prevent claims on their estates from remote family members. The family court denied the petition on the grounds that there was no preexisting parent-child relationship between them. Sorrels appealed.

ISSUE: Is a preexisting parent-child relationship required in order for one adult to adopt another?

HOLDING AND DECISION: (Moore, J.) No. A preexisting parent-child relationship is not required in order for one adult to adopt another. Delaware state law does not contain such a requirement, and a court may not engraft language that has been clearly excluded from a statute. Although no court should permit an adoption designed to further a fraudulent or illegal purpose, there is nothing inherently wrong with an adoption intended to confer an economic benefit on the adopted person. Since Sorrels's petition was within the scope of the statute, it should not have been denied. Reversed and remanded.

▶ ANALYSIS

This case represents the prevailing trend among jurisdictions to uphold adoptions for the purpose of improving the adoptee's inheritance rights. Statutory language setting criteria for adoptions is typically quite general, leaving courts with broad discretion to permit adoptions no matter the age difference. However, the New York Court of Appeals held that a fifty-seven-year-old man could not adopt his male lover, concluding that adoption was not a quasi-matrimonial device to provide unmarried partners with a legal imprimatur for their sexual relationship. See *Matter of Adoption of Robert P.*, 471 N.E.2d 424 (1984).

Glossary

Common Latin Words and Phrases Encountered in the Law

A FORTIORI: Because one fact exists or has been proven, therefore a second fact that is related to the first fact must also exist.

A PRIORI: From the cause to the effect. A term of logic used to denote that when one generally accepted truth is shown to be a cause, another particular effect must necessarily follow.

AB INITIO: From the beginning; a condition which has existed throughout, as in a marriage which was void ab initio.

ACTUS REUS: The wrongful act; in criminal law, such action sufficient to trigger criminal liability.

AD VALOREM: According to value; an ad valorem tax is imposed upon an item located within the taxing jurisdiction calculated by the value of such item.

AMICUS CURIAE: Friend of the court. Its most common usage takes the form of an amicus curiae brief, filed by a person who is not a party to an action but is nonetheless allowed to offer an argument supporting his legal interests.

ARGUENDO: In arguing. A statement, possibly hypothetical, made for the purpose of argument, is one made arguendo.

BILL QUIA TIMET: A bill to quiet title (establish ownership) to real property.

BONA FIDE: True, honest, or genuine. May refer to a person's legal position based on good faith or lacking notice of fraud (such as a bona fide purchaser for value) or to the authenticity of a particular document (such as a bona fide last will and testament).

CAUSA MORTIS: With approaching death in mind. A gift causa mortis is a gift given by a party who feels certain that death is imminent.

CAVEAT EMPTOR: Let the buyer beware. This maxim is reflected in the rule of law that a buyer purchases at his own risk because it is his responsibility to examine, judge, test, and otherwise inspect what he is buying.

CERTIORARI: A writ of review. Petitions for review of a case by the United States Supreme Court are most often done by means of a writ of certiorari.

CONTRA: On the other hand. Opposite. Contrary to.

CORAM NOBIS: Before us; writs of error directed to the court that originally rendered the judgment.

CORAM VOBIS: Before you; writs of error directed by an appellate court to a lower court to correct a factual error.

CORPUS DELICTI: The body of the crime; the requisite elements of a crime amounting to objective proof that a crime has been committed.

CUM TESTAMENTO ANNEXO, ADMINISTRATOR (ADMINISTRATOR C.T.A.): With will annexed; an administrator c.t.a. settles an estate pursuant to a will in which he is not appointed.

DE BONIS NON, ADMINISTRATOR (ADMINISTRATOR D.B.N.): Of goods not administered; an administrator d.b.n. settles a partially settled estate.

DE FACTO: In fact; in reality; actually. Existing in fact but not officially approved or engendered.

DE JURE: By right; lawful. Describes a condition that is legitimate "as a matter of law," in contrast to the term "de facto," which connotes something existing in fact but not legally sanctioned or authorized. For example, de facto segregation refers to segregation brought about by housing patterns, etc., whereas de jure segregation refers to segregation created by law.

DE MINIMIS: Of minimal importance; insignificant; a trifle; not worth bothering about.

DE NOVO: Anew; a second time; afresh. A trial de novo is a new trial held at the appellate level as if the case originated there and the trial at a lower level had not taken place.

DICTA: Generally used as an abbreviated form of obiter dicta, a term describing those portions of a judicial opinion incidental or not necessary to resolution of the specific question before the court. Such nonessential statements and remarks are not considered to be binding precedent.

DUCES TECUM: Refers to a particular type of writ or subpoena requesting a party or organization to produce certain documents in their possession.

EN BANC: Full bench. Where a court sits with all justices present rather than the usual quorum.

EX PARTE: For one side or one party only. An ex parte proceeding is one undertaken for the benefit of only one party, without notice to, or an appearance by, an adverse party.

EX POST FACTO: After the fact. An ex post facto law is a law that retroactively changes the consequences of a prior act.

EX REL.: Abbreviated form of the term "ex relatione," meaning upon relation or information. When the state brings an action in which it has no interest against an individual at the instigation of one who has a private interest in the matter.

FORUM NON CONVENIENS: Inconvenient forum. Although a court may have jurisdiction over the case, the action should be tried in a more conveniently located court, one to which parties and witnesses may more easily travel, for example.

GUARDIAN AD LITEM: A guardian of an infant as to litigation, appointed to represent the infant and pursue his/her rights.

HABEAS CORPUS: You have the body. The modern writ of habeas corpus is a writ directing that a person (body) being detained (such as a prisoner) be brought before the court so that the legality of his detention can be judicially ascertained.

IN CAMERA: In private, in chambers. When a hearing is held before a judge in his chambers or when all spectators are excluded from the courtroom.

IN FORMA PAUPERIS: In the manner of a pauper. A party who proceeds in forma pauperis because of his poverty is one who is allowed to bring suit without liability for costs.

INFRA: Below, under. A word referring the reader to a later part of a book. (The opposite of supra.)

IN LOCO PARENTIS: In the place of a parent.

IN PARI DELICTO: Equally wrong; a court of equity will not grant requested relief to an applicant who is in pari delicto, or as much at fault in the transactions giving rise to the controversy as is the opponent of the applicant.

IN PARI MATERIA: On like subject matter or upon the same matter. Statutes relating to the same person or things are said to be in pari materia. It is a general rule of statutory construction that such statutes should be construed together, i.e., looked at as if they together constituted one law.

IN PERSONAM: Against the person. Jurisdiction over the person of an individual.

IN RE: In the matter of. Used to designate a proceeding involving an estate or other property.

IN REM: A term that signifies an action against the res, or thing. An action in rem is basically one that is taken directly against property, as distinguished from an action in personam, i.e., against the person.

INTER ALIA: Among other things. Used to show that the whole of a statement, pleading, list, statute, etc., has not been set forth in its entirety.

INTER PARTES: Between the parties. May refer to contracts, conveyances or other transactions having legal significance.

INTER VIVOS: Between the living. An inter vivos gift is a gift made by a living grantor, as distinguished from bequests contained in a will, which pass upon the death of the testator.

IPSO FACTO: By the mere fact itself.

JUS: Law or the entire body of law.

LEX LOCI: The law of the place; the notion that the rights of parties to a legal proceeding are governed by the law of the place where those rights arose.

MALUM IN SE: Evil or wrong in and of itself; inherently wrong. This term describes an act that is wrong by its very nature, as opposed to one which would not be wrong but for the fact that there is a specific legal prohibition against it (malum prohibitum).

MALUM PROHIBITUM: Wrong because prohibited, but not inherently evil. Used to describe something that is wrong because it is expressly forbidden by law but that is not in and of itself evil, e.g., speeding.

MANDAMUS: We command. A writ directing an official to take a certain action.

MENS REA: A guilty mind; a criminal intent. A term used to signify the mental state that accompanies a crime or other prohibited act. Some crimes require only a general mens rea (general intent to do the prohibited act), but others, like assault with intent to murder, require the existence of a specific mens rea.

MODUS OPERANDI: Method of operating; generally refers to the manner or style of a criminal in committing crimes, admissible in appropriate cases as evidence of the identity of a defendant.

NEXUS: A connection to.

NISI PRIUS: A court of first impression. A nisi prius court is one where issues of fact are tried before a judge or jury.

N.O.V. (NON OBSTANTE VEREDICTO): Notwithstanding the verdict. A judgment n.o.v. is a judgment given in favor of one party despite the fact that a verdict was returned in favor of the other party, the justification being that the verdict either had no reasonable support in fact or was contrary to law.

NUNC PRO TUNC: Now for then. This phrase refers to actions that may be taken and will then have full retroactive effect.

PENDENTE LITE: Pending the suit; pending litigation under way.

PER CAPITA: By head; beneficiaries of an estate, if they take in equal shares, take per capita.

PER CURIAM: By the court; signifies an opinion ostensibly written "by the whole court" and with no identified author.

PER SE: By itself, in itself; inherently.

PER STIRPES: By representation. Used primarily in the law of wills to describe the method of distribution where a person, generally because of death, is unable to take that which is left to him by the will of another, and therefore his heirs divide such property between them rather than take under the will individually.

PRIMA FACIE: On its face, at first sight. A prima facie case is one that is sufficient on its face, meaning that the evidence supporting it is adequate to establish the case until contradicted or overcome by other evidence.

PRO TANTO: For so much; as far as it goes. Often used in eminent domain cases when a property owner receives partial payment for his land without prejudice to his right to bring suit for the full amount he claims his land to be worth.

QUANTUM MERUIT: As much as he deserves. Refers to recovery based on the doctrine of unjust enrichment in those cases in which a party has rendered valuable services or furnished materials that were accepted and enjoyed by another under circumstances that would reasonably notify the recipient that the rendering party expected to be paid. In essence, the law implies a contract to pay the reasonable value of the services or materials furnished.

QUASI: Almost like; as if; nearly. This term is essentially used to signify that one subject or thing is almost analogous to another but that material differences between them do exist. For example, a quasi-criminal proceeding is one that is not strictly criminal but shares enough of the same characteristics to require some of the same safeguards (e.g., procedural due process must be followed in a parole hearing).

QUID PRO QUO: Something for something. In contract law, the consideration, something of value, passed between the parties to render the contract binding.

RES GESTAE: Things done; in evidence law, this principle justifies the admission of a statement that would otherwise be hearsay when it is made so closely to the event in question as to be said to be a part of it, or with such spontaneity as not to have the possibility of falsehood.

RES IPSA LOQUITUR: The thing speaks for itself. This doctrine gives rise to a rebuttable presumption of negligence when the instrumentality causing the injury was within the exclusive control of the defendant, and the injury was one that does not normally occur unless a person has been negligent.

RES JUDICATA: A matter adjudged. Doctrine which provides that once a court of competent jurisdiction has rendered a final judgment or decree on the merits, that judgment or decree is conclusive upon the parties to the case and prevents them from engaging in any other litigation on the points and issues determined therein.

RESPONDEAT SUPERIOR: Let the master reply. This doctrine holds the master liable for the wrongful acts of his servant (or the principal for his agent) in those cases in which the servant (or agent) was acting within the scope of his authority at the time of the injury.

STARE DECISIS: To stand by or adhere to that which has been decided. The common law doctrine of stare decisis attempts to give security and certainty to the law by following the policy that once a principle of law as applicable to a certain set of facts has been set forth in a decision, it forms a precedent which will subsequently be followed, even though a different decision might be made were it the first time the question had arisen. Of course, stare decisis is not an inviolable principle and is departed from in instances where there is good cause (e.g., considerations of public policy led the Supreme Court to disregard prior decisions sanctioning segregation).

SUPRA: Above. A word referring a reader to an earlier part of a book.

ULTRA VIRES: Beyond the power. This phrase is most commonly used to refer to actions taken by a corporation that are beyond the power or legal authority of the corporation.

Addendum of French Derivatives

IN PAIS: Not pursuant to legal proceedings.

CHATTEL: Tangible personal property.

CY PRES: Doctrine permitting courts to apply trust funds to purposes not expressed in the trust but necessary to carry out the settlor's intent.

PER AUTRE VIE: For another's life; during another's life. In property law, an estate may be granted that will terminate upon the death of someone other than the grantee.

PROFIT A PRENDRE: A license to remove minerals or other produce from land.

VOIR DIRE: Process of questioning jurors as to their predispositions about the case or parties to a proceeding in order to identify those jurors displaying bias or prejudice.

Casenote® Legal Briefs